JESUS AND THE OTHER NAMES

JESUS AND THE OTHER NAMES

Christian Mission and Global Responsibility

Paul F. Knitter

ORBIS BOOKS

Maryknoll, New York 10545

Library of Congress Cataloging in Publication Data

Knitter, Paul F.
    Jesus and the other names: Christian mission and global
responsibility / Paul F. Knitter.
      p.   cm.
    Includes bibliographical references and index.
    ISBN 1-57075-053-X(alk. paper)
    1. Christianity and other religions. 2. Catholic Church—
Missions. 3. Missions—Theory. 4. Catholic Church—Relations.
5. Religions—Relations. I. Title
BR127.K56 1996
266'.001—dc20   95-48262
                                              CIP

Printed on recycled paper

For my friends
in the Society of the Divine Word,
past and present

CONTENTS

FOREWORD
Harvey Cox   *xi*

PREFACE   *xvii*

1. MY DIALOGICAL ODYSSEY   1
    An Autobiographical Introduction

    STAGES IN THE ODYSSEY   3
    Missionary Beginnings: Exclusivism   4
    Vatican II and Karl Rahner: Inclusivism   5
    Exploring the Other Side: Pluralism   7
    Pluralism and Liberation   9
    Necessity Becomes Opportunity   12
    THIS BOOK: CONTINUING THE ODYSSEY   15
    *A Globally Responsible, Correlational Dialogue among
        Religions*   16
    Still a Missionary   19
    A Preview   21

2. ADDRESSING THE OTHER NAMES   23
    A Correlational, Globally Responsible Theology of Religions

    A THUMBNAIL SKETCH   23
    Constructing a Theology of Religions   26
    CULTURAL SUPPORTS FOR A CORRELATIONAL,
    GLOBALLY RESPONSIBLE MODEL   27
    Awareness of Others   27
    Awareness of History   29
    Awareness of the Moral Imperative of Dialogue   31
    Awareness of Responsibility for the World   34
    CHRISTIAN SUPPORTS FOR A CORRELATIONAL,
    GLOBALLY RESPONSIBLE MODEL   36
    Doctrinal Incentives: The Nature of God   36
    Ethical Incentives: The First Commandment   38
    *Scriptural Incentives: Balancing the Universal and the
        Particular*   40
    Pastoral Incentives: A Question and Cry from the Heart   44

3. **IT ISN'T CHRISTIAN**   46
    The Critics Speak

    BELIEVING IN CHRIST   *47*
    FOLLOWING CHRIST   *52*
    RESISTING IN CHRIST'S NAME   *55*
    PROCLAIMING CHRIST'S NAME   *57*

4. **UNIQUENESS REVISED**   61
    A Correlational, Globally Responsible Christology

    THE MEANING OF FIDELITY TO JESUS THE CHRIST   *63*
    The Bible and the Daily Newspaper   64
    Right Belief (Orthodoxy) Is Rooted in Right Action
    (Orthopraxis)   65
    The New Testament Language about Jesus   67
    No Other Name?   69
    What about the Religious Pluralism of the
    New Testament World?   70
    "TRULY" DOESN'T REQUIRE "ONLY"   *72*
    Full, Definitive, Unsurpassable? No!   73
    Universal, Decisive, Indispensable? Yes!   76
    A Relational Uniqueness   80

5. **UNIQUENESS REAFFIRMED**   84
    How Jesus Is Unique

    WHAT DOES "UNIQUE" MEAN?   *84*
    UNIQUENESS AND THE HISTORICAL JESUS   *86*
    The Reign of God—Focus of Jesus' Message   89
    Spirit-filled Prophet—The Focus of Jesus' Titles   92
    A HISTORICAL GOD CALLING FOR HISTORICAL
    ENGAGEMENT   *93*
    A God of History   94
    A God of the Oppressed   96
    A God of Promise   97
    AGAIN A RELATIONAL UNIQUENESS   *98*

6. **MISSION REVISED**   102
    A Correlational, Globally Responsible Church

    SUSTAINING CHRISTIAN COMMITMENT AND COMMUNITY   *104*
    A Committed Faith and Following   104
    A Mature Faith   106
    THE MISSIONARY MANDATE REVISED AND REAFFIRMED   *108*
    From Church-Centered to Kingdom-Centered Mission   108
    The Spirit and the Church—Ecclesiology and
    Pneumatology   111

Seek First the Kingdom of God   *115*
The Religions: Agents of the Kingdom   *118*
What about Conversions?   *121*

A ROMAN CATHOLIC INTER-MISSION   125
Dialoguing with Vatican Views of Mission

VATICAN OBJECTIONS   *127*
VATICAN CONCERNS AND AMBIGUITIES   *130*

7. MISSION REAFFIRMED   136
Mission as Dialogue

A DIALOGICAL CHURCH AND MISSION   *136*
Another Vatican Milestone   *136*
An Unclear Milestone—A Wobbly Paradigm Shift   *140*
Mission Is Dialogue   *142*
The Result of Mission-as-Dialogue: A World Church   *147*
*From Supercultural to Supracultural to Crosscultural
    Mission*   *148*
THEOLOGY AS DIALOGUE   *154*
Christian Theology Cannot Be Just Christian   *156*
*Theology and Religious Studies: A Globally Responsible
    Marriage*   *159*
To Make It Work   *161*

AFTERWORD   165

NOTES   167

WORKS CITED   179

INDEX   189

FOREWORD

Harvey Cox

As the first months of 1996 begin to unfold, I am aware that I have now been teaching and writing about Christian theology for over thirty years. During those three decades, two urgent movements have shaken me to my roots and required me to rethink my theology from the ground up. The first was liberation theology, which first hit me like a freshening but disturbing wind from the south in the late 1960s. The second was the Christian response to other faiths, which, like a gentler but persistent breeze, began to claim my attention about ten years later. Both presented formidable challenges, not only to "traditional theology," but also to my own work, which was in many ways quite untraditional. Over three decades I have continued to struggle with these two demanding movements. Both were invigorating and complex. But as the years went by, it became increasingly evident to me that the most besetting intellectual test they exacted was the question of *how they related to each other*. On this front the outlook seemed particularly unpromising, and for some years I almost despaired, thinking that no one else shared this perplexity with me. Then I met the work of Paul Knitter. But let me start at the beginning.

When I first encountered liberation theology in the late 1960s, it was after the publication of my book *The Secular City*, which was quickly translated into Spanish and Portuguese. But I got a totally unanticipated wave of responses from such Latin American theologians as Gustavo Gutiérrez of Peru and Juan Luis Segundo of Uruguay. Gutiérrez even invited me to lecture at the Pontifical Catholic University in Lima, the first non-Catholic theologian ever to speak there. But both he and Segundo—while appreciative—were also quite critical of my book, and it soon became evident to me that they understood the issue of secularization in a very different way. They saw it not from the angle of the skeptical "modern man," but from the perspective of the poor and marginated. Still, I learned a lot from them and was quickly swept up in the excitement and energy of the early days of the liberation theology movement. So convinced was I that this was the most promising theological current I had ever experienced that I spent a summer in Mexico learning Spanish and then returned year after year to Brazil, Argentina, Nicaragua, and Mexico to learn more about liberation theology. I also began teaching courses and seminars on the subject at Harvard.

At first very few students were interested, and there was virtually no material in English for them to read. In my first seminar there were nine students. Now, however, twenty-five years later, thousands of students in colleges and seminaries study the various expressions of liberation theology, including Korean Minjung theology, African and African-American theologies, feminist liberation theology, "Dalit" theology arising from the so-called "untouchables" of India, and others. Also, thanks in no small part to the devoted labors of Orbis Books, there is a wealth of material they can turn to. There can be little doubt that, although it was treated dismissively at first by both academic scholars and church officials, liberation theology has made a tremendous impact on the entire theological world.

At the same time that I was teaching these courses, however, I also felt myself being ineluctably drawn into the growing interfaith dialogue and the efforts Christian theologians were making to rethink Christian theology in the light of religious pluralism. Part of this was due to the presence on the Harvard campus of the Center for the Study of World Religions, which each year brings men and women who are both scholars and practitioners of the great spiritual traditions to teach and live among us. Some, including Hindus and Muslims and Jews, began taking my courses on liberation theology, and I found myself trying to think with them about what a comparable theology drawn from the resources of their own traditions would look like. But like Paul Knitter, I also had met wonderfully impressive Buddhists, including Thich Nhat Hahn, during my work in the anti-Vietnam war movement. Then, in the mid-1970s Chogyam Trungpa Rinpoche, whom I had gotten to know when he gave a talk at Harvard, invited me to spend a summer teaching Christianity at the Naropa Institute in Boulder, Colorado. There at the foot of the Rocky Mountains—reminiscent to Trungpa of his beloved homeland—I immersed myself completely in Tibetan Buddhism while teaching a course on Christianity that strongly emphasized liberation theology to the mainly Buddhist students. It was a potent brew.

The trouble was that at this point in both my teaching and my writing I seemed to be participating in two quite different conversations. By and large the people with whom I conversed about issues of liberation theology were simply not interested in interfaith dialogue. Some even spurned it as a luxury or a diversion. They were understandably so absorbed with the raw wounds of the homeless and hungry, and with how to bring to bear Christian insights on their plight, that they simply did not have time for what seemed to be the possibly interesting but not so pressing problem of being Christian in a world of many religions.

Likewise, the people I talked with about a Christian theology of religious pluralism sometimes viewed liberation theology as a narrow and particularistic Christian movement that was unsophisticated or naive (or maybe even disingenuous) about the other world faiths. Some suspected it might be a newer and better disguised form of the same old Christian triumphalism. I rarely, if ever, met anyone in either of these circles having anything to do with the other one. At the American Academy of Religion meetings the two interest groups met on different floors or in different buildings. The two movements seemed to be almost two separate worlds. Yet I sensed that there must be some link, something to hold them together. Still, I could not say just what it was.

Then I met the work of Paul Knitter. Immediately I knew that I was not alone in my dilemma. But I also saw something else. Beginning with *No Other Name?*, and continuing through *One Earth Many Religions,* in various articles and talks, and now culminating in this book, Knitter has demonstrated beyond any doubt—and better than I could have hoped to—that concern for the "suffering Other" and for the "religious Other" *belong together.* More, he has shown that they need each other, and that the one without the other will be crippled and ineffective. Indeed, Paul Knitter is the principal figure to bring these two seemingly disparate streams of theological construction together. He simply has no peer in this enterprise.

How has he done it? Knitter, it seems, had been just as baffled by this problem as I had. But he had thought and lived his way through it in a remarkable way. Starting as a missionary in the Society of the Divine Word, Knitter began with the problem of religious diversity and then later encountered the imperative of liberation theology. Quite accurately, he judged that the most important contributions of liberation theology were its insistence that we reconceive the Christian tradition from the perspective of the poor and its "hermeneutics of suspicion." It was Knitter who first applied these insights to the so-called theology of religions, and this quotation from his contribution to the collection entitled *The Myth of Christian Uniqueness* published in 1988 illustrates how he does it:

> How much has traditional theology of religions especially its christological base, served to cloak or condone an unconscious theological desire to maintain superiority, or to dominate and control, or to devalue other traditions culturally or religiously . . . to justify the subordination and exploitation of other cultures and religions?

Here we have something close to the kernel, the *cogito ergo sum* of Knitter's theological method. From then on I knew he was a thinker from whom I could learn much. To my mind, Knitter's work took its most original turn when he moved from the christocentric and then theocentric emphases of his earlier thinking into the soteriocentric focus of his more recent writings. This was the key because it pointed toward the *future*. It pushed us to focus on the goal, the "omega point" of any tradition. It is also a strategy that enables all the participants in an interfaith dialogue to approach it on an equal footing. It was an inspired move.

The soteriological framework also, of course, is particularly inviting to liberation theologies, in which the central gospel category of the Reign of God is pivotal. In these theologies, the character of God, the ministry of Jesus, and the mission of the church are all understood from the perspective of the in-breaking of a new reality that vindicates the poor and includes the wounded and the excluded in the new community.

The "soteriological turn" draws the two movements together because when we talk with members of other religious groups a little less about their origins and rituals (although these are important) and more about what they are striving and hoping and praying for, then whole ranges of new possibilities appear. I know this for a fact, because I have seen stalemated interfaith conversations come alive when the focus shifted in this way.

There is much still to be done. There are many questions I hope Paul Knitter will take up even as this remarkable book is finding the audience it so richly deserves. For example, surely we must all begin to think more critically about the language of "reign" and "kingdom," realizing that both terms are central to the gospel, yet also being aware that in our time they tend—if inadvertently—to perpetuate hierarchical and subordinatist models of human community. It seems significant, for example, that Konrad Reiser, the general secretary of the World Council of Churches, has written in his provocative book *Ecumenism in Transition* that he believes "kingdom language" must give way to a "koinonia" idiom, so that a more egalitarian and reciprocal model of human life in envisioned.

Also, the widely heralded "return to experience" in theology will put even more serious questions to those of us who believe liberation theology and the theology of religions belong together. In this volume Knitter begins this vast task by reminding us in the closing pages just how much our definitions of what "experience" is have been shaped by social location, gender and race. It is also critical, I believe, to remember that among both the "suffering Other" and the "religious Other," experience is rarely thought of as individual, and there is often a recognition that the "religious" may not be a separate experience at all, but rather what my great teacher Paul Tillich called "the depth dimension of all human experience."

The present book not only moves Paul Knitter's work to a new and magisterial summit, it also begins to gnaw away at the questions that remain. But, wherever the argument leads, we can be sure that in the future no responsible Christian discussion of the suffering Other can take place without realizing that the religious Other has to be taken into consideration as well. And no theology of religions can proceed without consideration for the wretched of the earth. For that step forward, we have no one to thank more than Paul Knitter.

PREFACE

Since this book is of a piece with *One Earth Many Religions: Multifaith Dialogue and Global Responsibility,* the litany of thank yous that I sang in the preface of that book should be re-sung here. Just about all the people who stood supportively or critically behind that book so stand behind this one. But since the purpose of this book is more pointed, the thank yous need to be more precise. This book will try to pick up the theological pieces that the previous book set aside (or scattered). In the pages that follow, I hope to gather, ponder, and respond to some of the gnawing problems that Christians feel when they try to reconcile their religious beliefs and practices with a correlational (or pluralistic), globally responsible (or liberative) dialogue with persons of other faiths. Most of these problems focus on how to listen to "the other names" while confessing that there is "no other name" (Acts 4:12)—or, how to live out traditional beliefs in the *uniqueness* of Jesus and the *mission* of his church and at the same time affirm the validity of other religious paths.

In gathering and assembling the fragments of such theological issues, there have been particular friends in the academy but especially in my broad Christian community who have provided special help—both when I asked and when I didn't ask for it. Foremost among them is the international family to which this book is dedicated and of which I still feel a part: the Society of Divine Word Missionaries. Especially since the publication of *No Other Name?* back in 1985, I have realized ever more clearly and gratefully how much the vision and values that I absorbed during my twenty-three years with the "SVDs" have remained with me. After laying out, in 1985, my conviction that Jesus is not the *only* saving Word God has spoken, I have, over the past decade, come to realize more clearly the need to affirm Jesus as *truly* God's saving Word.

I confronted one of the most challenging realizations that the questioning of "only" can and must be joined with the affirmation of "truly" when I was invited to participate in a symposium of Divine Word Missionaries entitled "Dialogue and Mission," organized by my old classmate Jim Knight, S.V.D., and held at Tagaytay City, Philippines, in December of 1988 (see Mercado and Knight 1989). In this gathering of missionaries from all over Asia and the South Pacific, I witnessed an incredible and incorrigible openness to other religions and cultures combined with a joyful, natural commitment to Jesus and his Kingdom. I discovered an even more concrete and inspiring example of how missionaries can combine commitment and openness, or teaching and learning, during my visits with another seminary classmate, Vicente Castro, S.V.D., as he went about his parish work with the people of Ipil in Mindanao; Vince is as rock-solid, sometime old-fashioned, in his devotion to the gospel as he is ready to explore the latest idea, whether in pig-farming or concept of God. What I saw in these S.V.D. missionaries, and in many others whom I met during my five-month stay in India (like Jacob Kavunkal, S.V.D., and Anto Poruthur, S.V.D.) was something I had to translate more expressly into theological reflection: a humble recognition that they have much to learn from others together with a deep conviction that they have something important to say.

Further prodding to better balance a pluralistic embrace of other names with a particular embrace of Jesus and his message came from another missionary friend—a one-time SVD like myself—my Orbis editor, Bill Burrows. There was a leitmotif in all the commentaries that Bill would send back on the various installments of this book: any "new" Christian understanding of religions, or of Christ in light of other faiths, that does not flow from and nourish a sharing in Jesus' experience of Abba will not play in Christian "Peoria"—nor should it. For Bill's patience with my slow (or guarded) learning, I am grateful. Eugene Hillman, C.S.Sp., another tough-tested missionary and scholar, offered me similar advice about how to blow one's own bugle while listening to that of others. From colleagues in the academy with whom I have discussed the contents of these pages, I heard, and tried to take seriously, a common message; in differing ways, Schubert Ogden, David Tracy, John B. Cobb, and William Placher all admonished me to "go slow"—to proceed more cautiously and tentatively in assessing the truth of one or many religions, or in determining differences between religions, or in stating how Jesus is or isn't unique. They'll let me know whether I've listened.

I want to speak a special word of appreciation to some new dialogue partners who have also helped with this book. Over recent years, in conversations and in his writings, Harvey Cox has urged me and other so-called liberals not to neglect the dialogue with our Evangelical sisters and brothers, for they have valid concerns in this matter of relating Christianity to other religions (Cox 1988). When I hesitantly took up Cox's advice and began such conversations, I found among Evangelicals not only genuine concerns but an eagerness and gentle passion in talking about them. From my Evangelical friends John Sanders (1992), Clark Pinnock (1992), Paul Eddy (1993), and S. Mark Heim (1995)—who differ in the way they are "evangelical"—I hope I have learned a few things, especially from the way their deep personal devotion to Christ both urges and limits their reaching out to others. In my efforts to state more clearly how Jesus is unique and why mission is necessary, I have tried to listen and speak to their concerns. Again, I'm eager to hear their response and carry on the conversation.

In a real sense, the desire to engage more effectively in interreligious dialogue that animates this book has been for me an occasion for a more extensive and intense intrareligious dialogue with fellow Christians. I'm hoping that this book will generate a little more light and energy for carrying on both kinds of dialogue.

1

MY DIALOGICAL ODYSSEY

An Autobiographical Introduction

The title of this book announces its intent. It seeks to join together what, some would say, God (or history or psychology) has separated: Jesus and the other Names. I hope to show that if there are good reasons why Christians can and must continue to declare that there is "no other Name" (Acts 4: 12), such reasons do not remove the possibility—indeed, the necessity—of carrying on conversation and cooperation between Jesus and the other religious figures of our history and contemporary times. A genuine dialogue is possible and necessary between those who invoke the name of Jesus and those who invoke many other Names. In other words, I hope to persuade the readers of this book of what has become my own Christian persuasion over the years—that there is no contradiction, indeed there is a natural compatibility, between carrying on the message and mission of Jesus and valuing and taking seriously the religious vision and mission of other persons.

With such an intent, this book is the sequel to *One Earth Many Religions: Multifaith Dialogue and Global Responsibility.* In that book my hopes were to show that for a dialogue between religions to work it has to be a *correlational* (or pluralistic) encounter in which both sides really listen to and really speak to each other; I went on to urge that nowadays the best way for a correlational interreligious dialogue to work is for it to be *globally responsible* (or liberative)—based on a shared commitment to promoting eco-human well-being. *Jesus and the Other Names* is, in a sense, a *theological* Act 2 to *One Earth Many Religions.* Taking up the theological questions and challenges left over by the first book, I will try to show that when Christians engage in such a correlational, globally responsible dialogue (I'll be explaining these terms more amply below), they are not being "unfaithful" to Christian convictions about the uniqueness of Jesus and

1

the mission of the church. Indeed, such a dialogue can lead Christians to a clearer understanding of what makes Jesus unique, to a more committed following of him, and to a more meaningful carrying out of his mission to the world.

That last sentence announces what might sound like a rather audacious agenda. For me, it's not just a theological, academic agenda; it's also been an integral part of my own faith journey. So before getting into the theological content of the rest of the book, I want, in this chapter, to offer an overview of that personal journey. What follows in this autobiographical introduction replays, with some modifying adaptations, the first chapter of my *One Earth Many Religions*. I've decided to rerun this interplay between my theology and my biography since I've come to realize, thanks especially to my feminist friends, that to try to understand a theologian's "thinking" without also looking at her "living" is like a biologist attempting to understand an animal species without any regard for its environmental niche. And since not everyone who picks up this book will have read the other (although that's highly recommended!), I feel happily obligated to provide this overview of the biographical environment that has nurtured and limited my theology.

Back in 1985, in the opening sentence of the Preface for *No Other Name? A Critical Survey of Christian Attitudes toward World Religions,* I wrote: "All theology, we are told, is rooted in biography" (Knitter 1985, xiii). I could well have used the same words to begin this book. Once again, and even more so, I can stand back in happy awe at the way my theological ploddings have followed the flow of what has been going on in my life. My work as a Christian theologian—that is, my efforts to help my community mediate between our Christian tradition and our culture(s)—has been surprisingly, painfully, usually fruitfully, affected by the people and the events that either have been invited or have broken into my life. Certainly I have drawn up my own plans and made my own decisions—but always those plans and choices have been occasioned, stimulated, limited, reversed by people who meant something to me or events that challenged my mind or touched my heart. There have been particular people and events that have especially shaken and directed me over the past ten years since *No Other Name?*

But as I look at these past ten years, I realize that they are both piece and product of a larger picture—or better, of a larger journey that has been going on in my life since my high school years, back in the '50s, when I entered what was then called a minor seminary. It's been a movement that can best be described as a "journey with the other" or a "dialogical odyssey." Of course, everyone's life can be so depicted. As relational beings, we've all had "significant others" brightening and bending our lives. When I say "other" to describe my journey, I mean the *really different*, the unexpected, the unthought, the surprising, the jolting. I'm talking about people or events that didn't seem to fit into the world that I had experienced and understood. My life, especially as a Christian and theologian, has been enriched, disturbed, and redirected by people who have encountered or embraced me with their differences, or by situations or events that I never dreamed could be or happen. These people and events have crossed over the patrolled borders of my life and made my world different from what it had been.

As I look back over the past decades, it seems there have been two primary "Others" who have so affected my life and my theology: the *religious Other* and the *suffering Other*. Up until the early '80s, the most significant Other in my social and theological life had been the religious persons from other traditions who challenged or upset many of my spiritual and theological categories and expectations. It was the impact of their entry into and settlement in my life that I reported on and responded to in *No Other Name?* But as I will elaborate below, the flow of world and personal events during the '80s took me into a different and bigger neighborhood of Others: the Central American refugees who invaded our southern borders fleeing economic injustice and oppression represented these new Others who entered redemptively, though perhaps illegally, into my life; they represented the thousands of people throughout the world who are suffering horribly, unjustly, unnecessarily. More recently I have come to understand, even feel, the suffering not only of humans but of all sentient beings, including Mother Earth. Human and ecological suffering has become an Other who has disturbed my life even more than the religious Other.

Happily, though often painfully, I have been invited, even forced, into conversation with these Others. I say this as a human being, but also as a Christian and a theologian. And so I have felt, ever more strongly and apprehensively, that I must speak with the religious and the suffering Others *as* a Christian and a theologian. If I can't make sense of my Christian experience and beliefs, if I can't carry on my theological task, in dialogue with and in a life-giving encounter with *both* of these Others, then my faith is not authentic and my theology is a distraction.

STAGES IN THE ODYSSEY

From the vantage point of hindsight, as I look back over the decades and milestones of my journey with the Other, I can detect in my own life a mini-recapitulation of what has been the journey and the struggle of many Christian churches who have opened themselves to

the genuinely other. The signposts, or stages, in my journey correspond roughly to what have been called models for Christian efforts
to develop a theology of and dialogue with other religious traditions.
Today many theologians and pastoral practitioners speak and argue
about the *exclusivist* or *inclusivist* or *pluralist* approaches to persons
of other religious ways (see Race 1983).[1] As with all models and with
all technical jargon, there are dangers of defining things too tightly
and of stuffing people into pigeon holes they only half fit. Still, these
three general perspectives do reflect widespread and differing Christian views of other religions. For me, as I look back over my life, these
models are not simply intellectual constructs or academic playthings.
Rather, they represent the personal and spiritual struggles as I felt my
beliefs and my practices shaken by the entrance of the religious and
the suffering Others into my life. Before I was even acquainted with
the technical terms of "exclusivism," "inclusivism," and "pluralism,"
I was wrestling with the realities that those terms try to indicate; in
my Christian, theological journey I found myself moving—or being
forced—from one perspective or model to another.

What follows is a brief account of that journey. In its meanderings
and in the direction of its movement, I suspect that it will reflect the
journey of many of my fellow Christians. Whether that's true or not,
this is the personal story that has brought me to the writing of this
book and its immediate predecessor (Knitter 1995). I hope that both
books may clarify and give better direction to the story—both mine
and that of others.

MISSIONARY BEGINNINGS: EXCLUSIVISM

My dialogical odyssey began pretty much as a monologue. Other
religious persons interested me not so much because I wanted to converse with them, but because I wanted to convert them. I wanted to be
a missionary. In 1958, after four years of seminary high school and two
rigorous years of novitiate "boot camp," I officially joined the ranks of
the Divine Word Missionaries (the "SVDs" or *Societas Verbi Divini*).
Though ambiguous in many ways, that decision was one of the most
fruitful of my life. It was my first step toward the religious Other.

Although this step was motivated by concern, even love, for others,
it was the kind of concern and love that exist, not between friends,
but between a doctor and an ailing patient. Five times a day, in our
seminary prayers, we stormed heaven with the invocation: "May the
darkness of sin and the night of heathenism vanish before the light of
the Word and the Spirit of grace." *We* had the Word and Spirit; *they*
had sin and heathenism. *We* were the loving doctors; *they* were the
suffering patients.

In those years of seminary training—late '50s, early '60s—there
was much talk about "accommodation" or "missionary adaptation."

This was an indirect, though still real, recognition that there wasn't total darkness in the world of other religions. As some German theologians of the time put it, there were also *Anknüpfungspunkte* within other traditions—points of contact where Christians could insert their saving word. Actually, "missionary adaptation" was somewhat equivalent to "getting a foot in the door"—recognizing where other religious believers resembled us Christians and where their transformation into Christians could begin. This was a small, self-interested step toward recognizing positive values in other traditions. For me, it was a first step.

I discovered more than I expected. Here was the first phase in which the religious Other actually intruded into my life. During those seminary years, there was a constant flow of missionaries returning home on furlough and passing through the various SVD houses to give talks to us future missionaries. In their slide lectures, in their colorful, often moving stories of encounters with Hindus, Buddhists, primal religious believers, I gradually realized that the SVDs were not really practicing or experiencing what they were praying about; these missionaries talked much more about the beauty of Hinduism, or the insights of the New Guinea Highlanders, or about the rich depths of Buddhist art and meditation than about their pervasive and perverse "darkness and sin."

I especially remember how moved and bewildered I was at the Indian dance team Father George Proksh, S.V.D., directed; they presented not just Christian beliefs decked in Hindu dance forms but also the beauty and mystery of the Hindu sense of the Divine. Added to this were the discoveries I made as a member of our college Japan Study Club; we were all expected to select one of the SVD "mission countries" in order to study its history, culture, and religion. It was my first taste of Buddhism, my first acquaintance with the history of Zen, the rigor of its practice, the claimed illumination and peace of the satori experience. There was much I couldn't fit into my Christian categories; there was much I liked.

As I finished my college studies in 1962 and tucked away my bachelor's degree in philosophy, I had the uneasy but distinct sense that the old exclusivist model of Christianity as light and other religions as darkness didn't fit the facts. What to do about that became clearer for me when I was sent to finish my theological studies in Rome.

VATICAN II AND KARL RAHNER: INCLUSIVISM

I arrived in Rome to begin my studies at the Pontifical Gregorian University just two weeks before the Second Vatican Council began on October 11, 1962. It was an exhilarating, hope-filled time to be in Rome. Pope John XXIII was not just opening long-locked windows in the Roman church, he was knocking through walls and indirectly calling for reconstruction of old models and practices! Part of the general opening of the Catholic church to the modern world was a recognition of other cultures and religions. I remember well the enthusiasm of the twenty-four SVD missionary bishops who were staying with us while they attended the Council when they discovered that there would be a statement about the church's relationship not just with Judaism but also with other religions. I shared their enthusiasm when one of the bishops, a veteran of decades in New Guinea whose Latin had grown more than rusty, asked me to help him read the text of the *sub secreto* (confidential) document on "The Declaration on the Relationship of the Church to Non-Christian Religions." Here were positive statements about the truth and values of Hinduism, Buddhism, and Islam that had never before graced an official church document; here, I realized, was a turning point in Roman Catholic theology of religions.

At the same time the Council fathers were meeting, I was taking courses at "the Greg" about and by one of the theologians who offered decisive help in opening the Catholic church's windows to other believers: Karl Rahner. In 1965 Rahner himself came to the Gregorianum as a guest professor. Listening to him, I realized clearly how, with his carefully crafted doctrinal arguments, he had laid the theological foundations for Vatican II's new, positive view of other religions. Even more than the Council's terse but revolutionary recognition of truth and goodness in the world religions, Rahner's theologically honed case that Christians not only can but *must* look upon other religions as "legitimate" and as "ways of salvation" was a breath of fresh, liberating air for me. It enabled me both to make sense of what I had been seeing in the religious world beyond Christianity and to shake free of what I felt was the ungrounded hubris of Christian claims to be the only authentic religion.

So after earning my Licentiate in Theology in Rome, I decided to move to the University of Münster, Germany, to write a thesis under Karl Rahner on Catholic attitudes toward other religions. After working with him for about a half year, however, I discovered, to my devastating surprise, that someone else, back in Rome, had just published a dissertation on the very same topic. Back in Rome to resolve my dissertational doldrums, I sought counsel with Monsignor Piero Rossano, then Secretary for the Vatican's Secretariat for Non-Christian Religions. He helped transform my setback into a new opportunity when he suggested that I do with contemporary Protestant theology what I had hoped to do with Catholic theologians.

His suggestion turned out to be an opportunity for the religious Other to knock again on my door—or better, I on theirs! I moved from my familiar Roman Catholic world of Rome and Münster to the

University of Marburg and to a Department of Protestant Theology founded under the Reformers. Here, under the direction of Professor Carl Heinz Ratschow, I wrote a dissertation entitled "Toward a Protestant Theology of Religions." Though I was the first Roman Catholic ever admitted into the doctoral program of Marburg's Department of Protestant Theology, I had the Roman audacity to criticize contemporary Protestant thinkers (even my own "Doctor-Father" Ratschow!) for not going far enough in their efforts to overcome the exclusivism of Karl Barth's neo-orthodox attitude toward religion. In their efforts to recognize the value of other religions, Protestant theologians, I claimed, were stymied by the Reformational insistence on "faith alone" through "Christ alone" (see Knitter 1975). Protestants such as Paul Althaus, Emil Brunner, and even Wolfhart Pannenberg could recognize "revelation" in other faiths, but never "salvation." This was, I concluded, to go only half-way in their efforts to reach out to other religious believers.

But my criticism of Protestant theologians was thoroughly based on, and limited by, my Rahnerian Catholic perspective. I was criticizing the Protestants for not having made the move that Rahner made with his new theology of religions, often epitomized in his theory of "anonymous Christians" (that is, non-Christians are "saved" by the grace and presence of Christ working anonymously within their religions). Yet if I could chide the Protestants for not being able to admit that there is saving grace mediated through other religions, I myself was not able to imagine that such wisdom and grace in other traditions could be anything else but "reflections" of the fullness of truth and grace incarnated in Jesus the Christ. Such reflections, I took for granted, could be brought to full light only in the gospel. Thus, while Rahner's theology of religions constituted for me a giant, liberating step forward, I did not realize at the time of finishing my doctorate that it was for me but the first step in a broader, even more liberating, process of reaching into the world of the religious Other.

EXPLORING THE OTHER SIDE: PLURALISM

In an image used by John Hick, Rahner turned out to be for me not a new paradigm, but a bridge (Hick 1980, 180-81). I first began to suspect that I might have to get off that bridge and onto the other side when, during my doctoral studies in Germany, I met Rahim. From Pakistan, Rahim was a bright, friendly, fun-loving, and caring fellow-student majoring in chemistry. He was also a devout Muslim who prayed five times a day and ordered apple juice when the rest of us called for beer. We became close friends and often discussed religion. I began to realize clearly what I could not explain theologically, even with Rahner's help. Personally, Rahim was entirely content with his Muslim faith; ethically, he surpassed most Christians I knew. In discussing our faiths, we learned much from each other. But if I were to speak about Rahim's need of being "fulfilled" through Christianity, it would have to be in the same sense that I needed fulfillment through Islam. Theologically, I could say that Rahim was saved; I could not call him an anonymous Christian. Rahner's bridge was shaking.

It shook even more when I returned to Chicago to begin my teaching career at Catholic Theological Union in 1972. Besides offering courses on theologies of religions and interreligious dialogue, I also began a serious study of other faiths by teaching courses on them, especially Hinduism and Buddhism. Strongly influenced by the method of "passing over" that John Dunne laid out in his *The Way of All the Earth* (1972), I tried, amid many limitations and frustrations, to lead myself and my students into a study of other religious ways that was both intellectual-historical and personal-experiential. When I moved to Xavier University in 1975 (having left the Society of the Divine Word) and continued teaching these same courses with the same methodology, I gradually realized that I had slid, unawares, off Rahner's bridge and was exploring, with a sense of excitement and apprehension, new religious territory. And I further realized that the new territory would eventually call for new theological maps.

Among my most trustworthy yet bold guides in this exploration were Raimon Panikkar, both in his theoretical directives (*The Intra-Religious Dialogue*, 1978) and in the way he passed over to Hinduism (*The Vedic Experience*, 1977), and Thomas Merton, in the way he brought Zen Buddhism to life and meaning (*Zen and the Birds of Appetite*, 1968). I also became more engaged in actual dialogue with Hindu and especially Buddhist practitioners. In the midst of, or because of, all this, I found myself returning after years of neglect to a daily practice of meditation, only now it was in the form of zazen. From such study, conversations, and practice, I realized that a dialogue of discovery and theological insight was unfolding—sometimes exploding—within me. There were particular experiences and insights that shook and then rearranged my theological perspectives: when I realized that perhaps the Hindu claim of nondualism between Brahman and Atman was not just an analog, but perhaps a more coherent expression of what Rahner was trying to articulate with his notion of the supernatural existential[2]; or when I realized that the Buddhist experience of *Anatta* (no-self), as much as I had understood and felt it, enabled me to better understand and, I think, live, Paul's claim "It is now no longer I who live but Christ who lives in me" (Gal 2:20).

The theological conclusions from all this exploration and discovery came to an initial focus for me when I read Hans Küng's *On Being a Christian* (1976). With his staunch criticism of the theory of anonymous Christianity, Küng had been for me another prophetic prod to get off Rahner's bridge. But when I came to the bottom line of his treatment of other faiths, which in my estimation both misrepresented and unduly subordinated them to what Küng termed the "finality" of the Christ event, I realized that moving off the bridge would require a bigger move than Küng, at that time, was able to make (Knitter 1978). (Since then, Küng has taken his own further steps without, however, loosening his hold on the finality of Christ.) In order to figure out for myself just how this bigger move might be made and what it would entail, I decided, not to hie off to an Indian ashram or Japanese Zen monastery, but to write a book (a more practical decision since I now was a husband and father). Before engaging in deeper dialogue, I wanted to try to sort out, for myself and others, the past efforts and the inherent potential of Christian theology to interpret the so-called new experience of religious pluralism.

No Other Name? (1985) was billed as a "critical survey of Christian attitudes." After the survey and drawing from it, I attempted to assemble a theological case that would convince myself and fellow Christians that one is not at all abandoning the Christian witness contained in scripture and tradition, but rather understanding it more deeply and thus preserving it, when one sublates (which does not mean leave behind!) the given christocentric approach to other believers with one that is theocentric. Though we Christians claim Jesus the Christ as our necessary and happy starting point and focus for understanding ourselves and other peoples, we must also remind ourselves that the Divine Mystery which we know in Jesus and which we call *Theos* or God, is ever greater than the reality and message of Jesus. Thus we are open to the *possibility* (and that's all I was arguing for in No Other Name?) that other religions may have their own valid views of and responses to this Mystery; thus, they would not have to be unilaterally "included" in Christianity. Rather, *all* the religions could be, perhaps need to be, included in—that is, related to—each other as all of them continue their efforts to discover or be faithful to inexhaustible Mystery or Truth. I had, indeed, moved off the bridge, from inclusivism to some form of pluralism. I was now exploring "the other side." And though I would want to clarify and correct particular arguments in No Other Name? (and will do so in the following pages), I have continued to move in the direction it set for me.

PLURALISM AND LIBERATION

In 1986, in order both to ascertain how widespread this pluralist turn was among Christian theologians and to expose it to further criticism, John Hick and I assembled a group of theologians who were moving, each in different ways, in this general direction of pluralism. The results of that conference were presented to the broader Christian and theological community in *The Myth of Christian Uniqueness: Toward a Pluralistic Theology of Religions* (1987). In writing my own contribution to that volume, I came to realize that my pluralist turn had taken a new twist. Again, it was a case of theology following biography. There were some new events and new people in my life. Since the early '70s I had been trying to follow the developments of the new liberation theology coming out of Latin America. My interest was fueled initially by my desire to be methodologically up-to-date. Then, in 1983, I met in Cincinnati two Salvadoran students; they were refugees because they had spoken up for human rights and were being pursued by their Salvadoran government supported by my United States government. Since that fortuitous encounter, my life, as they say, has not been the same.

The following year my wife, Cathy, and I became active members of the local Sanctuary Movement—a loose ecumenical bonding of churches and synagogues that, in defiance of U.S. government policy, were publicly providing shelter and support to Central American refugees fleeing the poverty and dangers of U.S.-sponsored wars in their country. This led to summer visits to El Salvador and Nicaragua over the next five years. Through these experiences—through working with refugee families in Cincinnati, meeting with base Christian communities in Central America, collaborating with Jon Sobrino and Lutheran Bishop Medardo Gomez in El Salvador, experiencing the pain of Salvadoran friends picked up by security forces and tortured—liberation theology became for me not just a "new method" but a matter of making sense of religion and of being a faithful disciple of Jesus. I experienced the fundamental option for the oppressed not simply as an option but a demand. It affected the way I do theology to the point that I could no longer go about a theology of religions unless it was, somehow, connected with a theology of liberation. And so my contribution to *The Myth* collection bore the strange title "Toward a Liberation Theology of Religions."

Since then, the suffering Other has continued to accompany and challenge my spiritual and theological journey. Their voices and their cries for justice remain with me not only through my continuing contacts with the people and churches of El Salvador as a member of the Board of Directors of CRISPAZ (Christians for Peace in El Salvador), but also through my participation in local peace and justice groups in Cincinnati, especially the Faith and Justice Base Community of Bellarmine Parish at Xavier University. One of the staunchest and most encouraging confirmations of the need for dialogue to include both the religious and the suffering Others came for me during my five-month sabbatical in India, July-December 1991. With my family, I found myself immersed in a land of incredible, sometimes overwhelming, religious richness—a land, also, in which religions have lived and dialogued (on the practical level) for centuries. But at the same time, India is a land of just as incredible, and always overwhelming, poverty.

If there was ever a country that has housed, so graphically and tensely, the "many religions" and the "many poor," it is India. During my months there, the voices of the religious Other and of the suffering Other, though distinct and sometimes at odds, merged and spoke to me with new urgency and with new hope.

The urgency came both from those who have long been involved in the Hindu-Christian dialogue (e.g., Bede Griffiths, Ignatius Hirudayam, and Ignatius Puthiadam) and from those committed to the liberation of the Dalits or oppressed classes/castes (e.g., Swami Agni Veesh, Samuel Rayan, and K. C. Abrahams). From both sides, despite their differences in procedure and strategy, I was told that in India "dialogue" and "liberation" must be two facets of the same agenda. To have one without the other is to live outside the Indian reality. Despite the difficulties of such a "liberative dialogue" in a country where religion is being used with horrible success to foster "communalism" or factionalism, my hopes were nurtured by the examples I did find of Hindus, Christians, and Muslims coming together to struggle against oppression or communalism, and to learn from each other in their common struggle. (I describe and analyze some of these examples in the final chapter of Knitter 1995.)

But as I already indicated, I have come to realize, especially during the last half of the '80s, that the suffering Other includes not just humans but also earthlings, indeed the Earth herself. And just as human and ecological sufferings have common causes, they will have common solutions. To speak of justice and liberation, therefore, one must intend eco-human justice and liberation. Intellectually and logically such a statement has become clear and convincing for me through the books and studies on the environmental crisis that have filled our bookstores and our awareness over the past decade. But personally and in the fibers of my feelings, the Earth has become an object of love and concern through my encounters with a particular religious Other—Native Americans. I am thinking especially of my meeting with elders and spokespersons from various North American nations in June 1993 at "The Land and the Human Presence" conference sponsored by Bucknell University. As we sat and talked around the circle in the woods or around the fire, in their stories, statements and especially rituals, my Native American sisters and brothers enabled me to pass over to the sense of the Sacred they find in the Earth and all its inhabitants. More clearly and intensely than ever, I saw that dialogue must include liberation, and that liberation must include the Earth, for here was a people who could not talk about the Sacred without talking about the Earth and who could not talk about the horrid sufferings they themselves have endured without talking about the sufferings of Earth and animals. For me, this has become a paradigm for all interreligious encounters.

I received further and encouraging support for such a paradigm from my more academic conversations with friend and colleague Hans Küng. Though we have had our differences on theological aspects of Christian dialogue with other believers, his recent project for a global ethic resonates with and expands my own sense that a concern for dialogue must be wedded with a concern for justice. For Küng, and for the many who have endorsed his proposal, the avalanche of dangers forming on the slopes of economic injustice, environmental devastation, and military build-up will not be stayed unless the nations of the world come together to formulate and endorse some kind of shared ethical convictions and guidelines. But such a task will not be accomplished unless the religions of the world, in dialogue, make their contribution. In other words, interreligious conversations must take as their most pressing agenda the ethical issues behind the mounting suffering of humans and Earth. That Küng's project received international endorsement from the World Parliament of Religions in Chicago in September 1993 is an indication that he is speaking to "the signs of the times." Despite certain reservations about *how* Küng is going about the implementation of his project, I want to step to his side in calling upon all religious persons to cooperate in promoting eco-human justice and well-being. So I have drawn the subtitle of this book from the title of Küng's book, in which he announced his project: "global responsibility" must be part of all interreligious conversations and of Christian mission (Küng 1991).

NECESSITY BECOMES OPPORTUNITY

So people and events in my life have led me, sometimes lured me, to what has become for me a moral obligation to join "pluralism and liberation" or "dialogue and global responsibility." The two somehow have to go together. I have to speak with and learn from the voices of both the religious Other and the suffering Other. If this isn't possible, if I can't listen to both, if I can't link my concern for interreligious dialogue with my concern for eco-human justice, then I have to make a choice. Were such a choice necessary, I would have to abandon dialogue and pursue justice and the alleviation of suffering. Fortunately, however, my experiences both in theological conversations and in dialogical encounters (especially in India, Sri Lanka, and Thailand) have assured me that such a choice need not be made. Indeed, I have gradually become aware that what I felt to be a necessity was also an opportunity.

My own limited dialogical experiences, and especially the experiences and reflections of my friend and mentor Aloysius Pieris, S.J., have brought me to the strong suspicion, if not conviction, that the *necessity* of linking interreligious dialogue with global responsibility provides the *opportunity* not only for a different kind of dialogue but also for an effectively better dialogue. (In chapter 9 of *One Earth Many Religions*, I describe how Pieris is creatively combining dialogue and liberation in his work in Sri Lanka.) The voice of the suffering Other, in other words, has informed and made more comprehensible to me the voice of the religious Other. The immediacy and urgency that is contained in the presence of the suffering Other has been an occasion and means for me to enter into and appreciate the mysterious depths of the religious Other. That's quite an assertion. Let me try to explain.

The longer I have tried to engage in interreligious dialogue, the more clearly I have realized how difficult it is. The reason for this, I suspect, is that the more one seeks to enter the world of another religious tradition, through personal encounters and through textual studies, the more one bounces up against the wall of differences that are, finally, incomprehensible. While similarities in religious experience and expression abound, the differences are even more abundant—and many of them are incommensurable. To describe who the religious Other has been for me and how it has affected me, I find Rudolf Otto's expression most fitting: it has been a *mysterium tremendum et fascinosum*—a mystery both frightening and fascinating. I have been unsettled, confused, often put off by what the religious Other makes known to me, but at the same time (or soon thereafter) I just as often find myself touched, lured, persuaded by the very strangeness that frightened me.

This is true of my experience of the Other in my long-standing dialogue with Buddhists, as it is of my meetings with Hindus during travels through India; it is even more true, surprisingly, of my more-recent experience of three-way dialogue among Jews, Muslims, and Christians. In trying to pass over, for example, to the Buddhists' experience of impermanence or to the Zen insistence on non-attachment even to God, and in trying to understand and appreciate the centrality of Halakhah for Jews or their sense of uniqueness and their wariness about dialogue, I have found myself trembling before the utter, or "frightening," Mystery of difference. It is a difference that I cannot comprehend, that sometimes threatens me, that chides or even laughs at my theories. I have thus experienced the religious Other as the *totaliter aliter*—the utterly Other, the incommensurable, the incomprehensible. And so I have been experientially convinced that facile talk of "common essence" or "common experience" are gossamer theories spun out by academicians who most likely have never felt the hard, obstructing reality of otherness. Confronting the religious Other as the utterly Other or overwhelming Mystery, I must bow in silence.

But at the same time, in a paradoxical process that I cannot explain, the religious Other, precisely by being an overwhelming Mystery, has more often than not become a "fascinating," inviting Mystery.

What was so utterly different that I could not comprehend it also engaged me, beckoned me, held forth the promise of enriching me. This is a process that can, I think, only be experienced, not proven or clearly analyzed. In the interaction of mutual presence, in speaking and listening, in witnessing the commitments, the values, the rituals of others—the incommensurable, incomprehensible, utterly Other *has become* for me the possible, the imaginable, the attractive. I cannot simply bow in silent respect before other believers; I must also learn from them, speak to them, somehow find myself in them. The cocoon of silence becomes the birthplace of the fragile but inquisitive butterfly of conversation. Having experienced total, mysterious otherness, I find myself experiencing relatedness, even though I cannot explain such relatedness or say where it will lead. This is where Panikkar's notion of "cosmic trust" becomes real—I find myself trusting that despite or because of our differences, we can and we must talk to, and learn from, and be changed by each other.

For me, the suffering Other has provided help and guidance in coming to feel that the frightening otherness in my dialogue partner is an inviting other. When religious persons *together* listen to the voices of the suffering and oppressed, when they attempt *together* to respond to those needs, I have found that they are able to trust each other and to feel the truth and the power in each other's strangeness. Others who suffer become mediators, as it were, or conduits of trust and comprehension, between differing religious worlds. As I acted together with Jews and Buddhists in the Sanctuary Movement, as I prayed or meditated with them before the Federal Building in Cincinnati to protest U.S. aid to the Salvadoran military, as I heard their witness about why they were engaging in these activities of protest and concern, I felt that their strangeness was an inviting and affirming strangeness, one from which I could learn.

And so my image of the religious Other as a frightening and fascinating Mystery has been complemented by an image of religious others as *fellow travelers*. By this I do not mean that we are traveling toward some kind of eschatological or otherworldly realization of truth or fulfillment. Rather, my experience—and my trust—is that as followers of various religious paths, we all can and do experience a common concern and a common responsibility to respond, *as* religious persons, to the widespread human and ecological suffering and injustice that are threatening our species and our planet. I am not saying that all religious persons are concerned about such this-worldly suffering and crisis. But I can say, from my own experience and from reading about the experience of others, that a growing number of believers from most religious paths *are* so concerned—and *are* experiencing themselves as fellow travelers and fellow actors with persons from other faiths.

THIS BOOK: CONTINUING THE ODYSSEY

This book, and its elder brother, *One Earth Many Religions* (1995), are both the product and the continuation of the dialogical odyssey I have just described. In *One Earth Many Religions,* I tried to clarify the *dialogical* journey I have been on—why it is necessary and how it can be carried out; in this book I hope to provide this dialogical journey with a more solid *theological* foundation and a firmer place in the Christian church's identity and mission. And I have sought to do all this in conversation with others who are also searching for truth and values—primarily with members of my own religious community, Christianity, but also with brothers and sisters of other religious paths, in the hope that what I am talking about and proposing will enlighten and guide their journeys. My suspicion is that persons in a variety of religious traditions are growing ever more sharply aware that to understand and live their faith-lives in our present-day world, they must be in a conversation both with other religious believers *and* with the suffering ones of this Earth.

To speak in Christian terms and especially to my fellow Christians, I am attempting to bring together the concerns of a theology of religions and a theology of liberation—or the concerns of a dialogue of religions and a dialogue of liberation. Edward Schillebeeckx has described the twofold challenge facing all Christians (I would say, all religious persons): "The 'standpoint' from which we, as Christians . . . begin to think is increasingly the ecumene of the world religions and the ecumene of humankind . . . really and finally the ecumene of suffering mankind" (Schillebeeckx 1990, 189). These words summarize what my dialogical odyssey has told me—that unless I allow the religious and suffering Others to enter into my life, unless I am responding to them from the center of my human and religious values, I am less a human being, less a religious believer, less a Christian.

That many Christians have felt these same challenges is indicated in two of the most significant developments within Christian theology over the past half century: the *theology of liberation* and the *theology of religions.* Each movement has responded to one of the two Others who have, willy-nilly, intruded upon and challenged the composure and security of the Christian churches. While each of these theologies has contributed disruptively and creatively to Christian clarity and conviction regarding the gospel, they have not, especially in the Western churches, had much to do with each other. Liberation theologians and theologians of religions or interreligious dialogue have been working in different corners of the Christian vineyard.

In both these books I am seeking to represent and develop the efforts of those theologians who, in both North and South, have over the past decade been attempting to build bridges between Christian efforts to respond to the religious Other and to the suffering Other. These efforts grow out of the mounting and ever-clarifying conviction that although the suffering Other may speak to Christians with a more urgent and immediate voice, even though the removal of suffering has a priority over the promotion of dialogue, still there is the clear and strong sense that an effective, enduring, really transformative dialogue with the suffering of this world will have to include a dialogue with the world religions. If the unnecessary suffering of humanity and of the Earth is to be addressed and removed, the religions are going to have to make a combined, cooperative, dialogical contribution. To be effective, a theology of liberation must also be a theology of interreligious dialogue. To be meaningful, an interreligious dialogue or theology must include a theology of liberation.

In this book I will try to lay the christological, ecclesiological, and missiological foundations for a theology of religions that will be liberative, that is, a theology that will grow out of and contribute to the salvation and well-being of suffering humanity and Earth; and of a theology of liberation that will be dialogical, that is, a theology that is able to embrace and learn from the potential of many religions for promoting human and planetary life.

A GLOBALLY RESPONSIBLE, CORRELATIONAL DIALOGUE AMONG RELIGIONS

More precisely, the purpose of this book is to explore the theological presuppositions and challenges for the *pluralistic, liberative dialogue of religions* that I proposed in *One Earth Many Religions*. But because words like "liberation" and "pluralism" have been so battered and blurred by academicians and politicians, I'm wary of using them. Despite admonishing clarifications, "liberative" or "liberation" is felt by many to mean primarily if not exclusively a Latin American brand of theology based on a particular economic theory (usually Marxist) and limited to social or political reform. "Pluralistic" is suggestive to many of an approach to religions that sees them all as equal and as differently colored containers of a homogeneous mystical experience; pluralist theologians, for many, want to pile all religions on a happy syncretistic bandwagon. In the popular mind, and in many theological minds, all "liberation" or "pluralist" theologians are stuffed into the same drawer, even though there are distinctive, sometimes opposing, differences among them. So even though I will be using the terms "liberative" or "liberation" and "pluralist" or "pluralism" in order to be understood in the theological conversation, I will also adopt, even prefer, other clarifying, distinguishing designations.

I prefer to call the approach or model I am supporting in this book a *globally responsible, correlational dialogue of religions.* I'll be explaining the nature and need of such a dialogue more expansively in the next chapter, but as an introductory statement of purpose, let me say here that in proposing a model for a "globally responsible" dialogue or theology of religions, I will be urging that religious persons seek to understand and speak with each other on the basis of a common commitment to human and ecological well-being. Global responsibility, therefore, includes the notion of liberation intended by traditional liberation theologians but goes beyond it in seeking not just social justice but eco-human justice and well-being. And it does so aware that such a project, in order truly to attend to the needs of all the globe, must be an effort by the entire globe and all its nations and religions. A globally responsible dialogue is one that is aware that any interfaith encounter is incomplete, perhaps even dangerous, if it does not include a concern for and an attempt to resolve the human and ecological suffering prevalent throughout the globe.

A "correlational" dialogue of religions affirms the plurality of religions, not because plurality is good in itself but because it is a fact of life and the stuff of relationship. A correlational model seeks to promote authentic, truly mutual, dialogical relationships among the religious communities of the world, analogous to the kind of human relationships we seek to nurture among our friends and colleagues. These are relationships in which persons *speak honestly* with each other and *listen authentically.* Far from requiring that everyone be the same, a correlational dialogue presumes that the religions are truly diverse; without genuine diversity, dialogue becomes talking to oneself in the mirror. Participants will witness to what makes them distinct, trying to show and convince others of the values they have found in their traditions. But at the same time, they will be truly, courageously, open to the witness of truth that others make to them. This is a mutual, back and forth, *co-relationship* of speaking and listening, teaching and learning, witnessing and being witnessed to.

For such a correlational dialogue to take place, the dialogical encounter will have to be carried out in an *egalitarian,* not a hierarchical, community. Though all religious participants will speak their mind and make truth claims to each other, none of them will do so from a theological position that claims that theirs is the religion meant to dominate or absorb or stand in judgment over all others. A correlational dialogue cannot begin with one religion claiming to hold all the cards or to be superior in all respects over the others or to have the final norm that will exclude or absorb all other norms. Just as a relationship between two human beings cannot thrive if one of them claims, before the relationship even begins, to be superior or always to have the final word, so too the relationship constitutive of interfaith dialogue is doomed to failure if one religion claims, a priori, general superiority over all others to the extent that it is not willing or able to learn from them.

If women are correct in insisting that life-giving relationships between women and men are impossible in a rigid patriarchy that subordinates women to men, it is also true that a dialogical relationship between religions is impossible in a religious hierarchy that insists that all other religions are to be subordinated to and fulfilled in only one of them. In the dialogue a particular religious belief or practice may be corrected or fulfilled in another, but that will happen *as a result of the dialogue,* not because it is dictated by a theological master plan.

In trying to bring together the voices of the religious and the suffering Others and in mapping out a theology of religions that links global responsibility with religious pluralism, I am furthering the project I laid out back in 1985 in *No Other Name?*. Even though I'm uncomfortable with the term, I am still a pluralist—though a chastened one. Since then, and also since the publication of *The Myth of Christian Uniqueness* (1987), a dark though life-giving cloud of critics has followed the project for a so-called pluralist (I prefer correlational) theology of religions. I hope these pages will make clear that I have tried to take seriously the danger signals or dead-end signs these critics have raised alongside this project's path. I believe that the best way to respond to the many criticisms about the way I am calling religious persons into a correlational dialogue is to include suffering persons and the suffering Earth in that dialogue. As I argued in *One Earth Many Religions,* the most effective way to carry on a correlational dialogue among religions is to make it a globally responsible dialogue.

In supplying the theological maps for such a dialogical journey, this book is still sailing toward the same destination as *No Other Name?*. However, it also brings certain changes in course. In *No Other Name?* I ended up proposing a "non-normative, *theocentric*" approach to dialogue based on the common ground of shared religious experience. To unwrap that theological language: I was seeking a dialogue in which God, and not the church or Jesus, would be in the center and in which Christians would no longer insist that in Jesus they have the only or the final norm for all religious truth; let all religious people come together on the basis of their different experiences of the one Ultimate Reality or God. Having been shaken by the voices of the suffering and by the voices of theological critics both from within Christian communities and the academy, I would like, in this book, to pursue the theological contours of the course I proposed methodologically in *One Earth Many Religions*—a course that can be called a multinormed, *soteriocentric* (that is, salvation-centered) approach to dialogue based on the common ground of global responsibility for eco-human well-being.

Rather than searching for the common God dwelling within different religious communities (since the "indweller" usually turns out to be *my* God), rather than presupposing a common core for all our individually wrapped religious experiences (since we can never really discard the wrappings), I am now following the lead of those who hold up the "salvation" or "well-being" of humans and Earth as the starting point and common ground for our efforts to share and understand our religious experiences and notions of the Ultimately Important. In such a dialogue, especially when suffering and its remedy are at stake and when concrete decisions and actions must be taken, norms are necessary. Religious persons will speak their convictions and make claims regarding what will or will not remove suffering and promote life, about what must or must not be done. But such norms will be multiple, correctable, expandable—and always established within the dialogue. What this means and how this might work I explored in *One Earth Many Religions*. In this book I hope to show that this soteriocentric or globally responsible model for a theology of religions is *not* a rejection, but rather a revision and a reaffirmation, of the "God-centeredness" and "Christ-centeredness" that are essential to the way Christians live and talk about their religious faith.

STILL A MISSIONARY

After reviewing my dialogical odyssey and after formulating what I am about in this book and its predecessor, I have to admit, to myself and to my readers, that in a sense I've come full circle. I'm still a missionary. In the theology contained in this book I have something I want to "preach," something I want to persuade people about—yes, convert them to. Both intellectually and morally I am convinced that I and other religious persons can and must open our minds and our hearts to the many religious Others and the many suffering Others who dwell and toil upon this Earth. Because I believe this deeply, I want others to believe it deeply too. Thus, in this book I will consciously, sometimes unapologetically, be indulging in apologetics, in advocacy, in an agenda. For traditional denizens of the academy, such conduct has been considered a blight on proper scholarly conduct. Research and publication are to be value-free, entirely objective, scrupulously neutral. "The facts, only the facts." Nowadays, I am not alone in recognizing that such value-free objectivity or facts-without-advocacy are *always* impossible and *often* immoral. So I want to be up-front about the values, convictions, and agenda that motivate me.

But, though a missionary, I remain a theologian. My missionary élan will, I intend, always be embodied in and tempered by reasoned and researched arguments showing that what I am urging is consistent with both the tradition of my religious community and the insights and needs of our contemporary context. Fueled sometimes by passion, my case for a globally responsible, correlational theology of religions will also be sustained by reasonability and coherence and by a knowledge of what is going on in the community of scholars. As already noted, my theological and philosophical peers have greeted this so-called pluralist project with a baptism of fire; they have laid bare what they think are its scriptural, doctrinal, cultural, philosophical, even political soft spots and dangers. I would not be honoring their concerns and talents, nor would I be properly carrying on the always communal task of theology, if I did not take these warnings and criticisms seriously and respond to them as adequately as I can. I hope, therefore, that though I am clearly and strongly advocating something in this book, I will also be making a case that will be taken seriously by my theological comrades.

And yet, although I certainly want to speak to and be taken seriously by my theological friends and foes, the main (and bigger) public I want to talk with and be heard by in this book is the many Christian women and men who are struggling to make sense of their religious heritage in a world of so many religious heritages and so many human and ecological problems. I'm master of the obvious in pointing to the many Christians who are painfully engaged in, and often overwhelmed by, the effort to reconcile what they hear and do in their parishes with what they see and feel in the wider world. Among their most tangled questions are the ones dealing with how to put together traditional Christian claims of being the one true (or the best) religion with the apparent truth in other faiths, and how to relate their religious values to sociopolitical issues like poverty or ecological devastation.

I want to address Christians with such concerns. If they can't hear me, and if what I have to say does not elicit some kind of positive (though critical) response, then there's something wrong with the way I'm plying my theological trade. Theologians have to be in fruitful conversation with their theological community, but even more so with their religious community—with what Christians call "the sense of the faithful." So while I'm concerned that this book will be taken seriously at the University of Chicago, I'm even more concerned that it will have something helpful to say to my St. Robert Bellarmine Parish, my base Christian community, and my undergraduate students at Xavier University.

To address successfully my intended diversified audience, I'm going to have to walk a stylistic tightrope. In order to be part of the so-called theological conversation and be understood and taken seriously by my peers, I'm going to have to speak "theolog-ese." A certain amount of technical terminology and jargon will be unavoidable. But

I intend to minimize such theological shop-talk, and when I use it, to explain it. This book may presume some theological interest in the reader, but it does not presume professional theologian status. So while I want to keep the language technically precise, I also want it to be clear and engaging. As for differing opinions and schools within the theological community, certainly I will have to mark off differences and "respond to critics," and so the nonprofessional reader will be invited to join the theological debate. But when the debate takes up academic niceties or bickering, I will try either to avoid it or confine it to footnotes. Over the years, I have grown ever more convinced that we theologians spend too much time talking to ourselves, in a language foreign to most people. We have to discuss the really important issues in a manner and language that will allow non-theologians to understand and have their say. I hope I can do that in this book.

A Preview

A sketchy preview of the coming chapters will provide, I hope, a picture of the main pieces in the theological case I'm trying to argue: that commitment to an authentic, globally responsible dialogue will enable Christians to both revise and reaffirm their understanding of the uniqueness of Jesus and the purpose of the church and its mission.

Chapter 2 will summarize the main reasons—both in cultural awareness and in Christian beliefs—why many Christians feel themselves called to, or are already embarked upon, the kind of approach to other religions that I have termed correlational and globally responsible.

In chapter 3 I want to listen, as carefully as possible, to my fellow Christians and theological colleagues who fear that a "pluralistic" or "correlational" dialogue dilutes Christian belief, undermines personal commitment to Jesus, and erodes missionary vision and zeal. What I have to say in the rest of the book will be carried out in a careful and grateful conversation with these critics.

Chapter 4 opens a discussion of one of the most neuralgic points in the Christian discussion of religious pluralism; it proposes a *revised* christology that has two primary ingredients: it is based upon a practical rather than a literal fidelity to the New Testament witness, and it suggests that for Jesus to be *truly* God's saving revelation, he doesn't have to be God's *only* saving revelation.

Continuing this christological exploration, chapter 5 attempts to make clear that such a revision of our understanding of Jesus is also a *reaffirmation* of his uniqueness. After a discussion of the nature and necessity of our knowledge of the historical Jesus, I try to show that for our contemporary world, Jesus' uniqueness can best be formulated in terms of the master symbol of his message: the Reign of God.

In chapter 6, I draw out the ecclesiological and missiological implications of the christology proposed in the previous two chapters. After suggesting how this kind of christology can sustain Christian piety and discipleship, I summarize and carry forward the recent turn in mission theology from a church-centered to a kingdom-centered understanding of Christian mission.

The book ends, in chapter 7, with a proposal that I think will clarify and strengthen the missionary commitments of Christians: If we take seriously the way dialogue is understood not only in contemporary theology but also in recent Vatican statements, then we can say that the church's mission not only includes but *consists of* dialogue. Mission *is* dialogue. Such a dialogical understanding will allow and enable the Western Christian church to become truly the World church, genuinely incarnated in the cultures beyond the Eurocentric umbrella.

ADDRESSING THE OTHER NAMES

A Correlational, Globally Responsible Theology of Religions

The preceding chapter has traced the basic contours of what we are calling a correlational, globally responsible model for interreligious dialogue. Before we move to the substance of this chapter, I would like to offer a thumbnail sketch of that model. Such a sketch has to include three essential lines: how this model views 1) dialogue, 2) religions, and 3) the world.[1]

A THUMBNAIL SKETCH

1) *Dialogue:* A correlational model presumes—which means it cannot prove rationally—that conversation among members of different religious communities is *possible* and that it is at least *profitable*, if not *necessary.* Contrary to what some religious fundamentalists (in churches) and some postmodern fundamentalists (in universities) hold,[2] this perspective believes—or trusts—that persons from totally different religious ("culturally-linguistic") backgrounds can talk to each other and understand each other sufficiently to make the conversation worthwhile, even enriching, maybe transformative. Any religious person who feels the need, maybe even the necessity, to talk to other religious people will feel at home in this correlational model.

But for the conversation to be good and profitable, it really has to be *correlational*; that is, it has to take place as part of a genuine relationship of equality and respect. That doesn't mean that what each participant has to say is equally true or valid, but that in the conversation all have equal rights and are treated equally. The dialogue has to take place on a level playing field. That means that no one can sit down to the table of dialogue with hidden cards or loaded guns, that is, with claims that will be whipped out and used to announce a God-given absolute truth meant to determine the validity of or absorb all other truths. Certainly in the dialogue, claims will be made, and some of them might have to exclude others, but that will take place *within* and as the *result of* dialogue, not as a divinely pre-established ordinance. Relationship is impossible when one side has the a priori conviction that it is fundamentally superior to and dominant over the other.

Yet in a real co-relationship of religions, participants are called upon to speak their minds. For the relationship to be vibrant and productive, religious persons participating in dialogue have to be fully who they are—believers, persons who are convinced and committed to what they hold to be true and good. So, in their conversation with other believers, they have to speak boldly and witness enthusiastically; otherwise, the dialogue is bloodless. But the vigor with which they speak must be matched by the humility with which they listen. In a correlational dialogue, the yin of speaking has to circulate with the yang of listening; one has to be as committed to receiving truth as one is to delivering it. To be as ready to be persuaded as one is to persuade is both the difficulty and the richness of a truly correlational dialogue.

2) *Religions:* To be able to function, a correlational dialogue has to presume that there can be, and most likely are, many true religions. If there were only one true religion, then a correlational dialogue between given religions would be neither possible nor worth one's time and energy; instead of being correlational, the dialogue would be either excluding (intent on removing the false religions) or including (absorbing the false or incomplete religions into the one true religion). For the dialogue to be a two-way or co-relationship rather than a one-way or top-down relationship, all the participants have to believe that they can learn something, that is, that there is, or can be, truth on both sides. (Whether they *do* learn something or whether there *is* truth on both sides can be known only in the dialogue.)

But in affirming that there can be many *true* religions, the correlational model does not want to collapse or contort the *many* religions. The possibility, or the fact, that many religions share truth does not in any way remove the equally important fact that they share in this truth in *very different ways.* Contrary to what is generally thought, in a correlational model for calling religions to dialogue, differences are maintained, recognized, cherished; they are not boiled away in order to create some kind of common religious soup. Differences among religions are affirmed and guarded not simply because, as anyone who has studied the world of religions will confirm, that's the way things are, but also because differences are the stuff of dialogue. If religious differences are submerged into some kind of common essence or common mystical experience, all one can do in dialogue is swim around in a pool of common essence or experience and yet never get beyond the borders of the pool.

In affirming real differences, correlationalists are convinced—or better, they hope—that although such differences can sometimes be at loggerheads, they also, and for the most part, can be complementary. Again, one must be careful not to think that such a statement buries differences under complementarity. Rather, there is real complementarity *because* there are real differences. But the otherness existing between the differences is experienced as a communicative otherness; difference speaks to difference, other to other—and it's good! Correlationalists believe that even in the case of apparently incommensurable differences between two religions, if these differences are transformative and life-giving for their practitioners, then the differences cannot be totally alien to each other. If the Buddhist is transformed into a person more at peace with himself and others through the image of *no-self,* and if the Christian is similarly transformed though her experience of being a *new-self* in Christ Jesus, the evident contradiction between no-self and new-self must, in some way, be complementary; the Buddhist and Christian can speak and share, and be better off for doing so.

In affirming the reality and the incorrigibility of differences between the religions, the correlational model agrees with the postmodern reminder that there simply does not exist any universal (or "meta-religious") standpoint from which one can stand outside the different religions in order to look down on and evaluate them all. There's no one mountain top to which all religions lead and from which one can understand and assess them all (no matter how many Ph.D.s in religious mountain climbing one may have!). We are always looking out over the valley of religions from a *particular* elevation or standpoint. And that particularity will always limit our view and keep it from ultimate universality. But where the correlational model differs (incommensurably!) from many postmodern perspectives is in its understanding of the particular standpoint. Standpoints are not isolating; they do not lock us in a cultural-linguistic prison. Rather, with a trust built on the experience of conversation, correlationalists believe that our particular standpoints do not condemn us to silence but enable us to speak *and* to listen to persons at other standpoints. Particularity does not exclude universality; we are particular in order that we might reach out beyond particularity and connect with others. To deny that possibility is to balkanize humanity.

But this dialogical movement from particularity toward universality—toward ever better connectedness—will never be fully and finally achieved. We can never shake loose our particularity. And therefore, although through dialogue we may be able to see more and to connect better with others, we will never be able to see and say it all. Every new insight or every new "universal" connection will still be dressed in particularity. As Alfred North Whitehead put it succinctly: "The many become one, and are increased by one" (Whitehead 1957, 26). This means, practically, that in the dialogue and in the connections that we make and delight in, we will never be able to arrive at *the* universal. No matter how convincing and satisfying and transforming our "truth" may be, there is always more to learn. This is a "condition for the possibility" of a correlational dialogue of religions—that all the participants admit to themselves and each other that no matter how sure they are of what they know, there is always more to know. The possibility of learning something new in conversation with others is *always* real. To deny that is to make our particularities not only boring but dangerous.

3) *The world:* The correlational model links its understanding of religions to a particular understanding or sense of the world. This sense of the world will be described in greater detail below, so here I can state it simply and succinctly: the world is in dire need, and religions have a responsibility to respond to that need. The need surges forth, painfully and implacably, from the reality of pervasive and unnecessary suffering, both human and ecological. Such suffering is life-threatening for both individual sentient beings and for the entire ecosystem. If "salvation" or "enlightenment" or "walking the straight path" means anything among the religious traditions, it must have something to contribute to dealing with this suffering. By virtue of the world we live in and of what can be found within the scriptures and teachings of most (if not all) religions, religions do have a global responsibility to address global needs.[3]

Therefore, a model for developing a dialogue of religions must be not only correlational, enabling genuine conversation between religious persons; it must also be globally responsible: the content of the conversation has to include, in some way and to some degree, the suffering and needs of our world. Indeed, as I stated in the previous chapter, the model I am proposing urges that the best way for religions to be correlational is to be globally responsible.

CONSTRUCTING A THEOLOGY OF RELIGIONS

In the rest of this chapter I want to lay out the reasons why I, and a goodly number of other Christians, are finding that the model I have just sketched for understanding religions is becoming not only a viable option but a persistent imperative. In other words, this chapter attempts to assemble the main pieces of a *theological* foundation for a correlational, globally responsible Christian dialogue with other religious communities. I want to show that such a dialogue rests on sound theological supports. To do that, we must first ask where one can find the materials to build such supports. What are the sources for any Christian theology?

Theologians today speak of *two* sources for theology: contemporary *human experience* as mediated through historical context or culture, and the *Christian tradition* as it has been formulated in the New Testament and passed on through Christian teaching and practice (Tracy 1975). By appealing to both sources—experience and tradition, or culture and the Christian religion—I hope to show how this correlational, globally responsible model for a theology of religions is both *adequate* or responsive to our present-day realities and challenges, and also *appropriate* or consistent with the Christian witness (Ogden 1972). In chapter 4 I will say more about just how this interplay between experience and tradition works in the area of christology.

There are, in other words, both *cultural* and *inner-Christian* reasons why, in the words of David Tracy, a mounting number of Christians are coming to the conviction that "some envisionment of radical religious pluralism . . . [is] a live option" (Tracy 1986) and that "in any attempt to honor the pluralism of religions through genuine conversation . . . we cannot retreat from the praxis concerns [i.e., global responsibility] which impinge upon all religions in all situations" (Tracy 1987b, 145). Because of what they see in the world and what they hear in the gospel, Christians are searching, in seems to me, for a correlational, globally responsible way of relating to persons of other faiths.

CULTURAL SUPPORTS FOR
A CORRELATIONAL, GLOBALLY RESPONSIBLE MODEL

I'm going to try to describe my experience of what is going on in our present-day world in a way that will reflect how others, at least in Western cultures, are also experiencing it. If this is the way many Christians see and feel the world whirling around them, as I think they do, then something like a correlational, globally responsible theology of religions will make eminent, perhaps imperative, sense. I will describe my view of this "common experience" in terms of common awarenesses.

AWARENESS OF OTHERS

The awareness I am speaking about here is the kind I tried to describe in my own experience in the previous chapter—a personal, existential awareness of the other. By "existential" I mean experiences that we register in our feelings, our heart, our sensitivities—experiences that provide us with reasons for action or insight that goes beyond reason. I think most readers can identify in their own lives what I am talking about: to feel the beauty, authenticity, power, inspiration—yes, the truth—of another religious tradition embodied, not in a book or film, but in the person of a friend or colleague can touch us in the depths of our own religious identity. Through such encounters, the depths of who we are as humans and Christians are touched and challenged.

To so stand before the beauty and power of another tradition does not necessarily call into question our own religious truth, but it does necessarily announce the limitations of our truth. In sharing an office, dinner table, school program, maybe even a marital bed with a person who is a committed follower of another religious path, and to witness how that following has enriched and transformed that person's life—in view of such existential relationships, we cannot, we simply cannot, continue with the traditional Christian assertions that ours is the only true religion, not even with the modified claims that our religion is the final word for theirs, meant for their fulfillment. Whatever the theology or scriptural foundations for such traditional claims, we *feel* that they cannot be right, for they are a personal and therefore a real offense to the colleague, friend, spouse whom we know in his or her unique human and religious identity.

This is how the reality of religious pluralism has invaded, exploded, and transformed the religious world of many of us—through the eyes and voice and touch of a religious other who is part of our lives. I have explained this reality as a Westerner, a member of a culture that is predominantly Christian. What I have described as a new experience of the other is, in countries like India and Sri Lanka, the way things have always been. As I was told again and again by Indian Christians, in India—especially before power-lusting politicians began exploiting religion to promote communalism or factionalism—Hindus, Muslims, and Christians have had to live together, to form and grasp their religious consciousness in relation to each other. That "my truth" cannot be the "only truth" has long been part of the Indian religious subconscious. Here the West is catching up as the plurality of religious truth invades and reshapes its consciousness.

This expanding consciousness of religious pluralism, mediated existentially through personal encounters, has also alerted us to the dark side of ours and other religions—to the corruption, ugliness, and manipulative and exploitative power of religion. Still, it seems that Edward Schillebeeckx is right when he concludes that given the way people experience their world today, pluralism has become a "cognitive reality"—part of the way we perceive ourselves and our world. We are "beings with divergent possibilities" (Schillebeeckx 1990, 50). To say that ours is the only possibility for grasping religious truth is, in Schillbeeckx's view, to live in a "time warp" (ibid., 51). "The unshaken certainty that one continues to possess the truth oneself while others are mistaken is no longer a possibility. So pluralism is not just institutional; pluralism is to be found within us as cognitive reality" (ibid.).

Therefore, pluralism is now sensed to be not just a "matter of fact" but a "matter of principle"—the way things are supposed to be. "Logically and practically, multiplicity now takes priority over unity . . . the multiplicity of religions is not an evil which needs to be removed, but rather a wealth which is to be welcomed and enjoyed by all" (ibid., 163, 167). To relate this existential intuition to the world of biology, Klaus Klostermaier concludes "that differences in religions are not only an empirical fact but perhaps necessary for their mutual good. An environment with too few species is ecologically unstable. Lack of extra-specific pressures on further progressive development induces regression and produces a suicidal intra-specific competition. If religions are truly alive, they also follow the laws of living organisms." Religions must live with, interact with, learn from each other (Klostermaier 1991, 60-61).

Schillebeeckx, wise and cautious from years of theological give-and-take, can draw the daunting conclusion that many Christians feel but hesitate to state: "There is more religious truth in all the religions together than in one particular religion . . . This also applies to Christianity" (Schillebeeckx 1990, 166). Schillebeeckx, like many Christians, has affirmed the pluralist option.

AWARENESS OF HISTORY

The personal-existential consciousness that there are *many* religions leads to, or is reflected by, the historical consciousness that all of them are *limited*. This is one of the most compelling and clear paths toward a pluralist-correlational view of other religions. Historical consciousness, simply and yet disturbingly, is the awareness that insofar as every existing reality is historical, it is limited. We are caught in our historical context—that doesn't mean confined by it, but it does mean influenced and therefore limited by it.

Why? Because every piece of knowledge that we acquire, every truth that we profess, is always, unavoidably, *interpreted*. There is no such thing, we know today, as factual knowledge; it is always interpreted knowledge. Facts in themselves don't exist; only interpretations of facts do. But because knowledge is always interpreted, the interpretation will always come out of the particular historical situation we are in. We read the world through the glasses history gives us; that means through one, limited, changing vantage point.

So theologians like Langdon Gilkey remind Christians of what they probably already know: in order to preserve their integrity, they must accept *theologically* what they have long accepted *culturally*. Given the context-conditioned, "theory-laden," socially-constructed interpretative limitations of every grasp and statement of truth, and given also the ever-changing, always-confining flow of history, Christians (and all religious persons) have to admit honestly that within our human condition, there can be no final word, no one way of knowing truth that is valid for all times and all peoples. In Gilkey's confession: "No cultural logos is final and so universal (even one based on science); no one revelation is or can be the universal criterion for all the others (even, so we are now seeing, one based on Christian revelation)" (Gilkey 1987, 48).

The sobering, even frightening, implications of historical consciousness that were first described by philosophers and cultural analysts such as Nietzsche, Heidegger, and Troeltsch have gradually seeped into the mind-set of the Western world. Cultural anthropologists, perhaps the fiercest proponents of historical consciousness, generally recognize that a cultural system can be judged successful not on the basis of any universal principle but only if it is functionally viable in its immediate domain. According to literary theory, strongly influenced by the deconstructionist claims of Derrida, one no longer seeks after the inherent meaning of a text that was given once and for all by the author in his or her context; rather than a central logos or meaning in a text, there is a kaleidoscopic interplay of meanings to which we have to abandon ourselves in order to understand the text. Among contemporary philosophers, historical consciousness has been embraced and expanded into what can be termed the school of "anti-foundationalism." Philosophers such as Richard Rorty and Richard Bernstein challenge us to face the fact that there is no one center for the quest for meaning, no one, unchanging foundation on which we can stand and draw our sustenance. Rather, we must bravely cast out into the deep of a multiplicity of constantly changing points of view, casting anchor where we can but realizing that we will have to hoist it tomorrow and continue the voyage.

To a great extent theology has accepted and absorbed this historical consciousness. Two of the most influential theologians during the '80s have clearly given voice to a historical consciousness that recognizes the inherent limitation of all truth and all cultural systems. (Each, however, responds to or acts out of this consciousness very differently!) George Lindbeck in *The Nature of Doctrine* (1984) and David Tracy in both *The Analogical Imagination* (1981) and *Plurality and Ambiguity* (1987a) remind their fellow Christians that to think that they have a fixed source of truth, an unchanging criterion they can apply in all cultural situations in order to decide what is true or good, a foundation that transcends the process and pluralism of history, is to fly in the face of reality, to lust after the unreal. There is no fixed place of truth outside the fray of historical process and continuous dialogue (see also Omann 1986), which means that Christianity is one of the *many, limited* religions of the world.[4]

AWARENESS OF THE MORAL IMPERATIVE OF DIALOGUE

For many Christians, a pluralist-correlational model for understanding and approaching followers of other religious paths is not just a challenge stemming from their personal-existential experience, not just an intellectual conclusion from their historical consciousness; it is also an obligation based on their ethical or moral responsibility. It's a matter of conscience. Their conscience speaks to them from two sharply felt realizations: that interreligious dialogue is itself a moral imperative, and that previous Christian attitudes impede such dialogue, whereas a correlational model seems to foster it.

David Lochhead speaks of "the dialogical imperative" (Lochhead 1988). The term reflects both the popular and the philosophical awareness that unless we enter into genuine dialogue or conversations with those who are different from us, we are, individually and socially, lost. The foundations for this awareness are found in what we have said already about personal and historical consciousness. We have realized that there are many expressions or manifestations of truth, not just one. Therefore, as Schillebeeckx observed, we are going to find more truth by opening ourselves to the many than by staying locked in the "security" of our own house. From another perspective, we realize that these many expressions of the truth are not just limited and imperfect; they are also valuable, good, maybe even necessary for us. In other words, every historical expression of the truth is *sadly limited* but *happily related*. We can overcome our *limitations* through *relations*; that is, by opening ourselves to and entering into a conversation with the many. Thus, if we are serious about our pursuit of the truth, we *must* talk with others. Conversation becomes an ethical imperative. "Dialogue among the religions is no longer a luxury but a theological necessity" (Tracy 1990, 95).

This imperative is an expression of what philosophers might call the conversational or dialogical nature of truth. Truth is the result of communicative praxis (Habermas 1979, 1984; Tracy 1987a). If we are not talking and listening to others, we are not learning. Dialogue becomes the escape from or solution to the inherent limitations of our own viewpoint. Through conversation with the genuinely other, we can expand or correct the truth that we have. Our efforts to know the truth, therefore, must be both *critical* and *corporate*: critical in that they have to be based on our own efforts to experience, to understand, and to judge (following Bernard Lonergan's steps of critical consciousness) (Lonergan 1973, 3-25), and corporate in that they are carried out together with other people who are also trying to experience, understand, and judge the truth (see W. C. Smith 1981, 94ff.).

If truth is corporate, dialogical, conversational, then it is much more a shared search and journey than an individual discovery and possession. Yes, we discover what is good and true and beautiful, but it is never once and for all, never the last word, and never just our own experience. In the words of Charles Sanders Peirce, our searching journey is carried forward by a trusting to "the multitude and variety of arguments rather than to the conclusiveness of any one" (in Bernstein 1983, 224).

To find our own truth, therefore, we must dialogue with the truth of others. But we can also say that *to be protected from our own truth*, we must dialogue with the truth of others. Thanks to the criticisms of religion and of culture that have come from the so-called "masters of suspicion" (Nietzsche, Freud, Marx), as well as from the waxing voices of women and other oppressed groups, today we are more clearly and uncomfortably aware of how much the worm of *ideology* can eat into the beautiful fruits of truth that we have stored in our cultural and religious heritages. Ideology is the prevalent, really unavoidable, tendency that we all have to use our "truth" as a means to promote our own welfare (economic or societal) at the cost of others, or to use our own advantage or prestige as the subconscious criterion for determining what truth is.

When preachers proclaim that our place in heaven will be higher if we have suffered much on this Earth, is that what they really find in the scriptures or is it because such a message keeps the masses happy while exploited and the preachers well paid by the lords or landowners? When Catholic theologians or bishops insist that Jesus wants only men to be his ministers, is that the result of a critical study of the New Testament or a subconscious desire to maintain their own power? For whatever reason (original sin? ignorance?) we bear the irresistible proclivity to use our truth as a means to promote ourselves or manipulate others. As Walter Benjamin has said, "Every work of civilization [we could add, every work of religion] is at the same time a work of barbarism" (in Tracy 1987a, 69).

We cannot preserve ourselves from this barbarous or self-indulgent abuse of our own truth. Just as we need someone else to tell us when our breath is bad, so we need others to tell us when our religious truth has become ideological abuse. We need conversation with others; we need to open ourselves to the views of others who see the world differently than we do, who can therefore look at our truth differently and tell us not only what it looks like but how it *affects* them. Perhaps they will even point out how our truth has excluded, demeaned, or exploited them. Alone, in our own backyard, we cannot recognize the distortions of our own truth. Max Müller has said of religions that to know only one is to know none. We can join his dictum to Walter Benjamin's insight and let it read: to know only one religion is to turn it into a work of barbarism. So, once again, dialogue becomes a moral imperative.

What are the requirements of this imperative? What do we have to do in order truly to dialogue with another religion? Much has been written on the nature, method, and prerequisites of dialogue (see Swidler's "Dialogue Decalogue" in Swidler 1990, 42-46; Knitter 1985, 207-13; Knitter 1990a, 19-25). One of the crispest statements of the rules for effective conversation comes from David Tracy:

> Conversation is a game with some hard rules: say only what you mean; say it as accurately as you can; listen to and respect what the other says, however different or other; be willing to correct or defend your opinions if challenged by the conversation part- ner; be willing to argue if necessary, to confront if demanded, to endure necessary conflict, to change your mind if the evidence suggests it (Tracy 1987a, 19).

It is precisely in trying to follow these rules that many feel the clash between the dialogical imperative and traditional exclusivist or inclusivist Christian models for approaching other religions. How can one genuinely "respect" the possible truth in another's views, espe- cially, how can one be "willing to correct" one's own opinions and "change" one's mind—how can one really *hear*, much less be taught by the dialogue partner *if* one enters the dialogue convinced of having God's exclusive truth, or final word, or all-inclusive criterion for truth? (Of course, this applies as much to Hindus and Buddhists as to Christians.)

No matter how much I acclaim your merits and my desire to learn from them, if I am pre-convinced that your truth is meritorious only insofar as it is included and fulfilled by mine, then such a dialogue, as others have observed, is bound to end up as a dialogue between the cat and the mouse (Maurier 1976, 69-70). No matter how finely and pleasantly I dress it up, my "final word" either negates or subordi- nates your word. The mouse ends up "fulfilled" when "included" in the cat! Absolute revelations and final norms, therefore, seem to be an impediment to the moral imperative of dialogue. What prevents moral conduct is open to the suspicion of being itself immoral.

Please understand what is being said here. I am not denying that it is important, even necessary, for each partner to enter the dialogue with firm positions, with universal claims, with the deeply felt con- viction that his or her perspective on a given issue is better than others. Such is the stuff of dialogue, which keeps it from decompos- ing into chit-chat or mere exchange of information. But there is a difference, a decisive difference, between speaking out of deeply felt and divinely guided convictions, on the one hand, and speaking out of a God-given final revelation, on the other. In the first case I am, at least theoretically, open to criticism and change; in the second in- stance, if I budge I'm being unfaithful to God. "Privileged" with God's final, unsurpassable revelation, Christians have all too often been unbudgeable.

Not only have they been unbudgeable, they've been downright nasty. Not only have Christians, armed with God's final word, been unable to dialogue; they all too often have felt, consciously or unconsciously, entitled or obliged either to stamp out or "make use of" the contents of other religions. This is one of the most unsettling ethical reasons why many people within the Christian churches are uncomfortable with what they have been traditionally taught about the superiority of God's revelation in Christ: it has condoned, if not caused, an attitude of God-granted superiority that has led, all too frequently, to acts of imperialism, ethnocentrism, and exploitation over other cultures and religions. Certainly we don't want to blame all the colonial and imperial sins of the West on traditional Christian theology of religions, but neither can we deny the links (Hick 1987 and Ruether 1987, 141). Some feminists have observed that just as holding up male experience as the universal, focal norm for what it means to be human has led to the patriarchal subordination of women in most societies, so the holding up of Christ and Christianity as the universal, final norm for what it means to know and serve God has led to the imperialistic subordination of other religions (Suchocki 1987, 149-51).

For this reason, Christian missioners decry the "crypto-colonialism" of contemporary inclusivist theologies of other religions. The inclusivists' generous openness to other religions veils a lingering "better-than-thou" attitude and has been one of the main reasons for lack of missionary success. Our "crypto-colonialist theory of religions . . . keeps our [Christian] revolutionary rhetoric from resonating in the hearts of the Third-World non-Christian majorities," Sri Lankan Aloysius Pieris tells us (Pieris 1988a, 88; see Puthiadam 1980, 103-5). Because we have not genuinely dialogued, we have not genuinely witnessed.

The correlational model for dialogue I am proposing, with its openness to the truth in other religious cultures, with its view of religions as inherently in need of each other, and with its understanding of truth as many-faceted and in movement, would seem to respond to the ethical inadequacies of the earlier exclusive or inclusive perspectives. If dialogue is an imperative, so is something like the correlational model.

Awareness of Responsibility for the World

A final ingredient in the contemporary awareness of many Christians (and of many religious persons) gives the pluralist model we're talking about its *liberative* or globally responsible orientation. Such awareness can be called cosmological. "Political" might have been another fitting adjective, but "cosmological" connotes the necessary breadth of what I mean. Thanks to the Enlightenment, thanks to modern science, thanks to both the successes and the breakdowns of our technological age, thanks also to the critics of manipulative religion, there is an increasingly clear, even compelling, realization among Earth dwellers that 1) we are vitally and decisively responsible for the welfare of our world, and 2) the resolution of the crises draining the lifeblood and life-spirit of humans and the planet constitutes the number one item on the human agenda.

Let me speak for myself, though I know I am speaking for many. I feel deeply that in all the "important" things I do, I must at the same time be doing something to overcome the life-threatening problems of hunger, inhuman living conditions, ecological devastation—and the injustice that feeds these monsters. I cannot go about life as usual—family, education, theology, recreation, travel—unless somehow, in different ways in different situations, I am aware of and addressing the threatened state of the world. Yes, I need distractions, I need balance in my activities and concerns, but if these distractions or this balance diverts me from my responsibility for the world, then I cannot continue with them.

Juan Segundo calls what I am talking about an "anthropological faith," which we find given in our human condition and awareness, prior to—or better, more basic than—our religious faith and convictions (Segundo 1984, 60-66). I prefer to call it cosmological faith: our fundamental commitment, animated by an often inexplicable hope, to overcome what threatens and to advance what promotes human and ecological well-being. Such cosmological faith need not have an explicit religious basis. Humanists will experience it as the responsibility and calling they feel when they realize that evolution has reached a point where we now must play a key role. The entire evolutionary process on Earth will be impeded, or at least set back, unless we humans exercise our intelligence and our freedom responsibly and morally. The process of natural evolution will not do it for us, or despite us.

Religious people feel this cosmological faith as God's call to and God's need of our cooperation. The Divine Source of life, who is the "within" and the "ahead" of the cosmogenesis we are part of, will not take over for us. As much as religious people feel the need to experience the sustaining, hope-giving presence of the Divine, they also know that in some real sense the Divine must be "aided" by them. Raimon Panikkar has spoken of this experience and awareness as the "theanthropocosmic" Mystery—the vital, sustaining, interdependent, growing unity between the Divine (*theos*), the Human (*anthropos*) and the World (*cosmos*) (Panikkar 1993).

This cosmological awareness or faith both calls people to interreligious dialogue and makes them critical of it. Such faith functions as a *basic criterion* for religion in general. Simply and starkly stated, it tells, and warns, people that authentic religion—religion coming from its divine or transcendent source—will promote the well-being of humanity and the Earth. How do I know that? By faith. I just know it. I feel it. As Luther would put it, here I stand, I cannot do or say other-wise.[5] Yes, such faith or awareness is the result of my cultural condi-tioning, of my social status as a white, middle-class male, of my edu-cation, of my ability to travel; yes, it comes from my commitment to Jesus Christ. It is all of these things together and yet not any one of them individually.

More generally, or more deeply, I can say that this cosmological faith is the result of my efforts *to be human* in the world as I find it; as a religious person, I add that it results from the way the Spirit is touch-ing people in our threatened global world. It is a faith mediated and specified through my historico-cultural-religious context, but it is a faith, I feel, that has its roots in my humanity. Thus it is a faith that I can share with others—I dare say, with all others, if we keep talking and acting together.

Such a cosmological faith is foundational to the correlational, glo-bally responsible approach to dialogue and theology that this book is exploring. Such an approach understands and evaluates both religion and dialogue according to the criterion of this cosmological faith-awareness. According to this criterion, just as I would have to say that a religion that does not promote eco-human well-being (or, a fortiori works against it!) is not from God, so I must say that a dialogue that is not in some way concerned with addressing ecological and human suffering cannot be from God. Not that such concern must be a part of every single religious or dialogical activity; still, it must be present within the context, motivation, and ultimate goals of such activity. If it is not, then persons claimed by a cosmological faith will have seri-ous reservations, to say the least, about participating in such dialogue.

CHRISTIAN SUPPORTS FOR
A CORRELATIONAL, GLOBALLY RESPONSIBLE MODEL

If it is always difficult and dangerous to try to identify what is common in human-cultural experience, it is perhaps even more so when one attempts to locate what is common in Christian experience. But let me try. I do so not only because this is something that is part of a theologian's job description, but also because I do think that there are many common characteristics in the way Christians are hearing and living the gospel that are nudging or compelling them in the direc-tion of a correlational theology of religions.

DOCTRINAL INCENTIVES: THE NATURE OF GOD
Together with a number of my theological colleagues, I would like to suggest that the way we Christians have come to experience and

know God through Jesus Christ would nudge, if not push, us in the direction of a pluralistic theology of religions. The nudge comes from two essential characteristics of the Christian God: mysterious and trinitarian.

Historical consciousness, which warns us that all human knowledge is limited, has a flip-side in religious consciousness, which admonishes us that Divine Reality is unlimited. In other words, if historical consciousness tells us that every human grasp of truth is intrinsically finite and conditioned, religious consciousness—the fruit of religious experience—tells us even more assuredly that Divine Reality and Truth is, by its very nature, always more than any human can grasp or any religion can express. This realization is inherent in any authentic religious experience—the paradoxical sense that my particular, historical encounter with God is as mysterious as it is real, as ambiguous as it is reliable. The mystics and thinkers who have sensed and urged this recognition of God as utter Mystery populate the train of Christian tradition—Paul, Aquinas, Julian of Norwich, Eckhart, Luther—and one of the most recent witnesses to Mystery, especially in the last decade of his life, Karl Rahner (Rahner 1966b; 1978b).

Some concerned Christians might respond that this very Mystery of God has been revealed or made real in the *incarnation* of Jesus. Precisely! The Mystery has been *revealed* in Jesus, *not removed* or resolved. I suspect that Christian talk of the incarnation as "God in human form" or the "fullness" of Mystery in a historical being tends to violate the meaning of the incarnation more than preserve it. To say that all of the person of Jesus is divinized does not mean that all of divinity is humanized. Or stated positively, to say that divinity is made incarnate in Jesus means that God has taken on all that constitutes being human—and that includes being localized, particularized, and limited. If Jesus, as the incarnation of the Second Person, defines who God is, he does not confine who God is. Not to accept the limitations of the incarnation is to fall, implicitly but certainly, into a form of docetism—the heresy that so stressed the divinity of Jesus that it maimed and denatured his humanity. In fact, truly to comprehend and accept the reality of the incarnation in Jesus is to recognize that God cannot be limited to Jesus; divinity, while truly available in Jesus, is to be found beyond Jesus. In the words of Schillebeeckx, who has devoted his theological career to exploring the mystery of Jesus Christ:

> The revelation of God in Jesus, as the Christian gospel proclaims it, does not mean that God absolutizes a historical particularity (be it even Jesus of Nazareth). From that revelation in Jesus we learn that no single historical particularity can be called absolute and that therefore, because of the relativity present in Jesus,

every person can encounter God outside of Jesus, especially in our worldly history and in the many religions that have arisen from it (Schillebeeckx 1990, 184).

To recognize God, in Rahner's terms, as *schlechthinniges Geheimnis*—"absolute Mystery" (Rahner 1966)—requires us also to recognize that no religion and no revelation can be the only or the final or the exclusive or the inclusive Word of God. Such a final Word would limit and demystify God. But that, as Wilfred Cantwell Smith points out, is what we call idolatry. And so he gently reminds his fellow Christians that idolatry is a word that perhaps is much more applicable to Christianity than to its usual object: heathen religions. In reality, an idol is not something that mediates Deity—like a statue or a stone—but something that confines and limits Deity, like a magisterium or a book claimed to be the only or the final mediation of God (Smith 1987a). "Idolatry is the insistence that there is only one way, one norm, one truth. It is the refusal to be corrected or informed by the 'other'" (Driver 1987, 216).

This admission that the Mystery of God cannot be held by any one religion or revelation or savior becomes all the more demanding when one ponders, as many pluralist Christians do, that this Mystery is not simply one but *plural*! This is the deeper content of the Christian experience and doctrine of the Trinity: Deity is not only one but many. God is plural. If this is true of God *ad intra* (within the divine nature), it is also true of God's reality and creation *ad extra* (in God's external activity). God needs manyness to be God. Tom Driver is eloquent in describing what this means: "In pluralist perspective, it is not simply that God has one nature variously and inadequately expressed by different religious traditions. It is that there are real and genuine differences within the Godhead itself, owing to the manifold involvements which God has undertaken with the great variety of human communities" (Driver 1987, 212). Plurality is essential to all reality—from atoms to religions.

Panikkar states it clearly and pointedly: "The mystery of the Trinity is the ultimate foundation for pluralism . . . reality itself is pluralistic" (Panikkar 1987, 110). Therefore, just as God cannot be reduced to a unity that would remove eradicable differences among the three divine persons, can we also say that the world of religions cannot be reduced to the kind of unity that would do away with the real differences among the various traditions? This is not an air-tight logical argument but an indication based on analogy.

ETHICAL INCENTIVES: THE FIRST COMMANDMENT

If God's love *is* unbounded, ours *ought* to be. We are called upon to love each other as God loves us. This is, for Christians, the *first com-*

mandment—which means that this commandment takes priority over all other commandments in all aspects of life. It also means that, in situations where one has to choose, loving one's neighbor takes a prior place to proclaiming true doctrine or to formally worshiping God. No matter how important, even essential, orthodoxy and liturgy are, they cannot be made more important than loving our neighbor. We know the biblical images and refrains: *first* work things out with your alienated brother and sister, *then* go to church (Mt 5:23-24). Don't let the Sabbath observance, with its professions of faith and sacrifices, get in the way of doing good to your neighbor; better "break" the sabbath (offend God!) than fail in loving your neighbor (Mt 12:12).

In light of the primary, foundational role that love of neighbor plays in Christian life, I don't think I am alone in sensing that there is something wrong with traditional Christian views of other religions. I experience a painful tension, if not clash, between my desire and my obligation to love my neighbors in other faiths and the way traditional Christian theology has instructed me to look upon them and treat them. What, after all, does love mean? To love others means to respect them, to honor them, to listen to them with an authentic openness to what they are saying. It means to treat them as we would want them to treat us. It means to listen to them and their witness to truth as we would want them to listen to us and our witness. Yes, this means that I have to confront them when I think they are wrong, but I also have to be authentically ready to be so confronted by them. In other words, to love my neighbors I must be able truly to dialogue with them.

Yet previous Christian attitudes toward other believers—both the exclusive and inclusive models—seem to be obstacles to treating these neighbors in this way, and thus to loving them. Can we respect and be open to them when, before we even meet them, we must believe that our truth is better than theirs or that they are inferior to us in what they hold to be true and sacred? Can we affirm and love them when we are convinced, with a God-sanctioned surety, that they will have to agree with our truth if they are ever going to arrive at the fullness of God's truth? Whenever we hold up a truth or a revelation and insist that according to the will of God it is the only or the absolutely final norm in which all others have to be included, then we cannot treat them as our brothers and sisters in God. Such a norm does enable us to confront them, as love sometimes requires, but it does not allow us to be confronted *by* them, as love also requires. Whenever we are not disposed to learn as much from our neighbors as they can from us, we cannot love them. We may help them, we may build hospitals and schools for them, we may lift them from their poverty—but we are not loving them.

I think there is a growing awareness among many Christians of a discrepancy between their doctrine and their ethics—between the view of the other given by their beliefs and the conduct toward the other required by their ethics. It is a clash between orthodoxy—right beliefs—and orthopraxy—right behavior. Stating this same clash between doctrine and ethics somewhat differently, I suggest that many Christians are experiencing a tension, if not a contradiction, between the first commandment and the last commandment (or, final commission) of their faith. While Jesus instructed his followers to love their neighbors as themselves, he also gave them the last instruction to go forth into the whole world and make his message known. Christians are called upon to love their neighbors *and* to preach to them and make disciples of them. It seems that, for whatever reasons, Christians have made this final commission more important than, or the criterion of, the first commandment. In the way they have gone about preaching and making disciples, they have all too often not loved their neighbors. Given the exclusivistic or the inclusivistic understandings of *why* they must preach and make disciples, they have frequently not respected, listened to, or sought to affirm their neighbors in other religions as the nature of love requires.

There is a clash, then, between first commandment and last commandment, between ethics and doctrine, between orthopraxy and orthodoxy. But given the priority of the orthopraxy of loving one's neighbor over the orthodoxy of traditional theologies of religions, I suggest that the doctrines, the traditional exclusive or inclusive models for understanding the final commission, must be reviewed and revised. That is what the correlational or pluralistic model for a theology of religions is seeking to do.

SCRIPTURAL INCENTIVES: BALANCING THE UNIVERSAL AND THE PARTICULAR

The Bible also figures among the incentives and paths for a correlational theology of religions. But when I say this, I must admit that Sacred Scripture has not been a primary or original doorway to this new view of other faiths. Rather, as has generally been the case with the churches' use of scripture, pressures coming from outside—the cultural foundations we reviewed earlier—have provided Christians with new questions by which to explore, hear, understand, and submit to the Word of God. It's a new turn of the hermeneutical circle, of the ever-new effort to interpret the scriptures: new experiences in new contexts provide new opportunities to question and be questioned by God's Word.

In trying to summarize how so-called pluralist theologians of religions are treading this hermeneutical circle, I can offer here only some general perspectives or approaches, most of which will be expanded in subsequent chapters. I think the richest aspect of the biblical witness, which will not only allow but will require Christians to embrace a more correlational view of other believers, can be found in the pervasive and creative tension in the Bible between *the universal* and *the particular*.

One of the most salient and distinctive features of the Abrahamic religions—Judaism, Christianity, and Islam—is the way they discover and maintain their identities around *particular* events or persons. The God of Abraham, Jesus, and Muhammad is a God of history, a God who does particular things in particular situations. This God chooses a concrete people in order to carry out the divine plan for all nations; this same God actually takes flesh in a particular human being in order to bring salvation to all; and this God later finds voice through a particular Arab merchant and through a particular Holy Book resulting from his visions in order to make of all peoples one community. If the concrete particularity of the people of Israel, of the person and message of Jesus, of the vision and beauty of the Qur'an are lost, then the identity and the transformative power of these religions are also lost. These historical particularities of persons and events matter momentously; they cannot be lost or diluted in some grand scheme.

And yet, especially for Christianity (here I will not speak for Judaism and Islam), the grand scheme is also essential. The whole purpose of the particular is to make known or make possible the universal intent or activity of the Divine. The God revealed in Jesus is the God who antecedently has been within the world from the beginning, creating and saving and seeking to draw all things to God's self. This *universal* presence and intent is precisely what becomes clear and operative in the *particular* Jesus. The divine love and transformative justice that have become so powerfully and persuasively present in Jesus cannot be contained or limited by Jesus; God's self-manifestation is, rather, meant for all, available for all, operative throughout history. If, before knowing Jesus, Christians could only suspect this universal presence and offer of God's love, now they know it for sure. Thus, to lose touch with this universal aspect of the Divine Reality is also to lose touch with an essential ingredient in Jesus' message. If we must guard against subsuming the particular into the universal, we must be equally wary lest we limit or cloud the universal by overstressing the particular.

Yet throughout much of their history, Christians (perhaps because of understandable historical circumstances and limitations) have indeed limited or clouded the universal divine love and presence; they have so focused on the particularity of Jesus or of the church that they have lost sight of the universal God Jesus revealed. The present context of our intercommunicating but threatened world is providing an opportunity to correct this imbalance. Thus, the task of the correlational model laid out in this book: to explore ways in which the particularity of the person and work of Jesus can be brought into a more fruitful and mutually enhancing relationship with the universality of

God's love and offer of grace. The intent of this model is not to dismantle or replace the unique significance of Jesus, but to understand it in such a way that Christians will be genuinely open to the God who is present beyond Jesus. This presence of God within the world and within other religions will be one Christians will often have to clarify, maybe rectify, but also one that will surprise them and teach them new wonders. I am seeking an understanding of Jesus' particularity that will enable Christians to go forth to meet other religions both with something to say and with something to learn.

Therefore, among theologians exploring a pluralist perspective on other religions, there is a general preference for the Logos/Wisdom christology of John over the Paschal/Easter christologies of Paul. John's Prologue, for instance, starts with what God has been doing and is doing from the beginning, everywhere, and presents Jesus as a concrete, historical, normative manifestation of this universal presence and activity of God in the Logos (Word of God). Enfleshed in Jesus, the Logos is powerfully and lucidly encountered by Christians, but this same Logos continues to be encountered elsewhere, throughout the world.

On the other hand, an Easter christology, elaborated especially by Paul, identifies the historical ministry-death-resurrection of Jesus as the starting point or source of what God intends to do universally (see Schillebeeckx 1979, 432-36). In the currency of contemporary christological discussion, one might say that an Easter christology looks upon Jesus as *constitutive*—as the cause and source—of God's saving presence in the world, whereas a Wisdom christology views Jesus as *representative* of the divine love, which is there from the beginning and, in a sense, is the divine origin or cause of Jesus himself (see Ogden 1992, 83-104). So, by following a Logos or Wisdom christology, correlational Christians open the door to interreligious dialogue by locating the *particularity* of Jesus *within the universality* of God's self-revelation, rather than locating God's universality *within the particularity* of the historical Jesus.[6]

With the balance between universality and particularity gained by retrieving a Wisdom-Logos christology, Christians can affirm what has happened in Jesus without claiming that it happened *only* here. Hence we have Panikkar's trenchant and sobering axiom that while Christians can affirm that Jesus is the Christ, they cannot so easily announce that the Christ is Jesus (Panikkar 1981, 14). Interestingly, the pluralist theologians who are offering the boldest interpretations of traditional Logos christology are Asians such as Stanley Samartha of India (1991), Aloysius Pieris of Sri Lanka (1987), and Seiichi Yagi of Japan (1987), who are blending their christologies with Hindu and Buddhist images and experience.

Regarding the language, especially the titles and images with which the early Christians sought to articulate and proclaim the particularity of Jesus and his message, a number of theologians go about their search for more pluralistic models of dialogue by pressing what seems to be a fairly well-established hermeneutical principle for New Testament christology—that the titles and images given to Jesus by the early church are better understood as literary-symbolic rather than literal-definitive attempts to say who Jesus was for them. In other words, images such as Son of God, Word of God, Lord, Messiah, and Savior are to be interpreted as doxological or confessional expressions of personal-community experience of this man and his message and as exhortations to follow him, rather than as definitive, propositional statements about his nature or ontological status in the universe.

This is the tack taken by John Hick in his well-known but often poorly understood appeal to accept and live the incarnation as myth (Hick 1973, 120-47; also 1993). Rosemary Ruether and other theologians engaged in Jewish-Christian dialogue also follow this symbolic-poetic interpretation of New Testament images of Jesus when they suggest that his Messiahship places him not in the absolute center of history but on a leading edge, a paradigm of the future along with other paradigms (Ruether 1981, 31-43; Pawlikowski 1982, 8-35, 108-35). Once again, with this literary-symbolic reading of New Testament christology, Christians can enter the interreligious dialogue with clear claims of what God has done in Jesus without having to insist that God has done it *only* in Jesus. In firmly proclaiming Jesus as incarnate Son or Messiah, they are also open to the possibility of other sons and daughters who have incarnated God's grace and truth for others.

But what about the undeniable exclusive language that the early churches used to define the particular importance of Jesus for all peoples? The New Testament is filled not only with particularistic language but also with exclusive, normative claims made about Jesus. "There is no other name given to humankind by which we can be saved than the name of Jesus Christ" (Acts 12:4) is perhaps the most thunderous example. I want to take this language seriously and respectfully—which means I cannot simply take it literally. We must ask what kind of language this is. What is its purpose? What is its nature? To summarize grossly, concerning the *purpose* of this exclusivist language, I suggest that given the lack of historical consciousness in the early community of Jesus followers, given their threatened minority status, given the apocalyptic mentality that expected all to be over soon, their absolutist language about Jesus can be considered part of the historically conditioned *medium* by which they wanted to deliver their central *message* about Jesus. Simplifying, we might say that in their historical circumstances, in order to announce that God had *really* acted in Jesus, they had to say also that God had acted *only* in Jesus. Today, however, we can hold to the same central message of "really" without insisting on the medium of "only." (We shall explore such a New Testament hermeneutics more carefully in chapter 4.)

PASTORAL INCENTIVES: A QUESTION AND CRY FROM THE HEART

If, as has been claimed, the questions of the many religions and of the many oppressed are indeed invading the minds and the feelings of Christians more and more, then pastors, ministers, and theologians have an obligation to take up these issues in ways in which the people will feel that their questions are being taken seriously. In other words, the questions have arisen because the old answers don't seem to work any longer. Thus, new answers are needed (which doesn't mean *any* new answers). If, as most churches recognize, the *sensus fidelium*—the sense or insights or questions of the ordinary faithful—sets the agenda for the efforts of pastors, bishops, and theologians to interpret God's Word, then the issue of making sense of other religions, in a world of vast human and ecological suffering, remains on the top of the agenda. For many Christians, it is not being taken seriously. I have no statistical evidence to confirm my strong suspicion that among the variety of reasons why many people feel they can no longer maintain their intellectual or moral integrity within the Christian community and therefore must leave is the "problem" of traditional Christian claims to be the only or the superior religion willed by God.

To the charges that theologians who question the uniqueness of Christ are guilty of "scandalizing the innocent" among the people of God, I point out the equal, if not greater, guilt of "scandalizing the intelligent" incurred by those ministers and theologians who refuse to take seriously, or who provide pat answers for, the questions many informed, critical Christians struggle with in trying to reconcile their experience of other faiths with what they learned in school or hear in the pulpit. While pluralist theologians definitely must be careful not to commit "sins of commission" by *disturbing* the faith of sincere Christians, exclusivist or inclusivist theologians must recognize that they might incur "sins of omission" in failing to *nurture* the faith of thinking, searching Christians.

My description of the issue of other religions as a pastoral concern is based on my experience of the Western, North American churches. As I realized in recent travels, the concern is even greater and more pressing elsewhere. Among the Christian communities of most Asian countries, where Christians must understand themselves and interpret the gospel as small, even minuscule, minorities in a sea of other ancient, vigorous religions, the question of how to make coherent, practical, peace-producing sense of other traditions is a matter of daily awareness and struggle. In fact, as many Indian Christians are maintaining, the question is being turned around not only in urgency but in content: the uncomfortable question is not whether other religions can find any positive meaning for Christianity, but whether Christianity can have any significance in view of so many other life-giving, ancient, proven religious traditions. "The question has to shift from how can we as Christians relate ourselves to other religions to what is the place and meaning of Christianity in a religiously pluralistic Asian world . . . We cannot any more seriously enter into dialogue with other religions if our question is Christianity-centered" (Wilfred 1987, 33).

For many Christians, because of some or most of the reasons outlined in this chapter, something like a pluralist/correlational and globally responsible perspective on Christianity and other religions seems to be a direction they can explore in order to maintain integrity to their experience and fidelity to the gospel. Before we carry on with that exploration, however, we must listen more carefully to the many who warn of the dangers and pitfalls of such a perspective.

3

IT ISN'T CHRISTIAN

The Critics Speak

If Karl Rahner was correct in his claim that the Holy Spirit, as "the dynamic element in the church," is actively promoting the vitality and growth of the Christian communities not only through the gentle inspiration of individuals but also, and especially, through the clash of contrary opinions and programs, then the Christian churches are in pretty good shape (Rahner 1964). It is evident that nowadays the Spirit has an ample arena of clashing opinions and convictions in which to stir the churches to deeper faith and new growth.

One of the areas in which the clatter of differing views is most audible, and therefore most promising, revolves around the question of how to understand and deal with the reality of religious plurality. Though many religious others have always populated the environment in which the followers of Jesus have traveled and camped, their presence seems to be felt more expressly and disconcertingly in this century than ever before. Amid the variety of Christian efforts to deal with this presence, the move toward a pluralistic-correlational model for interfaith theology and dialogue has ignited a particularly colorful and forceful outburst of varying opinions. Whatever its final worth, the pluralist model is providing space for the working of the Holy Spirit and the dynamic element in the church.

But, as Rahner also pointed out, the Spirit can go about its creative work only if the differing claims and concerns are genuinely heard and responded to with love and commitment to the common good. The clash of views must be a loving struggle among brothers and sisters. To facilitate such communal, nurturing discussion, I will in this chapter try to summarize, as briefly but as accurately as possible, the main problems and pitfalls that many Christian ministers and theologians see in these new models for a more correlational dialogue and theology of religions. My focus will be on the critical

voices that have been raised over the past decade, especially in response to my *No Other Name?* (1985), John Hick's *An Interpretation of Religion* (1989), and our joint collection, *The Myth of Christian Uniqueness* (1987).[1]

The focus of these inner-Christian critics of the correlational model
is their valid concern that the pluralist model violates the identity and
integrity of the Christian religion. Can one be a pluralist *and* a Christian? That, essentially, is what these critics are asking. They believe
that a Christian cannot admit the possibility that other religious figures and religions may be as important in God's plan as are Christ and
Christianity. To assume the correlational standpoint, which allows the
possibility that Buddha may have as "saving" a word to speak as does
Christ, is, for these critics, to risk destroying the foundations of Christianity. More specifically, these critics warn that it seems impossible to
reconcile a correlational-pluralist theology of religions with the Christian commitment to *believe* in Christ, to *follow* Christ, to *resist* in his
name, and to *proclaim* his name to the ends of the Earth.

BELIEVING IN CHRIST

Theologians generally agree that in order to maintain the adjective
"Christian" before the noun "theologian," one must take seriously
and remain faithful to the original witness and ongoing tradition of
Christianity as one goes about the theological task of "reinterpreting"
and adapting the gospel to the changing times. This, in the opinion of
many, is precisely where Christians pursuing a pluralist or correlational theology of religions fail. I'll try to summarize the principal
reasons why many fear that such a theology cannot be reconciled with
traditional Christian beliefs.

Any attempt to recognize other equally valid saviors or revelations
alongside the message of Jesus risks diluting, if not destroying, the
very source and norm for Christian belief and tradition, the New Testament witness. The reason is clear to anyone who knows the Bible. If
there is any common thread running through the many-colored coat
of varying New Testament christologies, if there is a central chord
sustaining the harmonic variety amid the various images of Jesus that
have developed through the centuries, it is the claim and conviction
that Jesus is the only Son of God, that his name is above all others,
that there is no other way to the Father (Küng 1991, 99; van Beeck
1985; Geffré 1990, 67).

Adrian Hastings speaks clearly and with deep concern:

While the terms and images chosen for the formulation of Christ's
religious uniqueness vary, the affirmation of that uniqueness can

①
Based on
NT assertion

be found with basically equal weight in every New Testament writing as in all subsequent Christian creedal affirmations. That embarrassing claim to religious uniqueness on behalf of one man, Jesus of Nazareth, and a consequent ultimate universality of significance, have remained the central characteristic of the Christian tradition, formulate them as you will. Deny the uniqueness and defend Christianity as the appropriate folk-religion for the European west, and you are, I would hold, denying Christianity intrinsically, however many bits and pieces of Christian wreckage you may still find serviceable. Maintain that uniqueness and universality, in whatever linguistic form, and you maintain the continuity and the vitality of the Christian claim, however many bits and pieces you may discard as unserviceable (Hastings 1990, 27ff.).

Therefore, many Christians are deeply concerned when they witness attempts by some pluralist theologians to distinguish between the medium and the message of the New Testament—between the proclamation of Jesus as savior (the core message) and the exclusive, one-and-only language (the historically conditioned, changeable medium) (Knitter 1985, 182-84). To hold that one can still maintain the core message about Jesus' saving power and dispense with the medium about his being the only savior is, for many Christians, a very dangerous procedure. To cut away the adjective/medium "only" from the noun/message "savior" would have been both foreign and offensive to the New Testament authors and editors (Braaten 1981).

Even nonreligious philosophers of language would remind the pluralists that they cannot separate medium and message, or language and understanding, as neatly as they think. Language and understanding, cultural medium and essential message, though distinguishable, form an inviolable unity. One cannot reinterpret the one without in some way affecting the other. It is, therefore, naive to think that one can tamper with the New Testament's "one and only" language without tampering with the core of Christianity (Dean 1987).

There are also serious problems with the argument advanced by some representatives of the pluralist model that the reason the early Christians made so many claims about Jesus as the "one and only" was that they did not experience religious pluralism as we do today and therefore had a classicist mentality, thinking that in order for something to be true it had to be the only truth (Knitter 1985, 183). Is this really so? The world of the New Testament does not appear as classicist as pluralists maintain, for it was teeming with religions and religious encounter; pluralism was as much a problem and an option then as it is today. Therefore, according to Carl Braaten, when the early Christians declared that there was "no other name," they did so consciously and counterculturally; they were not merely dressing up their deeper message in a culturally conditioned and disposable medium. The early church faced an abundance of pluralist options and rejected them. Therefore, Braaten continues, the new pluralist theology of religions bears an air of déjà vu; it would be seen by the first Jesus-followers, as well as by Christians through the ages, as another warmed-over attempt to squeeze the image of Jesus into a mold that the early church expressly rejected (Braaten 1987, 19; Heim 1987, 14-15; van Beeck 1985, 29).

There was for the early Christians, therefore, an unbreakable link between God's salvation as *truly* present in Jesus and as *only* (or normatively) present in Jesus. Why? The reason has to do with a unique feature of Christianity. S. Mark Heim states it neatly: "Christians do not simply proclaim a message or a humane way of life of which Jesus is a model. Christians proclaim a *person* as one and the same with God's unique saving act . . . What Christians claim as the ultimate truth is a person not a proposition" (Heim 1985, 54, 56). Christianity, Paul Griffiths adds, does not simply proclaim a "timeless truth" about God and the human condition; rather, whatever timelessness there may be in the truth Christians announce, it can be grasped and appropriated only by reference to a historical person and a historical event in Palestine. Christianity therefore "closes off the path to 'timeless truth.'" This means that "a uniqueness that includes both universalism [meant for all] and exclusivism [manifested fully only here] is integral to both the syntax and the semantics of the Christian life" (Griffiths 1990, 170).[2]

This unbreakable link between truth and the person of Jesus is rooted in the very experience and message of Jesus himself. Heim argues that "it is not so much that Jesus calls himself God, as that he does not 'make room' for God . . . Jesus assumes that his own actions and presence *make* the kingdom of God present . . . He shows no intention to cut God's purpose free from his person" (ibid., 172-73). For Wolfhart Pannenberg, this was precisely the content of Jesus' consciousness of himself as God's *eschatological prophet*—the prophet who came at the end, who summed things up, who had a definitive, universal message. When Christians proclaim Jesus as God's exclusive and final word, they are but being faithful to what Jesus thought and taught of himself: "Since the impending future of God was becoming present through him, there is no room for other approaches to salvation besides him. Those who relegate the claim to uniqueness to the 'deification' of Jesus in later Christian interpretation do not take seriously the eschatological finality claimed by Jesus himself" (Pannenberg 1990, 100-101). For Pannenberg, therefore, Christian claims about Jesus' uniqueness as God's final Word did not arise from what *they* experienced him to be in their lives but, rather, from what *he* made known to them.[3]

Karl Josef Kuschel, speaking from his extensive studies of the New Testament, summarizes both the content and the existential meaning of the biblical claim that Jesus is unique: "This is clear: the definitiveness, finality, and normativeness of the Christ-event . . . are indispensable if one wants to ground one's belief that God has committed God's self to humanity and its 'new existence' in Christ, in this way and in no other way. This is what the uniqueness of Jesus is all about" (Kuschel 1991, 395).

In other words, according to Kuschel, in Christ God has provided humanity, all humanity for all time, a singular, credible expression of truth that can anchor individual and social struggles to know and live the truth in a world of uncertainty and postmodern confusion. With this appeal to what God has uniquely done in Jesus, Kuschel cures the postmodern "Cartesian anxiety" about not having, but needing, a firm footing for truth:

> A theology of religions that holds to a God who is ultimately an unknown, enigmatic mystery and who is revealed differently in different cultures has not understood the biblical witness about the one God who in creation and in revelation has willed to let God's self be known . . . The assertion that in the human condition there is no "final word" and no "firm place" for the truth is contrary to the bible and the church and downplays the decisive dimension of faith (ibid., 399-400).

According to Kuschel, the reliability of this "firm place" where we can know God's truth and mystery would be jeopardized if it were not singular. If I have understood him correctly, he holds that if there are multiple revelations of God that are as clear and engaging as the revelation in Christ, then God is no longer trustworthy or no longer really and clearly involved in humankind's search for truth and liberation. God had to reveal God's self fully and only once in order to redeem humanity. That seems to be the content of the following declarations:

> If it were otherwise, if the Christ-event were not definitive and normative, if there were besides or outside of Christ other possible incarnations or revelations of God just as complete as that of Christ, then God would remain in the final analysis an impenetrable riddle whose credibility would still be undecided.
>
> If it were otherwise, if Jesus Christ were *one* window [among others] looking out onto the ultimately ineffable mystery [of

God], then the foundation for the "new creation" would, in the final analysis, be rendered uncertain (ibid., 398-99).

The reasoning of Kuschel and other critics of the pluralistic model seems to be this: for an expression of truth to be reliable it has to be *final* and *singular*. As Küng puts it, in order to be *steadfast* in the truth, we must have a unique, definitive norm (Küng 1991, 94-101). If there are other equally engaging statements of truth, or if more may still come, our own decision to embrace this expression cannot be final and full.[4]

Contrary to the fears of pluralist Christians, such claims to possess the final and the full truth from God *do not* necessarily set up road-blocks to genuine dialogue with other believers. According to Frans Jozef van Beeck, in holding to Jesus as uniquely divine, as the final Word of God in history, Christians not only can but they must be open to what God has done, differently and uniquely, in other traditions. Van Beeck makes a distinction between superiority and sovereignty: "The affirmation of Christ's divinity puts Christ, not in a position of *superiority*, but in one of *sovereignty* . . . No one can bring Christ's divinity into play to defeat others" (van Beeck 1985, 29-30). Also Kuschel, despite his insistence on the singularity and finality of God's revelation in Jesus, holds to similar distinctions: we can claim for Christ "normativity without absoluteness, finality without exclusivism, definitiveness without superiority" (Kuschel 1991, 401, 396).[5]

It is precisely when Christians make their unique, final, definitive claims that the dialogue can really get started and generate results. Only by recognizing that many, if not all, other religions make similar final and normative claims about their truth, only by allowing a thousand final and normative flowers to bloom in the fields of dialogue, can we bring about "the crossing of new frontiers in interreligious dialogue" (Griffiths 1990, 170; Küng 1991, 101-3). In other words, these theologians maintain that one can be an inclusivist, proclaiming Christ as God's ultimate Word, without giving Christianity the upper, manipulative hand in the dialogue (D'Costa 1985, 117-37).

For some theologians and the Christian communities they represent, a pluralist view of Christ and other religions threatens the very integrity and vitality of Christianity. "The pluralistic religious paradigm opts for a theocentricity at the expense of the christological origins of the doctrine of the Trinity . . . The anti-christocentric theocentrists are prepared to speak of some other God than the One who identifies himself with Jesus of Nazareth" (Braaten 1990, 420; 1992, 109; Newbigin 1990). Therefore, the turn toward pluralism that seems to be seeping into Christian awareness, especially among academicians, is, in Carl Braaten's view, as serious a heresy as any that has diluted or deformed Christian belief and practice. "Just as the church in the third century could name and refute the heresy of Arianism, and just as the church in the twentieth century struggled against the apostasy of the Nazis' Aryan doctrine, so the church of the twenty-first century will be called upon to escape the deluge of neo-Gnosticism that places Jesus reverently into a pantheon of spiritual heroes" (Braaten 1992, 13; see also 51).

Most of the theologians who oppose the pluralist model do so not as a crusade against heresy but as a way of carrying on their theological task as they feel they must—*within* the Christian community. They fear that to "expect Christians themselves to demote the Christ Jesus to a provisional messiah and abandon the conviction of faith in the normative and definitive word of God given with Jesus Christ and called for by the New Testament, in favor of an identification of Jesus Christ with other bearers of revelation and bringers of salvation" would expose theologians to "the risk of parting company with their own faith-communities" (Küng 1991, 101; see also Dulles 1977, 78; van Beeck 1979, 385-95).[6]

Gregory Baum states the same concern by appealing to his own experience that prophets can change and open up the church only if they remain within it:

> It seems to me that churches become agents of political and cultural change only if their prophets, their daring thinkers, their innovators, speak from the center of the tradition. Their re-interpretation must verify itself in the religious experience of the people. The people must recognize in the new position the religion they have inherited. While I fully recognize the need for dialogue, brotherhood, and cooperation between Christians and members of other religions, I am not prepared to give up the Christo-centric perspective we have inherited (Baum 1987, 55).

Such critical concerns, coming from theologians such as Küng, Baum, and Hellwig, who have not hesitated to confront and challenge their communities on other issues, are especially sobering.

FOLLOWING CHRIST

This last concern, that of estrangement from the Christian community, spills into another and perhaps deeper problem with a pluralist or correlational view of Christ and other religions; namely, that it will not sustain what has been traditionally called the law of prayer (the *lex orandi*), one's personal devotion to the person of Jesus and one's commitment to follow him.

Voicing this concern and speaking from their own experience of Jesus the Christ, Denise and John Carmody maintain that the source of all Christian claims about Jesus' uniqueness is not theology or philosophy or worldview—but spirituality. To experience the full reality of Jesus and the role he plays in the God-human drama is to experience him as different from, and superior to, all other religious figures. Thus, the Christian claims for Jesus as the final or unsurpassable manifestation of God's reality and plan are basically a matter of the heart, not of the head. "The depths of Christian spirituality, as manifested in the prayer of the saints, go beyond the reasons dear to theologians" (Carmody 1990, 3). Such claims will be made heart to heart, not proven head to head.

From these evaluations of the role of *experience* in knowing Christ, the Carmodys move to assess the status of *persons* having (or not having) such experience. They conclude that Christians and theologians who advocate a pluralist christology must not have a very deep personal devotion to Jesus. "Here it becomes clear that those proposing the abandonment of traditional Christian claims about the uniqueness of Christ seldom speak from within the precincts of Christian devotion or spirituality. The love of the committed disciple carries no weight in their calculations, much to their loss" (ibid., 16).[7]

Others express concern on the basis of their own experience without drawing implications about that of others. Their main claim is that the decision or the impulse to follow Christ stems from the experience of him as a *decisive/definitive* and as a *universally meaningful* embodiment or manifestation of God. The terms "decisive" and "definitive" are used synonymously; to experience Jesus is to experience a call or a power that *decides* and *defines* one's life; it requires one to act and live in a certain way, a way that will "cut off" (*de-cidere*) and "mark limits" (*de-finire*) regarding other attitudes or lifestyles. And one experiences this encounter and the truth it contains as powerful and promising not just for oneself but for all persons; what is decisive is also universal.

Monika Hellwig, with her usual sensitive clarity, appeals to her fellow Christians to identify how their encounter with Jesus and their following of him is based on their experience of how he "makes a *definitive difference* in the possibilities for individuals and for human history as a whole" (Hellwig 1989, 480, emphasis mine). Christians are convinced that wherever "people implement the possibilities he opened up, there is growth toward fuller life, hope, community, and happiness" (Hellwig 1990, 115). Following Jesus means struggling to transform the world in the hope that such transformation is indeed possible. "But Christian hope for the fullness of redemption is directly linked to the definitive difference that Jesus makes in the possibilities of our history and that definitive difference in turn is linked inseparably to the claim that Jesus is uniquely capable of making that difference because what he does, God does" (Hellwig 1989, 480). In other words, Christians claim that Jesus can make such a definitive difference because of who he is—human *and* divine.

But Hellwig is very careful about how Christians make this claim in a world of many religions and ideologies. It cannot be propounded in a dogmatic, absolute way; nor can it be made purely on the basis of the Christian Bible or personal, devotional experience. Rather, she advocates that Christians join the table of dialogue with a *friendly wager* about Jesus—a wager that will prove itself if taken seriously. Christians should be as friendly toward and respectful of other religions as they are clear and firm about what they are betting their lives on; namely, "that Jesus is indeed at the heart of the mystery of existence and destiny, with a direct link to the source of all being that justifies us in referring to him as the enfleshed or personified Word of the transcendent God, uniquely Son of the Source that fathers all things" (Hellwig 1990, 111). Unless Christians offer other believers such a friendly wager about the *definitive difference* that Jesus can make in the lives of all men and women, "the Christian faith collapses," for while there have been Christians who have denied the divinity of Jesus ontologically, "none have denied that Jesus Christ as savior makes the definitive difference" (ibid., 109).

Edward Schillebeeckx makes this same point on the basis of the same appeal not just to what "the church has taught" but to "what Christians have experienced." "According to this experience of faith, Jesus is the place where in a decisive way God has revealed himself as salvation of and for men and women. Christians experience Jesus as the supreme density of divine revelation in a whole history of experience of revelation" (Schillebeeckx 1990, 26). But in appealing to experience, Schillebeeckx insists that in the dialogue with others, Christians are making claims not just about their own experience but about Jesus; they are announcing not just how they see Jesus but who and what he really is. "In the first place they want to say something about Jesus himself: that he is the supreme expression of God, and that precisely for that reason they have experienced salvation in him and continue to do so" (ibid., 26-27).[8]

To spell out the content of what Christians are claiming about Jesus and what their experience tells them about him, Schillebeeckx, like Hellwig, appeals to the Christian symbol of the Realm of God. Although Schillebeeckx affirms that God is bringing about this Realm of wholeness and justice in many other ways besides that of Jesus, he also holds that this Realm will not be realized in its God-intended fullness without Jesus: "To believe in Jesus as the Christ means at its deepest to confess and at the same time to recognize that Jesus has an *abiding and constitutive significance* for the approach of the kingdom of God and thus for the comprehensive healing of human beings and making them whole . . . For Christians Jesus therefore is the decisive and definitive revelation of God" (ibid., 121).

To say, as these theologians do, that Jesus makes a definitive difference in human history and that he has an abiding and constitutive significance for all peoples of all times means that Jesus must exercise a *normative role* not just for Christians but for all religions. Jesus, in other words, holds up standards or concrete forms of life that make claims on others and that offer criteria by which they can decide what is right or wrong. Thus, many of my fellow Christians have had grave reservations about the terminology I used in *No Other Name?*—namely, that a theocentric christology should be "nonnormative." Truth that is nonnormative cannot go anywhere, like a sailboat without wind. So the critics insist (and I have to agree with them) that any truth claim worth its salt must be normative[9] (see Küng, 1986b).

To be authentic followers of Christ and to have something substantial to contribute to the dialogue, Christians must, according to these critics, make known to their religious brothers and sisters, at least in the form of a friendly wager, their conviction that Jesus and his community can make a *decisive/definitive, normative* difference for *all* peoples in their efforts to know the Truth and transform the world. This is what Harvey Cox is getting at when he reminds his pluralist colleagues that while they properly hold up Jesus' declaration in John 14:2 that there are "many mansions" in God's plans for humanity, they should not forget what Jesus immediately adds in John 14:6: "I am the way, the truth, and the life; no person comes to the Father but by me." Cox delivers a challenge that every Christian seeking a more pluralist approach to other faiths must take seriously (as I hope to do in chapters 4 and 5): "From Jesus I have learned both that he is the Way and that in God's house there are many mansions. I do not believe these two sayings are contradictory. In fact I have come to see that only by understanding one can we come to understand the other" (Cox 1988, 19).

RESISTING IN CHRIST'S NAME

Expanding the concerns expressed in the previous section, others warn that the pluralist refusal to recognize absolute normative truth not only is unable to sustain Christian disciples in their following of Christ, but also cannot steel Christian prophets in their resistance against the powers of evil. Maybe, in their enthusiasm for peace through dialogue, those embracing a pluralist model forget that there is, indeed, evil in this world—realities that we must resist. If the term "evil" rings too religious, then perhaps the adjective "intolerable" will touch the feelings that overcome us in the face of starving children, the sexual or economic violation of women and children, the rape of nature, and the manipulation of innocent people by politicians or religious leaders. Also—perhaps we should say especially—in the realm of religion, we witness with horror and disgust how the intolerable can wrap itself in the sacred mantle of God's will. As Langdon Gilkey points out, affirming the plurality of religions means recognizing a plurality of both good and evil: "For within the plurality of religions that surrounds us are forms of religion that are intolerable, and intolerable because they are demonic. Toleration is here checked by the intolerable: and plurality means both" (ibid., 44).

Gilkey, himself a cautious pluralist, recognizes here the Achilles' heel of the model presented in the previous chapter. Absolute or intolerable evils can be resisted only on the basis of absolute, certain claims that such realities are indeed evil. The exploitation of women within one religious system can be resisted by another tradition only on the basis of truth claims that are held to be true across religious borders, "commensurably"—universally! Absolute evil calls for absolute resistance based on absolute truth claims. And there, for Gilkey and many pluralists, is the rub. Pluralism, according to its self-definition, allows no absolutes. "The rough parity of religions [the pluralist model], by removing the absolute starting point of each, seems to drain each of whatever it has to say and give to us, and so to leave us empty" (Gilkey 1987, 44).

Some kind of absolute or definitive convictions are needed not only when we confront evil or the intolerable, but also when it *confronts us*. When the pressure is on, when the structures of control and oppression make it dangerous to raise one's head above the herd, the Christian community needs clear, unquestionable norms. Here again the pluralist-correlational model seems to lack backbone. This is why Gregory Baum has not made the pluralist turn: "If we simply abandon a universalist norm, we are unable to detect the power of evil in the human world and unite with others in a common struggle against it. The liberal view of religious pluralism underestimates this power of evil" (Baum 1974, 15). Hans Küng in a number of public discussions in Toronto and Philadelphia has reminded me that during the threat of National Socialism in Germany it was mainly the "pluralists" who failed to take a clear prophetic stand. George Lindbeck puts this objection more positively and in terms that unsettle every true liberal's heart:

> The viability of a unified world of the future may well depend on counteracting the acids of modernity. It may depend on communal enclaves that socialize their members into highly particular outlooks supportive of concern for others rather than for individual rights and entitlements, and of a sense of responsibility for the wider society rather than for personal fulfillment. It is at least an open question whether any religion will have the requisite toughness for this demanding task unless it at some point makes the claim that it is significantly different and unsurpassably true (Lindbeck 1984, 127).

Pluralists, awash in openness, may not have the toughness to contribute to the kind of unified world they so desire.

PROCLAIMING CHRIST'S NAME

Another deeply rooted concern about the new correlational views of other religions is that such views can corrode or destroy one of the defining activities of the Christian church: its missionary outreach. The missionary enterprise, as theologians of all confessional colors will admit, is not just a peripheral pastime for the church, something that is taken care of after the main job is done. The Christian church not only *has* a mission to the world, but the church *is* mission, defining and realizing what it is in the activity of going forth to announce the gospel to the ends of the Earth. Remove or dilute this mission, and you have removed and diluted Christian identity.

According to voices coming from various Christian quarters, this is precisely what pluralist models for a theology of religions do. Carl Braaten, speaking out of the mainline Lutheran tradition, places his concerns squarely on the table: "The new pluralistic theology of the religions, if it gains ascendancy, will spell the death of both the ecumenical and the missionary movement." He goes on to explain why: "The pluralistic theologies relativize the universal validity of the gospel of Jesus Christ. They represent a radical shift in belief and a fundamental deconstruction of the trinitarian paradigm within which Jesus Christ, in his uniqueness and universality, has defined the nature and aim of the gospel's cross-cultural mission to the nations" (Braaten 1990, 419-20).

Pope John Paul II in his encyclical *Redemptoris Missio* (RM) echoes Braaten and underlines the alarm of many who are dedicated to

Christian missionary activity. He first identifies a situation of crisis, before which, as Cardinal Tomko of the Vatican Congregation for the Evangelization of Peoples notes, "the Holy See can no longer remain passive" (Tomko 1991, 754). "Missionary activity specifically directed 'to the nations' appears to be waning" (RM 2). Or, as the pope goes on to hold, it is being misunderstood, manipulated, malformed. A diagnosis of these ailments within the Christian body points to what the pope calls "incorrect theological perspectives" dealing with the salvific value of religions, the urgency of interreligious dialogue, the necessity of working for human development and liberation (RM 4, 35).

Like Braaten, Pope John Paul II locates the focus of these erroneous tendencies in a faulty christology that puts into question the unique and unsurpassable role played by Jesus in God's plan of salvation; for John Paul, the "definitive self-revelation of God [in Christ] is the fundamental reason why the church is missionary by her very nature" (RM 5). Question the definitive quality of that revelation, and you are undermining the foundations of mission. In other words, the malaise about mission in the churches today is nurtured, if not created, by the pluralistic-correlational theology of religions that has been developing within Christian communities over the past few decades.

We will explore these concerns more carefully in chapters 6 and 7. For the moment, I would like to point out what seems to be the core concern in these missionary reservations about a correlational view of religions. It is located in the prevalent understanding of the Great Commission itself: "Go therefore and make disciples of all nations, baptizing them in the name of the Father, Son, and Holy Spirit" (Mt 28: 19). The purpose of the "going" is twofold: to make disciples and to baptize. Traditionally, both goals have been understood as one; one can't make disciples without baptizing. Therefore, anything that would question the necessity and motivation for baptizing is contrary to the Christian missionary obligation. In other words, the missiological criticisms of the pluralist model are grounded in the conviction—sometimes stated, often presumed—that *conversion to the Christian community* constitutes the primary and determining purpose and raison d'être of missionary activity. It is the *sine qua non* condition for missionary identity—the goal without which all other goals are meaningless. Unless water flows and people are baptized, the good news is not being heard and disciples of Christ are not being made.

Pope John Paul II is explicit: "The mission *ad gentes* (to the nations) has this objective: to found Christian communities and develop churches to their full maturity. This is *the central and determining goal* of missionary activity" (RM 48, emphasis mine). Cardinal Tomko is even more precise: "There are *two primary and essential elements* [in the church's mission]: the proclamation of Jesus Christ and the gathering together of the believers in Jesus Christ, the Church. Without these primary elements, all other elements of Christian mission will lose their validity and cohesion" (Tomko 1990, 260).

If conversion is a "central, determining, primary, essential" goal of missionary activity, then of course both the christology and the soteriology (view of salvation) in the correlational, globally responsible model will be considered dangerous. This is what Cardinal Tomko had in mind when he tersely defined the difficulty: "Thus the missiological problem today is ultimately a christological and soteriological problem" (ibid., 241). To suggest that God's truth and saving presence can be communicated through other vehicles besides Jesus the Christ, to affirm the possibility that other religious figures or traditions may have a contrapuntal melody to play with that of Jesus in God's symphony—this is to erode, if not explode, the necessity of making all peoples explicit members of Jesus' community; it is to open the possibility that proclaiming the good news might have other purposes besides conversion to the church. Furthermore, to announce, as pluralists do, that a soteriocentric or globally responsible dialogue among religions can be considered by Christians an end in itself—that is, to hold up eco-human liberation and well-being as the primary context and purpose of dialogue and of Christian relations with other religions—is, for a conversion-centered missiology, an utter and ruinous reversal of priorities.

Thus we can understand the repeated warnings in the pope's, Tomko's, and Braaten's missionary critique of pluralism that such new views are "reductionistic," that they reduce missionary outreach to dialogue with others. Or, "the common foundation for all missions, Christian and other, could be reduced [by the pluralists] to soteriocentrism, understood as human well-being, wholeness, which in turn is salvation" (Tomko 1990, 241; RM 14-15, 58; Braaten 1992, 132-34). For the pluralists, as long as Christians are conversing and cooperating with others in advancing the soteria of eco-human well-being, they are carrying out their mission to the world. For the critics, this is to reduce Christian mission to something which, though included in Christian mission, can never constitute it.

•

The choir of critics that we have reviewed in this chapter may not always sing in harmony, but they do give voice to a wide spectrum of concerns, warnings, and accusations that Christians who are seeking a new, more open, and correlational approach to other religions must take seriously. If it is true that pluralist Christians undermine the very identity and integrity of Christian faith, then the model I urged in the previous chapter must be abandoned.

But I would consider such an abandonment to be, at least, premature and, at most, disastrous for the further and necessary evolution of Christian belief and practice. In the rest of this book I will try to state why I believe that one can be committed to what I am calling a correlational, globally responsible approach to other religions and at the same time be genuinely and resolutely committed to Jesus Christ and his mission.

4

UNIQUENESS REVISED

A Correlational, Globally Responsible Christology

Even though we may never be able to spell out neatly and conclusively what is meant by "the essence of Christianity," we do know that whatever it is, it has its foundation and focus in Jesus the Christ. Therefore, if we want to put the adjective "Christian" in front of what we have been calling a correlational, globally responsible dialogue of religions, we will have to show how such a dialogue, and the theology behind it, are consistent with and sustained by the role that Jesus the Christ has played, and must play, within the Christian community.

And there's the rub. As we heard in the previous chapter, there is a goodly company of theologians and ordinary Christian folk who view a correlational or pluralistic dialogue as a path leading away from commitment to Jesus and fidelity to the Christian witness. For them, any effort, expressly formulated or cleverly disguised, to set Jesus on the same level with other religious figures or saviors runs into the wall of what is clearly stated in the New Testament and staunchly maintained throughout the history of the churches. To place Jesus in a community of equals with other revealers is to steal the stamina of the Christian disciple's commitment and to dilute the courage of the Christian prophet's denouncement of evil. It may make for a comfortable community of religions, but at the cost of Christian identity.

But the rub goes both ways. If calls for a correlational dialogue seem to threaten traditional Christian views of Jesus, so many Christian claims about Jesus seem to set up roadblocks to the free and full flow of dialogue. Theologians holding to what has been called an "inclusivist" christology—that is, a view of Jesus as constitutive of or normative for all revelation and experience of God—claim that such an understanding of Jesus as the final, full, unsurpassable manifestation of God does *not* impede real dialogue. But as far as I have heard them, they don't seem to explain *how* this can be. For how can I really listen to your truth claims, how can I ever really be ready to admit that I am wrong and in need of correction, if I believe that God has given me (through no merit of my own) the conclusive, unsurpassable, self-sufficient revelation of divine truth. It is one thing to enter the dialogue with solid truth claims; it is quite another to place on the table of dialogue truth claims that are stamped with the divine seal of approval as final and unsurpassable. In the first case, my firm stand *is* open to correction and fulfillment (while standing firm, I'm ready to move if necessary); in the second case, to change my position is to violate the revelation God has given me. So it seems to me that traditional Christian announcements of Jesus as final, full, and unsurpassable must be, to say the least, a threat to dialogue.

For Christians, a threatened dialogue is (or should be) just as serious a problem as a threatened Christian identity. As was argued in chapter 2, a genuine dialogue between cultures and religions—in which all the partners are just as ready to learn as they are to teach, just as ready to recognize the truth of others as they are to speak their own truth—is felt today to be a *moral imperative*. Anything that makes such a dialogue problematic is a problem itself. Therefore, a Christian theologian-believer cannot first work out a christology or view of Jesus and *then* see how it applies to dialogue. A concern for the demands of dialogue with other religious communities cannot simply be a corollary or a special question that is taken up once a christology has been worked out. Rather, the reality of other religions and the demands of dialogue must be part of the preconditions for understanding who Jesus is. "Religious pluralism is part of the point of departure of a Christology which begins with Christian life and experience in our world today . . . [Religious pluralism] forms an *a priori* context for Christological thinking" (Haight 1992, 261).

There are also the continued reminders from Christians in what were previously called mission lands that, despite all the protests from European-American theologians to the contrary, the well-worn Christian language of Jesus as one and only universal savior and as God's final touchstone of all truth have confirmed, if not conceived, policies of cultural and religious imperialism. Samuel Rayan of India, responding to the Vatican's understanding of Jesus as absolute savior, poses a polite but pointed question: "We [Indians] ask about the subterranean connection between the Western conception of Christ's uniqueness and authority on the one hand and the Western project of world domination on the other" (Rayan 1990, 133). Therefore, Raimon Panikkar hopes that just as theologians speak of early notions of Yahweh as a "tribal deity," which were later purified by the Jewish prophets, so in the "third Christian millennium" theologians will recognize that many of the images of Christ made up a "tribal Christology," which can be purified by a revised christology that "allows Christians to see the work of Christ everywhere without assuming that they have a better grasp on or a monopoly of that Mystery which has been revealed to them in a unique way" (Panikkar 1990b, 122).[1]

In this chapter I will offer, in broad tentative strokes, some suggestions for such a revised christology, a correlational, globally responsible christology that will attempt to relieve some of the distress of the two-way rub just described: an understanding of Jesus and his abiding presence as the Christ in the Christian churches that will be, on the one hand, faithful to the original witness and conducive to Christian discipleship and, on the other, will nurture and orient a dialogue with other believers that is genuinely correlational and liberative. In this attempt, I want to keep ringing in my ears the voices of the critics reviewed in chapter 3; I want to meet their concerns, not just respond to their objections. To do this, my hope is to achieve, or take some first steps toward, the better balance envisioned in chapter 2 between the particularity of Jesus and the universality of what he was about. The question in this chapter is the tangled one of the uniqueness of Jesus. I trust it will be clear that my intent is *not to deny* that uniqueness but *to revise and reaffirm* it.

The proposal in this chapter for a correlational, globally responsible revision of christology has two components: First, I will explore just what it means to be faithful to the New Testament witness about Jesus and to the churches' reception of that witness through the centuries. Recognizing that we're always interpreting the witness of tradition, I ask about guidelines or criteria for doing so. Second, I will propose the formal qualities or attributes of a revised understanding of Jesus' uniqueness—what Christians mean, and what they don't mean, when they proclaim that Jesus is unique. This part will, I hope, generate the energy for a correlational christology, one that allows Christians to be as committed to Jesus as they are open to other religions. In the following chapter, we'll explore just what it is that makes Jesus unique—the material content of his uniqueness.

THE MEANING OF FIDELITY TO JESUS THE CHRIST

In posing the question of how one remains faithful to the original witness about Jesus, we are really asking about the nature of Christian faith and of Christian theology. I suspect that most Christians would agree that in speaking about their life of faith, it is more accurate to say one *lives* one's faith rather than one *has* one's faith. The same would be true of being "faithful to the gospel"—fidelity is not something that one has, but rather, something that one lives and practices day in and day out. But if this is true, if fidelity and faith are matters of *being* rather than *having*, of *living* rather than *affirming*, then I think it follows that the grounding or source for this faithful faith *cannot* be the gospel or the Bible all by itself. The Bible alone would suffice if faith were a matter of having or affirming; all we would need to do is understand what it means and then preserve that understanding. But if faith is primarily a matter of living and acting, then we have to relate or apply what we hear in the Bible to what is going on in our lives, to concrete situations as they change from day to day in our history.

THE BIBLE AND THE DAILY NEWSPAPER

Therefore, the data or the sources from which we are to live our faith and work out our fidelity are two: the experience we find and have in the *scriptures,* and the experience we have in our present-day, always-changing *world.* Or as Karl Barth used to say, to be a good Christian one has to read both the Bible *and* the daily newspaper. One needs both to practice the Christian faith: Without the Bible, Christians claim, they cannot understand what's being reported in the newspapers. But the reverse is also true—without the daily paper, one cannot really live and therefore understand the message of the Bible.

In the more academic and dry language of contemporary theologians, we can say the two sources for Christian theology are one's historically conditioned understanding of the Christian fact (scripture and tradition), and one's historically conditioned understanding of one's self and one's world. As was already stated in the beginning of chapter 2, these two understandings condition and nurture each other (Tracy 1975, chap. 2; Ogden 1972). A faithful Christian faith-life can therefore be described as the result of a *mutually clarifying* and a *mutually criticizing* conversation between the biblical witness and one's experience in the world (see Hill, et al. 1990, 251-61). Each side clarifies and criticizes the other.

At this point many Christians would object or call for greater clarity. It seems that such an understanding of fidelity to tradition and of theology is putting both sources—the Bible and human experience—on the same level. That exposes one to the danger of imposing one's own experience and understanding on the Bible, or of subjecting God's Word to human words and thoughts. Such a danger is always present. But at least it is recognized and confronted insofar as I want to affirm strongly that as much as God's Word may have to be "criticized" in order to be heard within the all-too-limited and sometimes beclouding human words in which it is written, as much as God's Word has to be clarified so it can speak to our present-day problems (many of which never existed in biblical times), still, once this divine Word is so clarified and criticized we expect that it will be a power that will also clarify and criticize our all-too-selfish and fearful ways of doing and seeing things. God's Word will be a force that not only reveals the august beauty of what we humans are, but it will also lay bare the pettiness and cruelty of the human heart. God's message in the prophets and in Jesus is both announcement and denouncement. If it is not denouncing, something is probably wrong with the announcing.

But even when the Word of God has to stand us on our head or set us in the opposite direction of the road we were traveling, even when God's Word "hurts"—we know it is true because our *human experience* tells us that this discomfort is for our own good. Therefore, when evangelical Christians insist that the Bible is their authoritative Word, that Jesus is their only savior, they are making such statements, it seems to me, on the basis of an authorization given by their experience. Jesus would not be their savior if they didn't find that he was saving them! The Bible becomes absolute for people because it "works" for them. Thus David Kelsey is not telling us anything revolutionary or bizarre when he states that the authority of the scriptures does not consist in any kind of extrinsic divine attribution (God declaring the Bible to be true) or because of any inherent cognitive content. Rather, the Bible is authoritative because of what it continues to *do* for people; it continues to transform their lives and the life of the community (Kelsey 1985; McFague 1987, 43-44).[2] We are faithful to the biblical witness, therefore, when we experience and affirm its transformative power in our lives and societies.

RIGHT BELIEF (ORTHODOXY) IS ROOTED IN RIGHT ACTION (ORTHOPRAXIS)

All this means that fidelity to the Christian tradition, especially to the "normative" scriptures, is primarily a matter of right action or orthopraxis and not simply of right words or orthodoxy. Notice, I said "not simply," for right words and doctrine and ideas are essential. But they are not primary. They are essential insofar, and only insofar, as they promote and flow from right action. One might say that Christians believe in the Trinity not simply because that is the truth of the way God is, but rather because it is the truth of the way God acts; or better, God *is* that way because God *acts* that way— God's being is God's doing.[3] We profess the truth of the Trinity not simply to announce the truth of how God is, but to act in the same way that God acts: in constant relationships of knowing and loving.

Again, to make such assertions about the primacy of orthopraxis over orthodoxy is nothing new for the Christian communities. From the first centuries there was the theological dictum *Lex orandi est lex credendi*, "the rule for believing is to be found in the rule for praying." In other words, Christians do not first have their beliefs all neatly lined up and affirmed before they *feel* the meaning of these beliefs, before they start praying about them and celebrating them. Creeds do not precede devotion. Rather, in devotion or in spirituality beliefs find their real form and power. As long as beliefs continue to stoke the fires of devotion and commitment and sense of Divine Presence, we can be quite certain that such beliefs are orthodox.

But the rule for praying (*lex orandi*) is in a sense incomplete, even dangerous, if it does not also include the "rule for following" (Latinists might say, *lex sequendi*). In fact, according to Jesus, it seems that the need to follow him has a priority over praying to or praising him. "Not those who proclaim 'Lord, Lord!' but those who do the will of the Father will enter the Kingdom" (Mt 7:21-23). And, according to John, when Jesus' potential disciples wanted to know more about him—where he lived and who he was—he responded simply: "Come follow me" (Jn 1: 35-51). In the following and the imitating of Jesus, Christians come to know him and to believe in him correctly. As Jon Sobrino puts it: "Faith in Christ is realized and actualized more as an invocation of Christ than as pure profession of Christ. As the locus of profession may be worship, the locus of invocation is practice" (Sobrino 1987, 59). The touchstone not only for right belief but also for right worship is therefore whether such beliefs and professions are flowing in and out of the following of Jesus—the *doing* as he did.

> To acknowledge Jesus as our Lord and Savior is only meaningful in so far as we try to live as he lived and to order our lives according to his values. We do not need to theorize about Jesus, we need to "re-produce" him in our time and our circumstances . . . so that our search, like his search, is primarily a search for *orthopraxis* (true practice) rather than *orthodoxy* (true doctrine). Only a true practice of the faith can verify what we believe (Nolan 1978, 139-40).

Stated most simply: "The proof of a map [its orthodoxy] is how well you can get around using it [its orthopraxis]" (Charles Taylor in Placher 1989, 129).

Again, I want to stress that in holding up the primacy of orthopraxis over orthodoxy, I am in no way trying to reduce one to the other, nor am I trying to minimize the necessity of orthodoxy. As soon as the community of Jesus-followers (or any religious group) begins to talk, among itself or with the broader world, about what it is doing and why, it needs to formulate statements, position and beliefs. But my point is that such formulations—especially in trying to clarify traditional beliefs or fashion new ones about the person, work, or uniqueness of Jesus—must flow from and nurture a saving experience of and commitment to Jesus (devotion and prayer) and a resolute following of him in the world (discipleship and practice). If they don't do this, they are heretical; if they do, they merit our serious consideration, if not acceptance. I shall be trying to follow such rules for fidelity in my suggestions for a correlational understanding of the uniqueness of Jesus.

THE NEW TESTAMENT LANGUAGE ABOUT JESUS

These considerations about the primacy of praxis—either devotional or ethical—over creedal formulations can help us in determining how we can understand and be faithful to all the marvelous things the New Testament says about Jesus, to the language the New Testament authors and editors use in their different christologies. This language can be not only inspiring and challenging but also overwhelming and, in an age of interreligious sensitivity, disquieting. I'm thinking especially of *titles* given to Jesus, such as Son of God, Savior, Word of God, which seem to put him in a category separate from and *superior* to all other religious founders and leaders. Even more pointedly, I'm thinking of adjectives and adverbs applied to Jesus and his message that seem to *exclude* all others, such as:

- "No one knows the Father, *only* the Son and anyone to whom the Son chooses to reveal him" (Mt 11:27—from the Q source).
- "There is *one* Lord, Jesus Christ, through whom are all things and through whom we exist" (1 Cor 8:6).
- He is the "*only*-begotten" Son (Jn 1:14).
- "*No one* has ever seen God. It is God the Son, who is close to the Father's heart, who has made him known" (Jn 1:18).
- There is "*one* Mediator between God and humankind, Christ Jesus" (1 Tm 2:5).
- "*Once-and-for-all*" (ephapax) (Heb 9:12).
- There is *no other* Name by which we can be saved" (Acts 12:4).

If we look at such language only as creedal or orthodox statements and forget that such confessions of faith (*lex credendi*) grew out of and were meant to nourish the practice of faith in devotion (*lex orandi*) and discipleship (*lex sequendi*), we are in danger of both misunderstanding and misusing it.

Following the insights of New Testament scholar Krister Stendahl, I have elsewhere tried to show that if we connect such language about "one and only" to its roots in the early Christians' practice of devotion, we can describe it as "love language" (Knitter 1985, 184-86). This cascade of praises and superlatives flowed out of the individual's and community's experience of salvation or transformation or well-being, which they had in and through this Jesus. As Schillebeeckx puts it: "A fundamentally identical experience underlies the various interpretations [of Jesus] to be found throughout the New Testament: all its writings bear witness to the experience of salvation in Jesus from God" (in Haight 1992, 264).[4] Their lives had been touched and transformed by this Jesus; they felt themselves, despite his death, in a living, enlivening relationship with him; they were devoted to him; they were in love with him. And they spoke the language of lovers—"you are my one and only."

This was not just a personal, individualistic relationship ("just me and Jesus"); it was a relationship they wanted to share, for they felt that others, too, could come to have the same experience of Jesus and to use the same love language.[5] Yet, if we take such love or confessional statements as "only begotten Son" or "one Mediator" and transform them into *purely* doctrinal or theological assertions, and if we then use these confessions for the negative task of excluding others rather than for the positive purpose of proclaiming the saving power of Jesus, we have, I fear, abused these texts. We have been unfaithful to them.

But if the roots of orthopraxis behind such New Testament talk of Jesus include not just the practice of devotion and spirituality but also, and especially, the praxis of following and doing as Jesus, then we can also describe such one-and-only declarations about Jesus as *action language,* or as the scholars put it, *performative language.* When the early Christians gave Jesus such lofty titles as Word of God or Wisdom of God or Son of God, they were not out primarily to present the world with a philosophical or dogmatic definition; rather, they were declaring themselves, and inviting all others, to be disciples of this Jesus, to follow him in loving God and neighbor and working for what Jesus called the Reign of God. The purpose of professing was to follow, not the other way around.

Therefore, as Jon Sobrino urges, we should look for what he calls the "praxic equivalency," that is, the motor-power, behind and within all the soaring language about Jesus' divinity and uniqueness. When the first disciples held up Jesus as savior and mediator, they were attempting to put into language their resolve to follow him and to carry on his way of living and loving. Calling Jesus the "only Son of God" was not meant mainly as an ontological, unchangeable definition of his nature, but rather, as a declaration of a way of life based on Jesus. "*Following* is the praxic form of accepting the transcendence of God; and following *Jesus* is the praxic form of accepting the transcendence of Jesus" (Sobrino 1988, 31-32).

If the primary purpose of the New Testament's "one-and-only" language was performative, a call to action, then "without any relationship to a redeeming and liberating practice of Christians" all talk of redemption or uniqueness "remains in a purely speculative, empty vacuum" (Schillebeeckx 1990, 44-46). "The history of Jesus' career must be continued in his disciples; only then is it meaningful to talk of the uniqueness and distinctiveness of Christianity" (ibid., 168). This is how Christians are to be faithful to all this exclusive-sounding language in the New Testament—by following Jesus and continuing his career in their own lives—*not* by excluding others. Any possible exclusion of others will come *only* as a necessary consequence of following Jesus, not as a prerequisite to that following.[6]

Even if the early Christians or the authors of the New Testament may have taken their own language literally and believed that there were no other names that could save (and I think they did), still this was not the primary intent, the essential content, of their language. It was action language, not exclusive language; or, they used exclusive terminology (like "only begotten Son") in order to call themselves and others to the practice of discipleship. Today, if it is possible to remove the exclusive implications of these texts and still preserve their call to act like Jesus, we are remaining faithful to this language. And that is what I am urging in this chapter—that fidelity to the New Testament confessions about Jesus is essentially and primarily a matter of acting with and like Jesus, not of insisting that he is above all others.

No Other Name?

It may be helpful to apply these guidelines for fidelity to the New Testament witness to a particular text. We can take one of the most exclusive-sounding statements in the New Testament: "There is no salvation in anyone else, for there is no other name in the whole world given to humanity by which we are to be saved" (Acts 4:12). The context itself already warns us against using this passage to rule all other witnesses out of court before we can present Jesus. The question at issue was "not one of comparative religions but of faith-healing"; that is, in whose power had Peter and John just healed the crippled man (Robinson 1979, 105), and more broadly, in whose power had the disciples undergone the transformation that was so evident to their fellow Jews? The passage delivers a clear answer: not Peter and John's own power, but the power contained in the name and reality of Jesus the Christ.

Good straightforward exegesis of language used; scenes public: not God? it is partly the language further: urges = praxis performance

The intent of the language, then, is not philosophical/theological—to define Jesus in relation to other religious leaders; rather, it is clearly praxic, performative—to call others to recognize and accept the power that is available to them in Jesus (Stendahl 1981; Starkey 1982, 69-71). Other passages from the story make this intent evident: "In the power of that name this man stands before you perfectly sound (Acts 4:10) . . . It is his name and trust in this name that has strengthened the limbs of this man" (Acts 3:16). The implication is evident: if we can trust in the power of this name, our limbs can also be strengthened for tasks that presently seem impossible, as impossible as that a crippled person should walk. Acts 3:23 makes it even clearer that Peter was talking about the power of Jesus, the prophet, who calls us to action: "Anyone who does not listen to that prophet [foretold by Moses] shall be ruthlessly cut off from the people."

Again, such language is telling us that we run a great risk if we do not listen to and follow this prophet. "No other name," as performative, action language, is really a positive statement in its negative couching: it tells us that all peoples must listen to this Jesus; it does *not* tell us that no one else should be listened to or learned from. The stress, then, is on the *saving power* mediated by the name of Jesus, not on the exclusivity of the name. If in our dialogue we find that this power of liberation is experienced through other names, then the spirit of this passage in Acts would call us to be open to them. Whatever can genuinely heal a cripple mediates this power. Certainly for Jesus—as well as for his early followers—the most important thing was that cripples be healed, not that they be healed only through the name of Jesus.

WHAT ABOUT THE RELIGIOUS PLURALISM OF THE NEW TESTAMENT WORLD?

But as we heard from the critics in chapter 3, the early Christians *did* exclude other religious ideas and leaders; they *did* use texts such as "no other Name" (Acts 4:12) as warnings to the community to keep its distance from other religious neighbors. As the critics remind us, the New Testament world was teeming with religious diversity, and the early Jesus-followers consciously responded to it with their crystal-clear assertions about the exclusive, or at least inclusive, uniqueness and normativeness of Jesus. The early disciples did not hop on the cultural band-wagon of religious mish-mash that was moving through much of the Roman Empire.

Such admonitions have to be taken to heart. In proclaiming the "new context" of a global village of differing religions, modern-day proponents of pluralism forget that the context is not that new; something quite similar crowded around the cradle of the newborn Christian religion. Yet in admitting this, I have to ask a further, and I think pivotal, question: *Why* did the early Christians seem to reject so much of this rampant religious pluralism of their age?[7] I would suggest that among the varied reasons that were evidently at play, one of the most powerful sources of this basically negative response to the then current religious pluralism arose from what we have been calling the performative or ethical content of the Christian communities' beliefs. This rejection, in other words, was more a matter of orthopraxis than orthodoxy.

The early Christians rejected the religious pluralism of their age not because it offended against their belief in the uniqueness of Jesus, but because it could not be reconciled with the right action or with the ethical-social vision contained in Jesus' message about the Kingdom of God. Soteriocentric or Kingdom-centered motivations, rather than christocentric or monotheistic convictions, brought about this rejection of pluralism—though these motivations would not have been laid out in the precise form or language that I am using now.

My central reason for suggesting this is another historical fact, neglected by some of the critics. As Frans Jozef van Beeck admits, "Modern pluralism is a far cry from the pluralism of the first century" (van Beeck 1985, 33-34). To equate the pluralism of the New Testament world with that of our own is, historically speaking, naive or ill-informed. The pivotal difference between the two worlds is that the pluralism of the first century was far more inclined toward—indeed, ridden with—relativism and/or syncretism. Religious tolerance was disposed to tolerate anything. Gods were accepted not because of inherent truth but because they were the local deities, or because they catered to one's religious fantasy, or because they were an absorbing distraction from either boredom or frustration. Differences really didn't matter, especially in the syncretistic cults.

This was why the early Christians found themselves repulsed by such religious diversity and tolerance. It would have simply absorbed and neutralized Jesus' new vision of the Kingdom; further, it would have tolerated, purely for the sake of tolerance, other visions that were opposed to that Kingdom. They rejected pluralism, then, not because it offended against the role or nature of Jesus Christ but because it offended against the kind of God and the kind of society that were integral to Jesus' vision of God's Reign.

If today, as the correlational theologians maintain, religious diversity can be affirmed without being sucked into syncretism or lazy tolerance; if, on the contrary, religious pluralism and dialogue can be an important, maybe even necessary, means of working for the eco-human justice that constitutes the heartbeat of Jesus' Kingdom—then we can expect that the early Christians might have been all for it. Again, the norms for deciding have to do primarily not with correct believing but with correct acting.

"TRULY" DOESN'T REQUIRE "ONLY"

In what follows, I will try to apply the guidelines we have just reviewed for faithfully passing on the Christian community's witness about Jesus the Christ. Recognizing that such fidelity is mainly (though not exclusively) a matter of orthopraxis rather than orthodoxy, understanding the New Testament and tradition's language about Jesus as primarily performative and action-oriented, I want to suggest now how Christians can understand the uniqueness of Jesus in such a way that they remain in faithful flow with Christian witnessing and at the same time are truly open to authentic conversation and cooperation with persons of other faiths. In this section I will describe the *qualities* or the *attributes* of Jesus' uniqueness— both the characteristics that *are* essential to making him unique and those that are *not*. This may seem like a rather dry, abstract exercise. It is not. What I'm trying to describe here is the way Christians actually do, or can, *experience* Jesus to be unique—how they *feel* his specialness, his saving role in their lives. Naturally, I'm speaking here, to a great extent, about my own Christian life and efforts to be a disciple of Jesus; I trust that my experience might reflect or clarify that of other Christians.[8]

The revision that I am urging can be formulated crisply and clearly, as I suggested in chapter 2, in terms of adverbs: *truly* but not *solely*. Christians can and must affirm within their own communities and before the world that all the marvelous things said about Jesus in the New Testament apply to him *truly*, but not necessarily *solely*. "Truly" is an essential ingredient in the Christians' experience of Jesus and in their faithfulness to him; "solely," I suggest, is not necessary and indeed, for many Christians, may not even be possible. What I am saying is nothing terribly complex or foreign to Christian experience; I would surmise that most Christians could verify these claims when they look calmly and honestly into their own experience of Jesus and his saving gospel.

Whatever it is that brings a person to be a Christian and follower of Jesus, by its very nature it must enable the person to say that Jesus is truly and effectively the vehicle of the Divine Presence in his or her life. For this person Jesus is truly the Son of God, the savior, mediator, word of God, messiah, the living one. Without the *feeling*—without an experiential awareness—that inspires the "truly," one cannot be, one would not want to be, a Christian.

But I don't think that is true of "solely." When one knows that Jesus is truly savior, one does *not* know that he is the *only* savior. One's experience is limited and has not been able to take in the experiences and messages of all other so-called saviors or religious figures.

But if Christians do not or cannot know that Jesus is the *only* savior, neither do they *have to* know this in order to be committed to this Jesus. The experience of Jesus that has enabled them to say "truly" enables them to keep following him. That there may be others is not an impediment to faithful following. Discipleship requires "truly"; it does not seem to require "solely."

FULL, DEFINITIVE, UNSURPASSABLE? NO!

The contents of this *truly/only* distinction need to be spelled out more carefully and clearly. Keeping to my grammatical tack, let me try to do so by means of adjectives. First, from a negative perspective, if Christians take seriously the possibility that Jesus is not the only self-manifestation of the Divine and not the only saving embodiment of God's truth and grace, then they will have to qualify or revise three adjectives that Christian preachers and theologians have attached to the way they speak about God's revelation in Jesus: *full, definitive*, and *unsurpassable*. I will summarize why to qualify or even to remove such terms from Christian proclamation of Jesus is not only permissible but may even be required by other things that Christians say they believe about God and about divine incarnation in Jesus.

a) In Jesus, Christians do not possess the *fullness* or the totality of divine revelation, as if he exhausted all the truth that God has to reveal. This statement is grounded, I believe, in both theological and biblical convictions. Theologically, Christians throughout their tradition would take it for granted that no finite medium can exhaust the fullness of the Infinite. To identify the Infinite with anything finite—that is, to contain and limit the Divine to any one human form or mediation—has biblically and traditionally been called idolatry.

But if this is idolatry, would not the Christian belief in the incarnation of the Divine in the man Jesus be idolatrous? Not really, for incarnation means that Divinity has assumed the fullness of humanity, not that humanity has taken on the fullness of Divinity. As Edward Schillebeeckx has recently reminded us, to believe in the incarnation is to believe that God has taken on all the *limitations* of the human condition (Schillebeeckx 1990, 164-68). Thus, if Christians want to affirm that the Divine has *truly* been "made flesh" in Jesus, they cannot, at the same time, hold that the Divine has *absolutely* or *totally* been made flesh in Jesus. Flesh cannot be made into a total container of the Divine. Also, in the biblical witness about Jesus, although he is often closely associated with the very being and activity of God—by being called the Son, Word, Wisdom of God—he is not identified with God.[9] So when we read in Colossians 2:9 that "the whole fullness of deity dwells bodily" in Jesus, it cannot mean that such fullness is exhausted by or restricted to Jesus, as if a human body or nature could confine the infinity of Divinity. We must interpret such texts without destroying the paradox that they contain. The fullness is really there, but it is not only there; or better, in Jesus we meet God fully, but that doesn't mean we have grasped the fullness of God.

Such a qualified understanding of fullness would seem to move in the same direction as the early patristic doctrine of the divine Logos or Word, even though it goes beyond that doctrine. In affirming and trying to grasp John's understanding of Jesus as the enfleshment of the Logos, early Christian theologians recognized that this Logos was not simply confined to Jesus; the Word was active in the world before Jesus and continues to be active after him.[10] Therefore, Christians cannot simply announce that Jesus is the fullness of the Word or of Divinity and leave it at that. Such claims must be qualified to recognize and affirm both the universality and the incomprehensibility of the Divine. Such an affirmation-with-qualification is expressed, I think, in the often-used distinction: Christians can and must proclaim that Jesus is *totus Deus*—totally divine, but they cannot claim that Jesus is *totum Dei*—the totality of the Divine (Robinson 1979, 104, 120).

b) Nor should Christians boast a *definitive* Word of God in Jesus, as if there could be no other norms for Divine Truth outside of him. Again, to claim definitiveness about anything is to hold that nothing essentially new or different can be said about it. To announce that one has the definitive Divine Truth is to imply that the Wisdom that surpasses all knowledge and the Love that is eternally creative have been deposited in a container to which nothing more can be added. Again, if that is what Christians mean when they say they have the definitive deposit of faith, then their deposit would seem to fit the definition of an idol.

Also, the way Christians talk about their revelation as definitive or as the norm that excludes all other norms seems to fly in the face of the essentially eschatological nature of the energizing truth that Jesus made available to humankind; the truth that he revealed, while utterly reliable and demanding our full commitment, was not a finished product. There was more to come; there will always be more to come as long as we continue in this terrestrial pilgrimage. For as long as the God whom Jesus revealed remains God, no one can have the final word on such a God.

Some Christian theologians have expressed the fear or the warning that when we so question the definitiveness or the exclusivity of the divine incarnation in Jesus, we are dismantling the central Christian belief in the Trinity (Braaten 1994). On the contrary, I think we are deepening and expanding this belief. While continuing to affirm the authenticity and reliability of the Divine Word's powerful presence in Jesus, we are also affirming that this Word cannot be restricted, that it can well surprise and instruct us elsewhere. Even Thomas Aquinas recognized the possibility that the Second Person of the Trinity could be incarnated in other human natures besides that of Jesus. "We cannot say that the divine person, in assuming one human nature, could not assume another."[11] Leonardo Boff attempts to make Aquinas's stunning statement a little less threatening:

> There is nothing repugnant about the other divine Persons being incarnate. The Mystery of the Triune God is so profound and so immense that it can never be exhausted by a single concretization like that which was realized within our earthly system . . . If this [God's incarnation in Jesus] need not be God's absolute communication with his creation, this does not take away its value for us. It means merely that we should keep ourselves open to the infinite possibilities of the mystery of God (Boff 1978, 216-17).

c) Therefore, God's saving word in Jesus cannot be extolled as *unsurpassable,* as if God could not reveal more of God's fullness in other ways at other times. To hold that God could provide a revelation that would so contain God's truth as not to allow anything more to be said would be analogous to that old mind-bender often dished out in grammar school catechism classes that asked whether God could create a rock so heavy that God could not pick it up! So, once again, it seems that to hold up a package of Divine Truth that is unsurpassable is to erect an idol. It would also seem to contradict, or rule out, the role of the Holy Spirit which Jesus, in John's gospel, affirmed: "I have many things to say to you, but you cannot bear them now. The Spirit of Truth, in coming, will guide you into all the truth" (Jn 16: 12-13). If we believe in the Holy Spirit, we must believe that there is always "more to come."

Therefore, even someone like Jon Sobrino, who is prophetically sensitive to any attempt to dilute or "pacify" the demands of Jesus and the Kingdom, warns against the dangers of what he calls a "mere jesusology" or a "christological reduction." By this he means a boiling down of the reality of the Reign of God to Jesus himself, so that in Jesus we would have the total or unsurpassable presence of the Kingdom. Sobrino reminds his fellow Christians that Jesus is not "the ultimate thing that God can intend for history" and that the incarnation of the Word in Jesus does not "represent the accomplishment of God's final will." Rather than a "christological reduction" we need a "christological concentration"—a focusing on Jesus that would call for commitment but that would not exclude the broader picture and power of the Kingdom (Sobrino 1984, 41-42; also 1987, 51).

The reason why Sobrino and liberation theologians are concerned about an unsurpassable reduction of the Kingdom to Jesus is not orthodoxy but orthopraxis—not doctrinal purity but Christian living. If

Jesus is absolutized as total, final, or unsurpassable, Christian existence is all too easily understood mainly as a confession of or a personal relationship with Jesus rather than as a commitment to work
with him for the Kingdom of God.

> When the person of Christ is turned into an unqualified abso-
> lute, it is often said that he *is* the Kingdom of God and that the
> encounter with the Thou of Christ is the ultimate reference point
> of faith. Such a view leads, with historical if not logical neces-
> sity, to locating the response to the gospel more in the line of
> faith and personal contact with Christ than in the line of the
> accomplishment of God's Kingdom (Sobrino 1984, 43).

UNIVERSAL, DECISIVE, INDISPENSABLE? YES!

But we can't stop there. Discipleship and fidelity to the New Testament witness require Christians to know and proclaim Jesus as *truly*
God's saving presence in history. If Christians no longer need to insist
on *only*, they must continue to proclaim *truly*. Unpacking the contents
of that "truly," we can say that Christians must announce Jesus to all
peoples as God's *universal, decisive,* and *indispensable* manifestation
of saving truth and grace. Once again, let me try to clarify briefly
what each of those adjectives contains.

a) God's word in Jesus is *universal* insofar as it is experienced to be
a call not just for Christians but for peoples of all times. I think this
runs through the multiple traditions of the New Testament—the insistence that the good news is good not just for a particular group of
Jewish faithful but for all peoples, and that therefore the followers of
Jesus have to go into the whole world, to all nations, to announce this
good news (Mt 28:19). To water down the universality of Christian
truth claims is to violate the biblical witness.[12] But it is also to violate
the way truth is experienced. If something is true, especially if it is a
truth that touches the core of how I see the world and live my life, it
cannot be true only for me. If it is true, it has to be true also for others.
Michael Polanyi's crisp declaration will, I suspect, feel right for most
people: "Any personal contact with reality inevitably claims universality" (quoted in Maguire 1993, 63). Granted, my grasp of truth is
always limited and conditioned. Still, what I am grasping is not confined by those limitations; it has to be "translatable" to other limitations and conditionings. Like salt that has lost its savor, truth that is
not universal is not worth much.

What we are saying about the universality of truth claims is embodied perhaps more convincingly in the contemporary discussion of
"classics." As the history of literature or any present-day college-level
literature program illustrates, a piece of literature that is deemed a

classic cannot be limited to its parent-culture (even though it is best appreciated and loved in its parent-home). As Gandhi discovered, a Hindu can find powerful truth in the gospels; Merton could say the same of the *Tao Te Ching* and the writings of Chuang Tzu (Merton 1969). Classics, we discover, have "perpetual contemporaneity" (Kermode 1975, 17-18). "By its nature, it [a classic] cannot be confined to one circle of appreciation. Its citizenship is humanwide . . . A classic is human conversation at its most communicable" (Maguire 1993, 63). To drink of the sources of truth is to want to share that drink with others, all others.

b) The revelation given in Jesus is also *decisive*. It shakes and challenges and calls one to change perspective and conduct. It makes a difference in one's life; this difference, often if not always, will "cut one off" (*decidere*) from other perspectives and ways of living. Therefore, to say that Jesus is decisive means that he is normative.[13] Such normativeness, according to Schillebeeckx, is a common tone in the various voices of the New Testament: "According to the witness of the New Testament, for Christians Jesus has a normative and essential relationship to the universal kingdom of God for all men and women . . . The quotations from scripture [those extolling Jesus] point clearly to the Christian awareness that in Jesus of Nazareth God has revealed himself in such a form as to manifest his will for the salvation of all humankind in a decisive and definitive way" (Schillebeeckx 1990, 144-45, also 121).

Notice that Schillebeeckx describes divine revelation in Jesus as decisive *and* definitive. That seems to make sense, for one may rightly ask how a truth can be decisive and normative without being definitive and unsurpassable; if the norm I have embraced is decisive and calls me to make a decision for this rather than that, such a norm surely requires a certain finality in the course of action I have chosen. Yes, this is true. But while such a norm calls me to a clear decision and way of acting, it does not at all rule out the possibility that I can also come to other insights and other decisions which, although they do not contradict my original decision, are very different from it. A decisive norm, in other words, may rule out *some* other norms, but it need not exclude *all* other norms. It is decisive, but not final or unsurpassable.[14]

Roger Haight makes this same distinction more clearly and concretely when he suggests that in relation to persons of other religious traditions, Jesus provides Christians with a *negative* rather than a positive norm. While Christians can imagine that God may have more to reveal to humankind than what has been made known in Jesus, they cannot imagine that such a revelation would contradict the central ingredients of the truth they have found in Jesus[15] (Haight 1989, 262; also Ogden 1992, 101-2). In serving as a norm, therefore, Jesus' good

good ✳⟩ news *defines* God, but it does not *confine* God; it reveals what Christians feel is *essential* to a true knowledge of the Divine, but it does not provide *all* that makes up such knowledge.

With such an understanding of how Jesus is decisive and normative, I think we can meet the concerns of those Christians who hold that the new views of Jesus' uniqueness run contrary to what they feel was Jesus' own self-consciousness as *the final prophet.*[16] Granting that Jesus did so see himself and that he was convinced that God's Realm was arriving in his message and person, I feel that an understanding of Jesus as delivering God's *decisive but not total* word enables Christians to be faithful to both the adjective *and* the noun in this title of "final prophet." When Jesus felt himself to be "final" (he never used that word), he was calling all people to take his message with utter seriousness, for it was calling them to take a stand, make a decision, for or against the Kingdom of God. But insofar as he sensed that he was a prophet (a word he most likely did use), he would want all those following him genuinely to be open to wherever and through whomever that Kingdom might be realized. His normative message did not necessarily exclude other messages.[17]

c) Finally, Christians continue to proclaim the truth made known in Jesus as *indispensable*. Although this quality of Jesus' uniqueness sounds more imposing than the other two we just examined, it flows from them. If I experience something to be true not just for me but for others, and if this truth has enriched and transformed my life, I automatically feel that it can and should do the same for others. So for Christians, to encounter Jesus as he who manifests God's reality and realm and who decisively calls them to cast their lot with this vision, Jesus' message is experienced as something "necessary," something without which we can't see the richness of who God is and what God is up to in the world. Again, in Jon Sobrino's words: "Jesus himself, then—what he does and says, what he suffers and what happens to him—becomes essential to an understanding of the approach of the Kingdom and the manner of realization of this approach" (Sobrino 1988, 30).

In other words, to know Jesus Christ is to feel that Buddhists and Hindus and Muslims need to know him too; this means they need to recognize and accept the truth he reveals (even though this does not necessarily mean that they will become members of the Christian community). Thus, it seems to me that inherent in the Christian experience of Jesus is the conviction that anyone who has not known and in some way accepted the message and power of the gospel is missing something in their knowledge and living of truth. Whatever other truth about the Ultimate and the human condition there may be in other traditions, such truth can be enhanced, clarified—maybe even corrected—through an encounter with the good news made known in Jesus.[18]

In a qualified but still real sense, persons of other religious paths are "unfulfilled" without Christ. One might even say that Jesus the Christ is "necessary" for them to have a more complete understanding of the human condition. This does not mean, I must stress, that such persons, without Christ, are imperfect, or inferior to Christians, or lost without Christ. John Hick has asked *how* or *why* Christ is indispensable: is it the way penicillin is indispensable for the dying person or the way vitamins are necessary for better health? (in Swidler and Mojzes 1996). I think Christ's (or, as I will add immediately in the next paragraph, Buddha's) indispensability is somewhere in-between. Maybe it is something like the illiterate person who is living a happy, satisfying life; when he learns to read, something is added to his life that was not there, something that doesn't demean what he had before but enhances it. One is somehow, but clearly, a fuller, a more aware human being—a better Buddhist or Hindu perhaps.[19]

This, then, is the skeletal outline of a reinterpretation of Jesus' uniqueness: he is not God's total, definitive, unsurpassable truth, but he does bring a universal, decisive, indispensable message. Notice that I said "a" rather than "the" in the last sentence, for if we no longer insist that Jesus is God's only saving word, we are open to the *possibility*—our Christian belief in universal revelation would suggest *probability*—that there are *other* universal, decisive, indispensable manifestations of divine reality besides Jesus.[20] Thus, if Christians are deeply convinced that whatever truth there may be in other traditions, it can be illumined, fulfilled, maybe transformed in the Word that has been given to them, they must be as deeply open to being enlightened, fulfilled, and transformed by the Word spoken and embodied for them in persons of other religious paths. Roger Haight illustrates how Christian theologians are seeking this balance between the particular and the universal, between asserting one's own norm and yet remaining open to other norms:

> If one maintains that Jesus is normative for one's own salvation as a human being, one must, by the principle of noncontradiction, assert that Jesus is universally relevant and normative for all human beings. But . . . the explanation of the status of Jesus must be such that it not be exclusive. It must also allow for the possibility of other figures of equal status and who may also reveal something of God that is normative. Indeed, if God is as Jesus reveals God to be, i.e. universal savior, one must expect that there will be other historical mediations of this salvation (Haight 1992, 280-81).[21]

This new interpretation of Jesus' uniqueness seeks to promote the transformation both of other religions *and* of Christianity. Just what this transformation will imply and how much it will affect other faiths and Christianity can be known only through dialogue.

A Relational Uniqueness

Those who relate to Jesus the Christ as truly but not solely unique—truly but not solely God's saving Word and Presence—will find themselves moving toward an image of Jesus' uniqueness quite different from traditional views, an image, I believe, more in harmony with the biblical picture of Jesus. For much of the history of the churches and for many Christians today, to picture Jesus as unique is to see him standing *by himself*. In the view of Jesus' uniqueness we have been discussing, he has to stand *with others*. We've been talking about a *relational uniqueness*, not a solitary uniqueness that pushes others out of the picture. To affirm Jesus as *truly* God's Word is to award him a distinctiveness that is his alone; to add that he is not *solely* God's Word is also to see that distinctiveness as one that has to be brought into relationship with other possible Words. Jesus is a Word that can be understood only in conversations with other Words.

I think this makes sound theological sense. The Christian trinitarian model of Deity understands God as self-communicating; God's nature requires that God be Word, which means that God speak or become Word. Applied to the finite, historical order, this means that the Divine Word must express itself in words; the Logos, in becoming enfleshed in history, will have to be the *logoi spermatikoi*—the multiple word-seeds cast upon the field of history. As Anthony Kelly puts it, the Christian affirmation of God as Word in history lays the foundations for a "global conversation" (Kelly 1989, 233-34). He expands the poetry of John's Prologue:

> Christian faith in the Word made flesh leads us progressively to the realization that the "flesh" is essentially a "conversation." Continuing revelation in history demands its times of listening as well as speaking, in the expanding world of mutual presence. The Word is not incarnate in an imperialistic shout drowning out other voices, but as an ever-original and healing address in the conditions of human speech. If the Word is God, the whole truth has not been heard. It is the whole truth that is the healing truth (ibid., 241).

A relational understanding of Jesus' uniqueness also makes good philosophical sense. As we said earlier, there is no such thing as a bare fact. That means that there is also no such thing as a naked word. All words, like all facts, come dressed in particular forms and cultures; they have to be *interpreted*. The meaning of a word is not simply a piece of fruit to be picked off the tree; it must, rather, be processed before it can be consumed and appreciated. Thus, as Frans Jozef van Beeck admits, if Christians believe that in God's Word in Jesus "God has definitively welcomed humanity and the world into the divine life," they must also remember that "the fulfillment of this divine commitment remains a matter of hope, that is, of a *profession of faith that remains true only to the extent that it is interpreted perspectivally*." Such a claim for a definitive revelation "rests entirely on discernment, that is, it operates on *interpretation*" (van Beeck 1991, 559).

God's "definitive" Word in Jesus must be interpreted—and interpreted perspectivally. That means: amid the multiple and changing perspectives of history; and that means: in conversation with many other Words within history. Without a conversation with other Words, Christians can't really understand what the "definitive" Word in Jesus means! That certainly makes "definitive" claims much less imperialistic and much more relational.[22]

What I am calling "relational uniqueness" has also been termed "complementary uniqueness" or "inclusive uniqueness" (Thompson 1985, 388-93; Moran 1992). For William Thompson, if we believe in a kenotic or self-emptying God, that is, that "the Divine has kenotically self-limited itself and disclosed itself within the necessarily limited, cultural forms of the varied religions and their founders," then we also have to recognize not only the uniqueness and "the possible decisiveness" of many religions but also their need to complement each other (Thompson 1987, 22-24). John Cobb points to the same complementary understanding of uniqueness when he answers his own question: "So am I affirming Christian uniqueness? Certainly and emphatically so! But I am affirming the uniqueness also of Confucianism, Buddhism, Hinduism, Islam and Judaism" (Cobb 1990, 91-92). Each unique religion, however, cannot stand alone:

> My exclusive [read: unique] claims for Christ need not conflict with the exclusive Buddhist claims for the realization of Buddhahood of which Gautama is the paradigm instance . . . We [Christians] should strive to share what has been exclusive to Christianity as we appropriate what has been exclusive to other traditions. This is what a Christianized Buddhism and a Buddhized Christianity are all about (Cobb 1984, 177).

Cobb states that Christ "need not conflict" with other unique claims. But Christ *can* conflict, and sometimes *must*. This is why I prefer the

term "relational" rather than "complementary" or "inclusive" uniqueness. "Complementary" or "inclusive" suggests peaches and cream;
"relational" allows for thorns and thickets. Insofar as Christians proclaim the "pure, unbounded love of God" at work in the world and
therefore do not insist that Jesus is God's full, final, or unsurpassable
Word, they expect that for the most part their relationships with sincere believers of other paths will indeed be complementary. But insofar as Christians also experience God's presence in Jesus to include
universal, decisive, and indispensable claims, they will also be ready
to take strong stands, sometimes in opposition, to the claims of others. If we always grow through relationships, the growth can often be
painful.

So, with John Cobb, we can describe Christian faith and discipleship succinctly and challengingly: Jesus is the way that is open to other
ways (Cobb 1990, 91). The kind of truth that Jesus enables us to
affirm and feel is a truth that tells us that there is, happily and excit-
ingly, more truth to come. To say yes to the God made known in Jesus
is to say yes to what that God has still to make known to us. The truth
that we know provides us with a confidence, even an eagerness, to
face whatever truth may still come, as surprising and disturbing as it
may be. So in a paradoxical sense, to experience that Jesus makes
known the "fullness" of truth is to be aware, at the same time, that we
don't know what that fullness contains. But we now have a place, a
confidence, to find out; here we stand, and that "standing" is a step-
ping stone from which we can move and stand somewhere else. The
"fullness" of God in Jesus, in other words, is one which opens us to
the "fullness" of God in others. Therefore, the text from Colossians,
"in him dwells the fullness of Divinity" (Col 2:9) "is not speaking of a
fullness of Christ the individual, but of a fullness that includes others"
(Sobrino 1988, 42).

To express this paradox differently, to be christocentric—centered
on Christ—requires one to be centered on others, to be open to and in
relation with others. If one is not looking out toward and in conversation with others, then one is not centered on Christ. "What you do to
the least of your brothers and sisters, you do to me" (Mt 25:40). Such
openness to others, such ability to dialogue, is an essential part of
what "being faithful" to Christ means. This requires having to balance the oft-heard admonition that following Jesus means turning one's
back on others; at the same time, one has to remember that to follow
Christ, one also has to follow—that is, be open to, in dialogue with—
others. Christ equips his followers with the firmness to resist, but also
with the humility to learn.

The question is then what Christ is doing in the world today. It is
not hard to think of that work as reminding us of our finitude

and breaking our tendency to think that our own opinions are final and adequate. It is easy to think of that work as calling us to listen to the truth and wisdom of others . . . To learn from others whatever truth they have to offer and to integrate that with the insights and wisdom we have learned from our Christian heritage appears to be faithful to Christ (Cobb 1990, 91).[23]

5

UNIQUENESS REAFFIRMED

How Jesus Is Unique

The previous chapter is incomplete. More needs to be said and pondered. It is not enough simply to declare that Christians can and should continue proclaiming Jesus to be universal, decisive, indispensable. We have to ask: *why*? What makes him unique? What moves his disciples to feel that his message is for all, that it calls one to take a stand, that all people need to know of this man and his vision? What is the *content* of Jesus' uniqueness?

WHAT DOES "UNIQUE" MEAN?

As pressing as such questions may be, they can also make people very uneasy and suspicious. To those outside the Christian churches, it sounds like another dressed up or disguised attempt to establish the superiority of Christianity and the need to hustle everyone into the Christian church. To those within the Christian community, such questions seem to be presupposing some kind of "essence of Christianity," an inner core of Christianity that never changes and that defines Christians once and for all. But as far as my judgments are accurate and my motives honest, the questions I've asked about the uniqueness of Christ are neither intended to, nor do they have to, prove Christian superiority or enshrine an essence of Christianity.

By "unique" I do not mean what someone has that no one else has. Rather, one's uniqueness is that which makes one special or distinctive—that without which the person would not be the person he or she is. What makes one unique is whatever others speak of first when they try to describe a person, or when they try to state what it is that always so delights or disturbs them when they interact with that person. Remove those unique qualities, and you are meeting a different *uniqueness as specific identity*

person. So the uniqueness of Jesus and the gospel is that without which Jesus would no longer act or speak the way he is portrayed in the New Testament, that without which we would no longer have the authentic, complete gospel.

In theological terms, what I understand by uniqueness is close to what has been called the canon within the canon—those truths or principles that are central to everything in the New Testament, those truths that can be used to adjudicate the truth of other contents of the Bible, those convictions and articles by which, in Luther's terms, the entire structure of the church "stands or falls" (the *articulus stantis et cadentis ecclesiae*).

So I agree fully with Roger Haight when he warns, "One should beware of the fallacy that the essence of Christianity is reducible to what is specifically different from other faiths" (Haight 1994, 231). Jesus' uniqueness is that which makes him who he is, not what necessarily makes him different from others (although his uniqueness may indeed make him different from many others). It is what gives him, and what should give Christians, their focus or their center for the way they see and understand and respond to the world. It is what provides "a centering, interpretative, and transforming effect on what the Christian affirms about things held in common with other religions" (ibid.). Therefore, what we mean by the uniqueness of Jesus will constitute his followers' distinctive contribution to the interreligious dialogue—that necessary ingredient without which Christians would no longer be speaking or acting like disciples of Jesus in their dealings with persons of other faiths.

But is there such a unique core or canon within the canon? The answer to that question has to be yes and no. No, if by unique core one means an unchangeable something, an always sparkling family jewel that is passed on from generation to generation. Yes, if unique core is viewed more as a treasure that has to be appreciated and invested differently according to the changing world of each generation. The core is there, the distinctive something that is the uniqueness of Jesus, but to get at it and to feel its transformative power, one has to approach it and apply it with the interpretative tools of one's own historical and cultural context. What makes Christianity unique is, paradoxically, ever the same but ever different. There is something that endures and doesn't change, but one cannot see and talk about it without using the differing lenses and languages of changing times and peoples.

I think that the history of Christianity bears out that the heart of the gospel or the core of Christian revelation is a pluriform, adaptive, changing reality. What Christians find to be most important or meaningful or saving in the good news of the living Christ has been experienced and formulated differently according to different stages of history and cultures. The living Christ is the same yesterday, today, and to-morrow, but his transforming power will work in and be perceived differently by a medieval European peasant than by a contemporary Salvadoran *campesino*.

UNIQUENESS AND THE HISTORICAL JESUS

Admitting that we will see the unique core of the Christian message differently as Christians plod their path through history, where do we begin looking? Where it all started, one would think: Jesus himself, or what the New Testament scholars and theologians have come to call *the historical Jesus*. But to look for the uniqueness of Christianity in the historical Jesus is to enter a mine field of scholarly dispute. I want to work only with those minimal assertions that most mainline New Testament experts would agree with (over the last decades, that mini-mum seems to be an expanding-contracting quantity). What do I mean?

Let me venture two general statements that I think will draw the basic assent, if not eager support, of the majority of New Testament scholars and theologians:

First, if we look at what we can know of Jesus based solely on historical or so-called scientific procedures, we have to recognize that we *can't* know enough to paint a crystal-clear, certain picture of who he was and what he said and did, but we *can* know enough to keep on the right track of following what he set in motion for ensuing history. First the "can't": we will never know the historical Jesus fully, conclu-sively, unambiguously. In a sense, the quest for the historical Jesus will never be over; we will always have to keep looking. As John Meier, certainly one of the most dedicated of the questers, tells us, there is much we can know about the historical Jesus, that is, "the Jesus whom we can 'recover' and examine by using the scientific tools of modern historical research." But results, though significant, will always be limited, piecemeal, open to further questions. "Of its very nature, this quest can reconstruct only fragments of a mosaic, the faint outline of a faded fresco that allows of many interpretations" (Meier 1991, 25; see also 21-23). We can attain only "a softly focused characterization of the pre-Easter Jesus" (Burton L. Mack, quoted in Borg 1994, 29). The reason is simple and generally recognized: the gospels, our chief source of knowledge about the historical Jesus, were not intended to give us a picture of the historical Jesus; to think that they were "trans-ports them in an exegetical time machine to the Enlightenment" (Meier 1991, 26).

But though the fresco is faded and the interpretations abound, we *can* see enough of what this Jesus was about to know whether our efforts to understand and follow him are basically on track or not.

Although there may be room for *many* interpretations, that doesn't mean that *any* interpretation goes. We will be able to say that some images of Jesus are, to put it bluntly, off the historical wall! (like the Jesus of apartheid, or the Jesus of the conquistadors, or the Jesus of the patriarchs, who invoke him to keep women from any positions of authority in the churches). Some would hold that our knowledge of the historical Jesus is sufficient to serve only as a kind of negative referee, which decides which served-up images of Jesus are out of bounds (Tracy 1980, 36-39). That's a minimalist view indeed, but still a quite valid and important one.

Others are more positive, holding that the general picture and message of this Spirit-filled prophet or cynic-critic is clear enough to give us a vision of what he stood for and how he would respond to a society like our own (see Borg 1987, 1994; Crossan 1991). If we can't know the "ipsissima verba" or "very words" of Jesus, we can know the basic contents of his "ipsissima intentio"—his intention or what he was up to (Nolan 1978, 10).[1] If we will never come to a clear picture of what Jesus thought of himself, we can achieve a reliable notion of why people were interested in him and responded the way they did, both positively or negatively (Segundo 1985, 13-21). If we don't have the script of his message, we can see clearly enough what he set in motion—his practice and the spirit with which he carried it out (Sobrino 1994, 51)[2]; and we can see that practice and spirit reliably enough to know when his followers derailed or obstructed his movement. If we don't have Jesus' own theology or christology, we do know basically who God was for Jesus and what values and concerns this God inspired in him. We can know enough about Jesus to feel his challenge and to know when we are turning our backs on it.

My second statement about how the historical Jesus enables us to know the uniqueness of Christ/Christianity: Even if we did have a picture of the historical Jesus that was clear, certain, unambiguous, such solid historical knowledge would still *not* be enough for the Christian community. For in a real sense, the historical Jesus has never existed purely and solely as the historical Jesus. Even during his earthly ministry, the Jesus of history—insofar as he was experienced as messiah or prophet or savior—was experienced and interpreted *within a community.* Jesus was interpreted by his followers from the beginning of his ministry, and this interpretation intensified after his death and the experience his followers came to call the resurrection.

This means that the historical Jesus was always seen, and must continued to be seen and understood, *together with* what has been termed the Christ of faith. Insofar as Jesus—who he was, what he said, and what he did—touched and transformed the lives of others, this Jesus became, and has remained, the Christ of faith. Therefore, even if we had a clear and certain picture of the historical Jesus, we would have to interpret, apply, and turn that knowledge into the power and presence of the Christ of faith. The relation between the historical Jesus and the Christ of faith is analogous to the way Christians have come to speak about the divinity and humanity of Jesus: distinct but never separate. You can't have one without the other, although you don't want to reduce one to the other (Thompson 1994).

Another term or symbol for the Christ of faith is the *Pneuma tou Christou*—"the Spirit of Christ" (2 Cor 3:17) or the Holy Spirit. Therefore, in order to determine what makes up the "uniqueness of the Christian message," we have to turn to *both* the data on the historical Jesus that is found in scripture *and* the guidance found in the pneumatic working of the Spirit of the absent but risen Christ in the church. If we appeal only to the data of the scriptures, we end up with a type of biblicism; if we are guided only by the Spirit, that Spirit can easily become the spirit of subjectivism. We need both—the New Testament witness felt and interpreted under the continued presence of the Spirit in the community (the historical Jesus and the Christ of faith). If Christians can't speak about God without christology, that is, without turning to the story of Jesus in the New Testament, they also cannot speak about christology without pneumatology, without recognizing the presence of the Spirit. "And it is impossible to speak about either christology or pneumatology without a living church community, and thus without at least an implicit ecclesiology" (Schillebeeckx 1990, 109-10).

So in the next section, when I will propose that the uniqueness of Jesus and his community has to do with "liberation" and the transformation of this world, I will be basing that claim on what we can know, with relative certainty, about the historical Jesus—*but not only* on the historical Jesus. I will also be appealing to and presupposing the way the Spirit of Christ seems to be active within the community, the way the Spirit is present in the community's efforts to understand and interpret the witness of the New Testament in *the world as it exists and is perceived today*. So I recognize that what I am proposing as unique to Christianity is not the only thing that could be, and has been, so proposed. The Spirit will blow differently (which doesn't mean in any old direction) in different contexts and needs.

More explicitly, I admit that when I, with so many other Christians, propose liberation or emancipation as the heart of the gospel, I admit that our contemporary need for liberation and global responsibility plays a key role in how I hear the gospel. But I am also claiming that there is something to be so heard; there are sound historical reasons to see Jesus as a liberator and to make historical claims that he sought the well-being of others, especially the suffering. I endorse the honesty of Mark Taylor's confession: "The primacy of emancipation [in Jesus and his message] can indeed be developed through direct discussion of the figure of Jesus, as of texts bearing witness to him . . .

However, . . . the primacy of emancipation emerges not just because Jesus or the Bible 'tells us so' but also because emancipation is needed by so many" (Taylor 1990, 180; see also 177-79).

THE REIGN OF GOD—FOCUS OF JESUS' MESSAGE

So what was primary for Jesus, what was the center or axis of his mission and message? On this question there is a surprising consensus among scripture scholars, both mainline and evangelical: According to the gospel record, the heartbeat of the being and practice of Jesus was what he called the Reign of God—the *Basileia tou Theou*. Dermot Lane summarizes what he holds to be a statement about Jesus that would be broadly endorsed as historically reliable:

> Indeed, everything that Jesus says and does is inspired from be-ginning to end by his personal commitment to the coming Reign of God into the world. The controlling horizon of the mission and ministry of Jesus is the Kingdom of God. The life, death, and resurrection of Jesus derive their meaning from the announce-ment of the Kingdom of God (Lane 1991, 11).

This means that the ultimate or the absolute or the norm that grounded and guided Jesus' life was not what many people would think. Jon Sobrino takes us through a step-by-step approach to Jesus' ultimate concern. First of all, he points out that "Jesus is not ultimate for himself . . . Any attempt to make Jesus the absolutely ultimate breaks down in the face of the evidence of exegesis, and not only [concerning] the historical Jesus but the risen Christ as well" (Sobrino 1988, 82). Second, and more surprising, "The ultimate for Jesus is not simply 'God'"; that is, "Jesus did not simply preach 'God.' 'God' is not simply and absolutely Jesus' ultimate pole of reference" (ibid.). Whenever Jesus referred to God, he was not speaking about a reality that, by itself, could be known or used as a criterion for judgment. There was something else that "mediated" the absoluteness of God and so was identified with this divine absoluteness. This was not, thirdly, "the church or the Kingdom of heaven" (ibid., 83-84). The reality of the Divine is not found primarily or ultimately either in heaven or in the church. Rather, Sobrino tells us finally, "The ultimate for Jesus is the Kingdom of God," that is, God not in relation to God's self but in relation to this Earth, to this history. For Jesus, as for any authentic Jewish prophet, "God is a God-*of*, a God-*for*, a God-*in*, never a God-*in-himself*" (Sobrino 1994, 69).

In contemporary theological parlance, we can say that Jesus was not ecclesiocentric or even christocentric; his primary intent was not to establish and fill a church or to bring all persons to recognize what he felt was his God-given mission (which doesn't mean that he would have been opposed to such endeavors; we're talking about what was primary for him). But we also have to be careful about announcing that Jesus was *theocentric*, God-centered. Certainly, Jesus' experience of and devotion to the God he called Abba was the dynamo of his life. Yet simply to bring people to believe in God or to adore and worship God would have been for Jesus not only incomplete but dangerous; the Abba whom Jesus proclaimed could not be known or worshiped apart from the *Basileia*—the Reign of God. "The final reality for him [Jesus] was not simply 'God' but 'the Kingdom of God.' . . . For Jesus even 'God' is seen within the wider reality: 'the Kingdom of God'" (Sobrino 1994, 68). To know God apart from this Reign was to know a false God. Jesus, we can say, was Kingdom-centered. More precisely, for him, in order to be God-centered, one had to be Kingdom-centered.[3]

But what does it mean to be centered on, committed to, the Reign of God? Again, no nicely chiseled, hard-as-rock answer can be given. Jesus never provided a definition of the Reign of God. As a symbol— indeed, his master symbol—its meaning will never be captured and will have to be explored and reappropriated through centuries and cultures. But amid this profundity and richness, one foundational quality of the Reign must be recognized as rooted in Jesus' message and must be preserved in all the subsequent interpretations: God's Reign is meant to be a *this-worldly reality*. Yes, it definitely was a promise for life after death, but just as definitely Jesus envisioned God's Reign as taking place in and transforming human beings and societies in this world. With his vision of the Reign of God, in experiencing that Reign arriving through himself, Jesus intended the betterment, the well-being, the fuller life of people around him, especially those who were suffering. It was a reality that would change both human hearts *and* human society. "Generally speaking, the kingdom of God refers to God's values and intentions for creation and history as revealed by Jesus' own preaching and ministry" (Haight 1994, 249). Or, more pointedly: "Jesus' listeners understood one thing perfectly: while the force behind the Kingdom . . . was for him the force of God, the reality of the Kingdom was something to be achieved on earth, so that society as a whole would reflect the will of God" (Segundo 1984, 88).[4]

Schillebeeckx offers a contemporary description of this Reign that is consonant with, and required by, what we know of the historical Jesus:

> The kingdom of God is the saving presence of God, active and encouraging, as it is affirmed or welcomed among men and women. It is a saving presence offered by God and freely accepted by men and women which takes concrete form above all

[Handwritten margin note: A majority of NT scholars no longer think Jesus preached an imminent K of G. Borg. A reversal of opinion here.]

in justice and peaceful relationships among individuals and peoples, in the disappearance of sickness, injustice and oppression, in the restoration of life of all that was dead and dying. The Kingdom of God is a changed new relationship (*metanoia*) of men and women to God, the tangible and visible side of which is a new type of liberating relationship among men and women within a reconciling society in a peaceful natural environment (Schillebeeckx 1990, 111-12).

For Jesus, God as God is present and active and revealed in any and all "Kingdom activity"—anything that promotes the welfare of humanity and removes suffering. Wherever such things start happening—wherever there is greater peace-love-justice and less hunger-war-exploitation—there is present the power and reality of what Jesus understood as the Kingdom of God (Sobrino 1988, 84-85; Lane 1991, 27-29, 46-49). In a sense, for Jesus, the announcement of Jeremiah was reversed and shown to work both ways: Not only is it true that "to know God is to do justice" (Jer 22: 13-17), but also "to do justice and work for the Kingdom is to know God."

Furthermore, from the evidence we have in the gospels, especially in Luke, it seems quite clear that although God's Reign was to embrace all people, it was especially meant for those who needed it most: those suffering needlessly, the many victims of the oppression resulting from a foreign domination working through local elites (Horsely 1985, 23-87). Perhaps the clearest indication that the table of the Kingdom would be open especially to those who were excluded from the well-laden tables of the establishment was Jesus' scandalous table fellowship (or open commensality) with the riffraff of Jewish society: beggars, prostitutes, tax collectors (Nolan 1978, 39-40; Crossan 1991, 261-64). There were sound historical reasons behind the accusations hurled against him that he was "eating with tax collectors and sinners" and that he was "a glutton and a drunkard, a friend of tax collectors and sinners" (Mt 11:19). The same priorities that moved Jesus to open his table to the marginalized moved him to overturn the tables of the money changers in the Temple. In this new Kingdom, victims are embraced, defended, and empowered.

Therefore if there is anything like a "hermeneutical key" that will unlock the central message of the scriptures, or if there is a "canon within the canon" that can serve to order, sort, and even revise the divergent voices that have gone to make up the Jewish and Christian testaments, I suggest that it is to be found in the symbol of God's Reign and its vision of a society structurally transformed through the spiritual transformation that has renewed the hearts of its members. Juan Luis Segundo explains how such a hermeneutical key can work:

According to Jesus, the key [for interpreting God] entails attending to the human being and placing oneself in the service of humanity's full and complete humanization . . . Only being in tune with the poor and their interests will open one's heart to the correct interpretation of God, of the law and the prophets, and ultimately of Jesus himself (Segundo 1984, 128, 131).[5]

SPIRIT-FILLED PROPHET—THE FOCUS OF JESUS' TITLES

Certainly, we must recognize that after the resurrection the Kingdom-centeredness of Jesus took on a new appearance.

The key word of Jesus' prepaschal preaching, "conversion," no longer has to do with understanding and pursuing his thoroughgoing criticism of an oppressive religious ideology; now it has to do with believing that Jesus is the Messiah (Acts 2:38). Now "salvation" in "the name of Jesus" takes the place of the "year of grace," that is, the realization on earth of the values of the Kingdom that will transform the plight of the poorest and most exploited members of Israelite society (see Acts 2:47; 4:10-12) (Segundo 1984, 186).

The proclaimer became the proclaimed. Jesus' own Kingdom-centeredness became the early community's Christ-centeredness. A litany of titles were heaped upon Jesus: Messiah, Christ, Savior, Mediator, Lamb of God, Word of God, and the title that eventually assumed center stage in Christian liturgy and doctrine—Son of God. All this was certainly an understandable, necessary, life-giving development, for it expressed the early community's experience that now the reality of the Kingdom was present to them and still possible through the ever-living Spirit of Christ. Yet christocentrism was not meant to replace but to enhance Kingdom-centrism. Being centered on Christ is the Christian way of being centered on the Kingdom. As Jesus would remind us: It is more important to focus on the Kingdom than to focus on him.

Therefore, just as the symbol of the Reign of God can be given a hermeneutical privilege and be used as the key to interpret the biblical message in general, so too, I suggest, can the title Spirit-filled Prophet be used as a hermeneutical flashlight to understand the many christological titles given Jesus in the New Testament. It can also be adopted as a hermeneutical litmus test to evaluate our ongoing understanding of these titles, including those that came to dominate Christian tradition and consciousness: (only begotten) Son of God and (one) Savior. From what I read of contemporary New Testament scholarship, this picture of Jesus as a Spirit-filled Prophet stands on a solid scriptural-historical foundation. As Marcus Borg surveys the present state of New Testament scholarship (and tries to respond to the Spirit of Christ alive in the church and world), he concludes that we can say four things with relative certainty about the historical Jesus:

1. The historical Jesus was a *spirit person*, one of those figures in human history with an experiential awareness of the reality of God.

2. Jesus was a *teacher of wisdom* who regularly used the classic forms of wisdom speech (parables and memorable short sayings known as aphorisms) to teach a subversive and alternative wisdom.

3. Jesus was a *social prophet* similar to the classical prophets of ancient Israel. As such, he criticized the elite (economic, political, and religious) of his time, was an advocate of an alternative social vision, and was often in conflict with authorities.

4. Jesus was a *movement founder* who brought into being a Jewish renewal or revitalization movement that challenged and shattered the social boundaries of his day, a movement that eventually became the early Christian church (Borg 1994, 30).

Basically, these traits come down to two: Jesus was a *spirit-filled mystic* and a *social prophet*. "Not only is he a witness to the reality of Spirit as an element of *experience*, but his passionate involvement in the culture of his own time—his social world—connects two realities which Christians have frequently separated" (Borg 1987, i). These two realities—Spirit and Prophet—have to be maintained in one's understanding and appropriation of all the other New Testament titles for Jesus; as explained in the previous chapter, these titles are best seen as calls to action (performative language). They are to communicate the same Spirit-experience to Christians and empower and guide Jesus' disciples in acting within our culture and social world. If such "calls" are not heard and felt in the way we understand Jesus as "the only Son of God" or as our "one and only Savior," then something is wrong, sadly wrong. But also, in our efforts to fashion new titles for Jesus or to reinterpret his uniqueness, as long as these efforts are enabling the Christian community to feel the power of the Spirit of Jesus and to act prophetically for the Kingdom of God in the world, we can have a basic confidence that our new interpretations are orthodox.

A HISTORICAL GOD CALLING FOR HISTORICAL ENGAGEMENT

After this hasty but I hope helpful review of how Christians can appeal to the historical Jesus and why the Reign of God forms the focus of his message, how might we formulate, for our contemporary context, the uniqueness of Christ and of Christianity? What is it in the message of Jesus that is essential for living this message in our present world? What *must* Christians bring to the table of dialogue if they are going to be faithful to what Jesus and Christianity are all about?

The answer to these questions will be fashioned out of what we have just said about Christian discipleship as a constant conversation between the historical Jesus and the Christ of faith. To hear and live Jesus' message about the Reign of God, to follow him as a Spirit-filled Prophet in our world of agonizing and threatening human-ecological suffering, Christians must realize among themselves and announce to others that in order to know God (or to experience the Transcendent, or to be enlightened to the Truth), one must also be taken up in a threefold commitment: 1) to be engaged actively in the life and struggles of this world, 2) in this engagement, to give special concern to those persons and beings who are suffering because of injustice and oppression, and 3) to carry out this engagement with a hope that despite failure and death this world can be changed for the better. Ultimate Reality experienced as the God of Jesus is a God who is *known in history*, who seeks the *well-being of the oppressed*, and who is *faithful* to those who work for God's Reign on Earth. To proclaim such a God, and the possibility of such an experience, makes up the uniqueness of Christian identity and of the Christian contribution to interreligious dialogue. Let me briefly discuss each of these three essential ingredients in Christian religious experience.

A GOD OF HISTORY

For Jesus, as for any good Jewish prophet,[6] God is a transcendent Reality that can't remain transcendent. By the very divine nature, God must get involved (express God's self) in the finite, in history. The philosophical rendition of the way Jesus always spoke of God in relation to the Kingdom is what we can call a *nonduality* between the Divine and the historical. This is not to reduce the Divine to the historical, but it is to affirm that in order to discover or be part of the Divine, one must do so through involvement in history. Jesus could not be Spirit-filled unless he was prophetically involved in his society. Though the two realities are different, they do not exist without each other. Indeed, from the perspective of human experience and awareness, it seems that for Jesus, the prophetic activity of loving one's neighbor had a certain epistemological priority; one feels the Spirit, one senses the presence or potential of God's Reign, by the praxis of historical involvement. Without historical praxis, mystical experience is somehow maimed, inadequate, even dangerous.

Christians must therefore speak of a "bipolarity" (Sobrino 1988, 4), or a "differentiated unity" (Gutiérrez in Sobrino 1988, 56), or "an unbreakable bond" (Schillebeeckx 1990, 171) between the Divine and the historical. Christian existence contains a historical element—the Reign of God, justice, knowledge, and service to human beings—and a transcendent element—God and the knowledge of God. The transcendent element is not directly accessible but must be reached through its historical mediation.

> One thing is perfectly clear: it is impossible to profess God without working for God's reign . . . There is no *spiritual* life without actual, *historical* life. It is impossible to live *with spirit* unless the spirit *becomes flesh* (Sobrino 1988, 4).

To describe the distinctiveness of Christian existence, therefore, perhaps the model of *ora et labora*—pray and work—is not entirely accurate, for it can suggest that the two can be neatly separated. Nor is the ideal of *contemplata tradere* exact—to communicate what one has contemplated—since it suggests that we first contemplate and only then communicate. More accurate for Christians is the goal *in actione contemplativus*—contemplatives in action. Divine reality is known and felt in the action of historical involvement. Therefore, if one tries to know the Divine only by contemplation in the silence of one's room or church, one is missing an essential part of what the Divine is; one must also, maybe first of all, contemplate in the action of historical involvement (Knitter 1987). "God is contemplated and practiced" (Gutiérrez in Sobrino 1988, 68).[7]

But what is the "historical involvement" we are talking about? Essentially, it is love of neighbor. This is why for Christians—also for Jews, I would say—the first two commandments—love of God and love of neighbor—are inseparable, two aspects of the same experiential reality. Love of neighbor is not just a commandment imposed on us by God; rather, in the very loving of one's neighbor, one is loving God. Two realities—neighbor and God—but somehow, one love, one experience (Rahner 1983, 71-74).

But as is clear from the example and message of Jesus, love of neighbor is not only a *compassion*, a feeling or suffering with, and not only a *communion*, a feeling connected with. It is also a *collaboration*, an acting with and for. Christian love seeks the well-being of others, and it does so *now*; if that well-being is hindered, then Christians roll up their sleeves and *act* in order to change the situation. Historical involvement, therefore, also means acting to change the conditions of this world; it means being an agent in history, not just a spectator. It means specific decisions, plans, undertakings in order to bring the world and history closer to Jesus' vision of the Reign of God.

Therefore, in their dialogues with other religious believers, Christians today will express their uniqueness by stating (better, by showing) that however else God or Truth may be experienced in other traditions, God and Truth *must* also be realized as a Call and Empowerment to transform this world from one of division and injustice into one of love and mutuality. "The transformation of the world to a higher humanity, to justice and peace, is therefore an essential part of the 'catholicity' or universality of Christian faith" (Schillebeeckx 1990, 171). Truth or God, as made known in Jesus, calls us to struggle for the betterment of human beings in this world, and as we realize today, human betterment is intertwined with ecological betterment. If Christianity at one time defined its uniqueness in the dictum *extra ecclesiam nulla salus* (outside the church no salvation), today it can find that uniqueness in the proclamation *extra mundum nulla salus* (outside the world no salvation). Unless we are realizing salvation or well-being in and for this world, we are not realizing the salvation announced by Jesus (ibid., 5-9).

A God of the Oppressed

With our image of a God involved in the mess of history, a God calling all persons to a practical love of all others, we still do not have the most striking colors in the picture of Christian uniqueness. This historical God, we must add, has priorities. The God of Moses and the God of Jesus is a God who has a special ear for the cries of the oppressed. What liberation theologians and the Catholic bishops of Latin America have termed the preferential option for the poor and oppressed is not a recent, politically correct pastoral or theological concoction. What scholars have discovered in the "softly focused characterization of the pre-Easter Jesus," especially in his open commensality, is a clear vein running through the sediment of the Jewish scriptures: any creature who cries out from the pain of slavery or exploitation can count on a special hearing from Yahweh/Abba.

The Judeo-Christian concept of God was first grasped from the perspectives of oppression and was constantly, even though not exclusively, refined by a critique of oppression from the point of view of the poor. This process of critical refinement is the main internal corrective of the Hebrew scriptures. The incarnation of Jesus was historically revealed by a life-praxis that favored the oppressed and crushed, just as his resurrection is constitutive of the eschatological vindication of the sufferings of the unremembered and the forsaken (O'Brien 1992, 121).

Throughout the biblical writings one can find "a primary interest in the emancipation of the culturally and politically oppressed" (Taylor 1990, 182). In his broad study on biblical hermeneutics, Croatto shows that a concern for the oppressed can be identified as a central motif of the Bible from three perspectives: *historically* in the very origins of the Jewish people when they experienced "salvation" as liberation from Egypt, *structurally* in the way the concern for liberation repeats and gives shape to the biblical witness, and *thematically* in that liberation is a focal element in what is proclaimed and practiced (Croatto 1987). So one can say, without exaggeration I believe, that "suffering humanity is evidently *the* chosen people of God" (Schillebeeckx 1990, 187). (This of course doesn't mean that God is not concerned about others.) "The option for the poor is a *datum* of revelation . . . The option for the poor is thus a question of orthodoxy" (ibid., 186).

The God of Jesus, and all those who invoke this God, are therefore in "emancipatory solidarity" with the oppressed of the world (Fiorenza 1975; Haight 1994, 249). A preferential option for the poor includes, by its very nature, a preferential concern for *justice*. One cannot hear the cries of the oppressed without crying out against the causes of their oppression. There is, in other words, an intrinsic link between love of neighbor and commitment to social and ecological justice. Especially today, when we are so aware of the millions of our neighbors who are poor and when we understand the socioeconomic reasons for their poverty, to announce that we love our neighbor without working for justice is to make a mockery of love.

So even if, as some cautious biblical scholars maintain, we can't be sure that the historical Jesus actually did show special concern for the poor and that he wanted to improve their lot in this world (Sanders 1985, 228-41), still his command to love one's neighbor as oneself (and we *can* be sure of that!) cannot be practiced in *today's world and today's consciousness* without an active commitment to justice. To love our neighbor is to want to relieve his or her suffering. Today, most of our neighbors are suffering from unjust political and economic policies and practices.[8] Today, therefore, we can say that "you will know they are Christians by their solidarity with the victims of the world."

A GOD OF PROMISE

A further distinguishing mark of the disciples of Jesus and co-workers in God's reign is that *they don't give up*. Here what Christians call the Paschal Mystery enters into their unique identity. The God whom Jesus has enabled them to know is a God who brings victory out of defeat, life out of death. So even when all seems lost and hopeless, there is hope and perseverance. This God is faithful to the promise that love, even love unto death, leads to life.

To translate into a syllogism the mysterious process and power of what Jesus imparted and imparts to his disciples: God desires that salvation take place in this world, that God's people be freed now. But God is faithful, trustworthy, infinite in resources and creativity. Therefore, no matter what happens, no matter what the odds, we can trust that the horrors we see around us can be changed and that this world can be brought closer to the Reign of God. In proclaiming this bold hope Jesus was carrying on, clarifying, and intensifying his Jewish heritage. "What is central and distinctive [unique] within the Israelite religion is that their history is governed by Yahweh, that Yahweh is always present to the people of Israel in their history, and that therefore history does have a purpose and goal, even if this purpose and goal seem to change from time to time" (Lane 1991, 14).

This is the vision and the conviction that Jesus of Nazareth affirmed and incarnated for his followers. One of the most pointed and hope-filled specifications that he gave to this vision is contained in the story of his passion, death, and resurrection—that the Reign of God cannot be realized without the kind of commitment and faith that opens one to suffering and death, and that, somehow, such suffering and death can contribute to the vision of new life and transformed humanity.

I dare say that this is perhaps the most important, the most distinctive contribution that the Judeo-Christian covenant has to make to the conversation of peoples and religions: history, this world, *can* be saved. The followers of Jesus make the bold claim to other believers that if a person thinks that in the end good and evil have a fifty-fifty chance (or that the human heart's capacity for selfishness is as strong as, if not more powerful than, its capacity for love), such a person *is an atheist*! (Nolan 1978, 85). "To believe in Jesus is to believe that goodness can and will triumph over evil. Despite the system, despite the magnitude, complexity, and apparent insolubility of our problems today, humanity can be, and in the end will be, liberated" (ibid., 140).[9] If Christians do not express and try to embody such hope, even as they face or embrace death and defeat, they are not representing the real uniqueness of Jesus the Christ.

AGAIN A RELATIONAL UNIQUENESS

This articulation of what, in our world as it is, makes Jesus unique— his experience and revelation of a *historical God* who calls us to an *active love that seeks justice* for the oppressed and who provides us with the *hope* that can overcome defeat and death—enables us to fill in the abstract claim, made above, that the uniqueness of Jesus is a *relational uniqueness* (see chapter 4 above, pp. 80-83). Certainly, this view of Jesus' uniqueness can connect with what in *One Earth Many Religions* I described as the world-affirming power or potential within all religions. To some degree, in some way, all religious traditions have to do with how we can make our life in the world more liveable and more satisfying (Knitter 1995, chap. 5). *How* they do that, how they understand the sores and the salve of what ails us humans, how important they see such concern for this world—all this makes for the undeniable and fruitful differences between the religions.

Let me suggest tentatively how the unique characteristics of the Christian effort to better or remedy the human situation in this world might differ significantly from and so converse with the efforts of other traditions. (I say tentatively because such suggestions can be verified only in an actual dialogue with persons of other religious communities.) What is distinctive and different in the way Christians seek to move humans from self-centeredness to other-centeredness? I think it has to do with the way Jesus, in his message and example, insists that an active love of neighbor is an essential part of the way we tap into the Power that will change this world.

What Aloysius Pieris has described as a striking difference between Buddhism and Christianity can well apply to differences between Christians and members of other traditions (especially Indic): in general, while for Buddhists *prajna* or wisdom exercises a certain priority in their practice, for Christians that priority goes to *agape* or love. Although both activities—wisdom and compassion—are crucial to both traditions, one of them seems to open the door to either the Buddhist or the Christian world. For Buddhist and many spiritualities (also within Christianity), the stress is placed on interiority, on sitting, on time in the temple; as enlightenment or inner transformation comes, a sense of connectedness with and compassion for others will flow. For Christians and many other spiritualities (also for some Buddhists), first steps must always include a reaching to one's neighbor; one must first set straight one's relationship with one's neighbor before one goes to the temple. *Agape* or love includes, but also has a practical priority over, *prajna* or wisdom (Pieris 1988b, 110-36).

For Buddhism, and perhaps generally speaking for the Asian and primal religions,[10] love of neighbor results from the experience of the Divine or of Enlightenment. For Christianity, and perhaps generally speaking for the Semitic religions,[11] such love of neighbor enters into, and conditions, the very experience of the Divine (Spretnak 1991, chap. 5). Such differences are extremely significant; they are not, however, simply exclusive of each other.

Also, there is something distinctive and particular about how Christians diagnose what's wrong with the world and what the remedy must contain. Having learned, with Jesus, from the Hebrew prophets, Christians would first tend to the sufferings of victims, to the oppressed (and today, they realize that includes the oppressed Earth); in doing so, they diagnose the cause of such suffering as having to do with the way *people* treat each other; and that means with practices and systems of *injustice*. If there are slaves, one must address the Pharaoh. If the temple has become a den of thieves, one must confront the chief priests and elders.

Therefore, although Christians would agree with their Hindu and Buddhist friends that the pain of the world has to do with how the individual's mind and heart see and feel the world, they would add, distinctively, that an analysis of the pain must also include the way human greed and ignorance lead to programs and systems of injustice. Both diagnosis and medicine must be *social*; one must examine not just the human heart but political and economic policies. Besides changing or enlightening the heart, one must also address the Pharaohs, the lawyers and chief priests, the kings, popes, and presidents.

I think Charlene Spretnak is correct in the way she describes the core teachings or the distinctive qualities of Christianity and its parent religion Judaism:

> Their scriptures teach that active opposition to exploitation, evil, and corruption is a matter of fulfilling a spiritual mission: justice and righteousness are the *ongoing conditions* of a people's communion with the divine creativity in the universe . . . waging justice is *not an outgrowth* of the spiritual practice but an *inherent component* of the core teachings. A sense of connection with those who suffer poverty and oppression is particularly emphasized (Spretnak 1991, 158-59).

> The core teachings of the Semitic traditions remind us that our spirituality is always tested: If you allow injustice, you fail to grasp the depth of communion (ibid., 195).[12]

To these descriptions of the Semitic religions' shared concern for justice and the oppressed, Christians would want to add their unique and important reminder: in struggling against injustice and seeking to bring about the righteousness of the Reign of God, one is going to face opposition, and that means one is bound to suffer and fail. But although such suffering and failure are never intended, even though they may drive one to feel abandoned by God, still, to so suffer and fail are often going to be part of the process of victory and greater life and love. We are back to the uniqueness contained in the Christian symbols of cross and resurrection.

In locating the uniqueness of Christianity in the experience of a historical God committed especially to victims—even in showing how this uniqueness perhaps *differs* from the way other religions seek to promote salvation or well-being—we are dealing with a uniqueness that demands relationship with others, both religious and nonreligious. For the Reign of God is meant for all, ready *both* to challenge and learn from all. Now I think we can understand why I said above that the uniqueness of Christ and Christianity is better described as a *rela-*

tional rather than a complementary or inclusive uniqueness, that it can produce thorns and thistles, not just peaches and cream.

Indeed, using the theological models we discussed in chapters 1 and 2, when Christians ground the uniqueness of Jesus in the Reign of God and in the symbol of his death and resurrection, they are establishing a relationship with other religions that can be exclusive, or inclusive, or pluralistic-correlational: *exclusive* in that this understanding of Jesus' uniqueness will challenge any religious belief or practice (also within Christianity) that does not promote a this-worldly engagement for love and justice, especially for oppressed persons and the oppressed Earth; *inclusive* in that it will clarify and fulfill the potential of other religions to further what Christians call the Reign of God; *pluralistic* in that it will recognize and be itself fulfilled by new insights found in other traditions as to how we can enable humanity and the Earth to have life and to have it more abundantly.

•

In order to explore how viable and practical this correlational, globally responsible christology really is, we turn in the next chapter to how it can be practiced within the Christian communities and how it can help Christians understand and live the role and mission of their church.

6

MISSION REVISED

A Correlational, Globally Responsible Church

As we saw in chapter 3, the uneasiness many Christians feel about the correlational, globally responsible dialogue we have been proposing has to do not only with Jesus but also—and perhaps more threateningly—with the church. To propose interreligious dialogue as a conversation of equal with equal, to suggest that a Buddhist or Muslim might be experiencing divine truth and salvation just as surely (though differently) as do Christians, to propose an encounter with other believers in which the primary concern would be cooperation toward eco-human well-being rather than conversion to the Christian church—all this is to darken or even evaporate the sense of identity that many Christians have had of themselves and their church.

This threatened sense of self-identity is focused for many around the issue of *missions*. Throughout all the centuries of its existence the Christian community has been animated and sustained by a sense of "being sent," of having to "go forth into the whole world," of having a *necessary* role to play in the unfolding of the drama of creation. If the contribution or purpose of the church is not something that is "necessary" for all peoples of all times, then missionary outreach becomes a peripheral pastime at most. It no longer is what it has always been: part of the heartbeat of the body of Christ. So, in a pluralistic or correlational view of other religions, is the church necessary? Is it missionary?

Pope John Paul II and recent Vatican voices would say no in answer to those questions. In chapter 3 we reviewed the "incorrect theological perspectives" that, according to the mission encyclical *Redemptoris Missio*, are contributing to the "waning" of missionary activity (RM 2, 4).

There seem to be two central concerns, or, as Cardinal Tomko of the Vatican Congregation for the Evangelization of Peoples, puts it:

"The missiological problem today is ultimately a christological and soteriological problem" (Tomko 1990, 241).

The christological problem: Because the "definitive self revelation of God [in Jesus] is the fundamental reason why the church is missionary by her very nature" (RM 5), and because "Christ is the one savior of all, the only one able to reveal God and lead to God" (RM 5), any christology that would allow other religions or religious figures to "be understood as parallel or complementary to him" would eviscerate the mission of the church.[1]

The soteriological problem: Any understanding of the Christian experience of salvation that would lead people to think that the purpose of missionary work can be limited or reduced to helping "people to become more human" and to building "communities capable of working for justice, freedom, peace, and solidarity" (RM 46) is drastically curtailing and maiming the missionary nature of the church. The pope speaks for many Christians, Catholic and Protestant, when he warns that unless one is proclaiming Christ as "history's center and goal" (RM 6) and unless that goal includes more than earthly well-being, one is not announcing the saving content and power of the good news.

The pope's concerns about undermining or diluting Christian identity and mission are clarified and confirmed by the Christian critics we heard from in chapter 3. They repeatedly warn that unless Jesus makes a "definitive difference" in the world, Christians will not be able to find the stamina and strength to take up their cross daily and follow. The kind of personal commitment that the gospel calls forth requires rock-solid convictions that Jesus delivers God's rock-solid truth. To follow Jesus truly and perseveringly, Christians have to be able to see and feel that he is more than a partial expression of God's truth; if they are going to leave everything behind, they have to know that what they are committing themselves to is not just another great idea that may have to be expanded or surpassed by a greater idea. This is especially so when living the values of the Reign of God will require disciples to resist cultural or governmental policies to the point of risking their reputation or their very lives. One does not lay one's life on the line if one is uncertain of the abiding value and dependable strength of that line.

So in order for a correlational, globally responsible view of other religions to secure its validity within the Christian community, it must make clear how it can nourish and sustain the life and commitments of that community. It must show its ability to form and nourish disciples able and eager to follow faithfully, to speak the truth of the gospel to the powers that be, and to go forth to the ends of the Earth to announce the news that they know is good for everyone. These last two chapters hope to show how this is possible with the proposed new model for understanding Christ and other religions. We will first explore how the correlational, globally responsible christology out-lined in chapters 4 and 5 can inspire personal commitment and hold together the fabric of Christian community. In the second section of this chapter I will suggest how this same christology, which is as com-mitted to the gospel as it is open to other religious paths, requires the revision of the missionary mandate but also promises its reaffirma-tion. In the next chapter I will draw a general, and perhaps at first startling, conclusion for ecclesiology and missiology: the church's mis-sion not only includes dialogue but can best be understood and lived *as dialogue*. Finally, in the second part of chapter 7, I will try to show why and how theology, one of the church's life-sustaining activities, can no longer be carried out "mono-religiously"; theology itself must be a dialogical and interreligious enterprise.

SUSTAINING CHRISTIAN COMMITMENT AND COMMUNITY

In this section I will be speaking from my own experience as a believing, practicing Christian. I am witnessing—or trying to witness—how my correlational or pluralistic understanding of Jesus as truly but not solely God's universal saving Word has arisen out of, and continues to sustain, an always faulty but determined devotion to Jesus and an effort to follow him. In doing this, I trust that what I witness of my own experience will reflect or clarify the experience of many of my fellow Christians. (If it doesn't, I'm in trouble, for every theolo-gian, like every Christian, must be sustained, at least to some extent, by his or her community.)

A Committed Faith and Following

Is it really possible to be totally devoted to Jesus even though I no longer affirm him as the one-and-only savior or Word of God? Yes—mainly because I continue to affirm that God has *really and truly* spoken a saving Word in Jesus, and the reason I can make such an affirmation is that I continue to *experience* it to be so. As explained in chapter 4, "truly" means decisively, universally, indispensably. I use such adverbs not simply because I find them in the New Testament, but also and especially because Jesus is the place in which I encounter God, the place in which my life is transformed and set in a new direc-tion. Also for correlational or pluralist Christians, the story of Jesus becomes their story, a story by which they now know that their lives are grounded in a God of love who calls and empowers them to love. In breaking bread and reading the scriptures, pluralist Christians can feel the Spirit of Christ alive in their communities and individual lives, a Spirit that de-centers them and enables them to feel that it is no longer they who live but Christ who lives in them (Gal 2:20). All this is what enables me, with my correlational christology, to say that God has *truly* acted in and as Jesus.

This means that even with my pluralist views, I have no difficulty whatsoever in announcing—indeed, I feel impelled to proclaim—that Jesus is truly the Son of God and universal savior. The recognition and announcement of Jesus' divinity remains integral and essential to a correlational christology. Out of my own experience I can endorse the explanations of what it means to call Jesus divine that have been proposed by Christian theologians such as Karl Rahner (1978a, 176-228), Paul Tillich (1957, Part II), Edward Schillebeeckx (1963), Hans Küng (1976, 117-65), and Monika Hellwig (1983). To feel and proclaim that Jesus is divine is to encounter him as God's sacrament, as the embodiment, the historical reality, the symbol, the story that makes God real and effective for me. To meet this Jesus is to meet the living reality of the Divine—the reason why the early Christians proclaimed him as God's Son and the reason why pluralist Christians continue to do so. Only someone who is utterly at-one with God can so communicate God to me and be God for me. This, too, is contained in the pluralist affirmation of Jesus as *truly* divine.

But as was stressed in the last chapter, the real test of fidelity to Jesus and his message is not whether one adheres to the proper titles for him or even whether one duly worships him; rather, one's fidelity and orthodoxy regarding who Jesus is has to be measured by one's ability and decision to *follow* him—to act as a disciple. And here, too, even though I do not feel it possible or necessary to affirm that Jesus is the *only* savior, I still so experience him to be *truly* a savior that I feel impelled to cast my lot with him. What he reveals of God's Reign, his vision of a humanity united in love and justice as children of a God of love and justice, the power of this vision as it lives on in the community after his death—all this calls me to believe in this Reign and to act for it, even if it should require of me what it required of him. Contrary to what others have suggested, a pluralist Christian has sufficient clarity about and commitment to the gospel values of justice and love to resist those who trample on these values, whether Nazis or the Salvadoran oligarchy. One does not have to affirm Jesus as the only Truth in order to die for the Truth that he does reveal.

Therefore, in the spirituality of a Christian who recognizes the possibility of other names, even of other sons and daughters of God, Jesus certainly remains unique. But as Gabriel Moran has suggested, his uniqueness is not a matter of superiority or arrogation of privilege; rather, it is a matter of distinctness, of specialness that will surely be different from, but not necessarily better than, others (Moran 1992). It is a distinctness that consists primarily and most importantly not in Jesus' ability to exclude or absorb others (although that can indeed happen) but rather in his ability to offer us a distinct, concrete, decisive way of knowing God and living God's life in this world. As William Burrows has put it, "The uniqueness of Christ and Christian life lies in a distinct structure of existence; the Christian manner of being a saint . . . is unique."[2]

A MATURE FAITH

To recognize that God may have enriched other cultures and peoples with revelations whose beauty and power stand alongside that given in Jesus need not, therefore, threaten the vitality of the Christian's faith and commitment to Christ; indeed, it can deepen one's Christian commitment and give it a more mature expression. If there is any truth to James Fowler's stages of faith (Fowler 1981), I think it is found in the recognition that the more one matures in faith, so much the more will one happily, if somewhat fearfully, embrace the mystery, the expansiveness, the pluriformity of truth. My own experience has been that the more I know of God and God's truth, the more I am able to know two things: 1) that this Truth is beyond anything I can put in human, historical forms, and 2) that it is utterly trustworthy—so that I don't have to fear whatever else this Truth may contain as it reveals itself in other human, historical forms. Here again we are teased by the psychologically tantalizing paradox of religious experience: the more deeply we experience and are committed to a *particular* expression of the Divine, the more we sense and are opened to the *universality* of the Divine. To feel and delight in this paradox is, I suggest, to mature in faith and religious experience.

This paradox reflects the psychology of human love and commitment: the deeper and more lasting one's commitment to a particular person or partner is, the more one is open to—and less threatened by—the beauty or truth of other paths and persons. In the marriage relationship—at least the way many of us experience it—there is a particularity of love and devotion that one feels for one's spouse and that cannot be shared with others; this specialness or particularity is evident in the sexual expressions of that love. But precisely by being so special, even exclusive (e.g., in sexual expression), such love for this one person frees or empowers one to notice, respond to, and affirm the lovable qualities of others. Secure in a committed, particular relationship to one person, one is better able to form relationships with others. Paradoxically, again, the more deeply I love my wife in a very special way, the more I am enabled to love others in different but nonetheless authentic ways.

This is a reflection of the paradox between the "relative" and the "absolute," (which I explored in *One Earth Many Religions*) (Knitter 1995, 129-32). Even though I well know how "relative" and limited my wife is, even though I admit that there are other women just as or more beautiful, honest, sensitive, strong—still, her limited particularity elicits my absolute commitment. She doesn't have to be "the best" or "the only woman I could ever marry" for me to love her and commit myself to her. If one had to find the "best" (the most attractive or honest or intelligent) person to marry, if each of us could marry only one particular person, few persons, I'm afraid, would get married, and those who did probably would not stay so. But when this finite, limited woman elicits my love and absolute commitment, she somehow enables me to appreciate the best and the absolute in others. Therefore, as was said in the previous chapter, to know and be fully committed to Jesus the Christ is to be open to and appreciate others. Christ is the way that is open to other ways.

From my limited experience in the undergraduate classroom and in parish adult education programs, I have found that what I have been suggesting in these last paragraphs rings true for many Christians. If asked to look into the inner workings and feelings of their faith-life, most people, I have discovered, have to admit that the reason they are committed to Jesus is not because he is the "one and only." If we take a pew count, or a religious education classroom count, I suspect we will find that the majority of Christians will admit that their ability to pray to or to worship Jesus, or to stand up for what he is all about, need not be jeopardized just because there *may* be others like him. They are committed because of what they have found in him, not because they are certain that they can find it only in him.

To require such certainty about having the one and only truth before committing oneself is to be exposed to the frustration of never being able to find what one thinks is necessary. And that frustration can lead down one of two very different avenues: *agnosticism*, in which one gives up the search for truth and commitment; or *fundamentalism*, in which one turns to whoever will offer the apple of impregnable (but also manipulatable) security and absolute, infallible certitude.

I have found that for the most part people in my classes or in adult education programs respond positively, if not eagerly, to an explanation of New Testament language about Jesus as praxis-oriented or performative language. They feel that such titles and terms as Lord, Savior, one and only Mediator, or only-begotten Son of God can become for them all the more meaningful, engaging, and liberating when understood not as doctrinal language meant to define Christ once and for all and to exclude others, but as confessional or action language meant primarily to call them to accept and live his message and to "go and do likewise." Such traditional language about Jesus, when understood as a call to action, has great pastoral power to arouse faithful response in people.

In general, it has been my experience that a correlational, globally responsible way of speaking about Christ and other religions, when it is presented carefully and with sensitivity, will be received by many in the community of the faithful as a way of strengthening their faith and community bonds. In all honesty, in my own activity as a teacher within the North American Roman Catholic and mainline Protestant communities, I have not found the warning that some colleagues have given me to be true—that to pursue a pluralistic or correlational image of Christ is to run "the risk of parting company with [my] own faith communities" (Küng 1991, 101; see also chapter 3 above, pp. 51-52). I have found that even though such views may indeed upset or scandalize some Christians, there are also many who accept this pluralistic image of Christ with openness and even gratitude, revealing that they have long had questions and suspicions in this area but never felt free to explore them. They have been scandalized that theologians and church leaders are not taking up these questions with sufficient honesty or candor. For many in our Christian churches, a Christ who is the way open to other ways is a Christ they can more readily follow.

THE MISSIONARY MANDATE REVISED AND REAFFIRMED

Just as a correlational, globally responsible christology offers an image of Christ that can more readily elicit the personal faith of disciples, so it also presents an image of the church's mission that can inspire disciples to go forth to the nations. In the context of the views of Christ and religions that this book has been proposing, missionary work has to be revised; but that revision, I feel, will lay the foundation for a reaffirmation and renewal of missionary commitment.

FROM CHURCH-CENTERED TO KINGDOM-CENTERED MISSION

The revision of mission theology (missiology) that has been taking place since the Second Vatican Council is built on the same biblical-theological foundation that sustains the revisions in christology summarized in the previous chapter: the centrality of the Reign of God in the message and practice of Jesus. Stated pointedly: If the mission of Jesus was the Kingdom of God, it cannot be otherwise for the mission of the church.

As we shall see in greater detail below, there has been a momentous shift in Christian, especially Roman Catholic, understanding of what the church is all about, a shift from an ecclesiocentric or church-centered understanding of mission to what the Roman Catholic bishops of Asia call a "regnocentric" or Kingdom-centered perspective (Dupuis 1993, 27). Today there is general agreement among both Catholic and Protestant theologians that the church and the Kingdom *cannot be identified*. Though these two realities are deeply and importantly related, they are not the same thing. The Kingdom is not only more extensive than the Christian church; it is also more important!

This means that Christians are coming to understand that the primary purpose—or what the scholastics used to call the *ratio sufficiens* (sufficient reason)—of being sent into the world is *not* to build the church but to build the Reign of God. In terminology that even the Vatican has used, the "servant" in the relationship between the two is the church (RM 20; DP 35). The church is to serve the Kingdom, not the other way around. The church, therefore, lives out its true nature when it is Kingdom-centered, not self-centered. Or, as the Pastoral Constitution of Vatican II, *Gaudium et Spes*, puts it: "The Church has but one sole purpose—that the Kingdom of God may come and salvation of the human race may be accomplished" (45).

To form a sense and appreciation of this Kingdom-centered shift, I offer a sampling of how various theologians are unpacking its meaning. From his experience in India and then in the central offices of the Society of Jesus, Michael Amaladoss, S.J., concludes that "the theology of evangelization is undergoing a Copernican revolution . . . the centre of the framework is shifting from the Church to the Kingdom" (Amaladoss 1986, 63). In terms of past debates on the purpose of missionary outreach, this means that the *primary* reason why missionaries are sent forth is not to establish and plant the church but to establish and build the Kingdom. Planting the church and establishing Christian communities remain important, but this importance is as a *means to an end*, not as an end in itself. The Asian bishops make this point with simple clarity: "The focus of the Church's mission of evangelization is building up the Kingdom of God and building up the Church to be at the service of the Kingdom. The Kingdom is, therefore, wider than the Church" (in Dupuis 1993, 27). Clarifying what he means by this Copernican revolution, Amaladoss makes the same point:

> It [the church] is called to a twofold service; one is to witness to the Kingdom and to promote its realisation in the world; another is to proclaim Jesus and to build up a community of disciples. *The second is a means of serving the first.* In doing the first service the Church discovers that the mystery of God is active everywhere, in various ways. It has no claims to exclusivity. It discovers a community of faith. It is called to dialogue and to collaborate. It makes its specific contribution to the integral wholeness of the Kingdom (Amaladoss 1985, 112, emphasis mine).

In a Kingdom-centered mission theology, Christians are better able to keep their priorities straight. The church "does not place herself at the center" (Asian bishops, in Dupuis 1993, 30). "The Church is not placed at her own service: she is entirely oriented toward the Kingdom of God that is coming. For only the Kingdom, as the fullness of God's manifestation, is absolute" (Claude Geffré, in Dupuis 1994, 158). To put the Kingdom at the service of the church is not only to mix up one's priorities, but it is, one can say, idolatry. As it was for Jesus, so it should be for the church. Only the Kingdom is absolute.

But we must avoid misunderstandings. All this is not to deny the importance of other goals for missionary activity; it is only to keep them in proper perspective. In order to promote the Kingdom, missionaries must be about many things, such as planting the *ecclesia*, establishing the community, proclaiming the Word, dialoguing with other faith communities. All of these tasks, it must be said, are *essential* to the purpose of mission. But in insisting that they are essential, we recognize that they are *subordinate* to the primary, focal goal of working for the Kingdom. They are essential means to the primary end; they can never become ends in themselves.

David Bosch, who in his magisterial review of missiology also recognizes the move to Kingdom-centeredness as a defining shift, offers a description of how differently people on either side of the shift view the church:

> Kingdom people seek first the Kingdom of God and its justice; church people often put the church work above concerns of justice, mercy, and truth. Church people think about how to get people into the church; Kingdom people think about how to get the church into the world. Church people worry that the world might change the church; Kingdom people work to see the church change the world (H. Snyder, quoted in Bosch 1991, 378; see also 377, 390-91).

I want to draw out the full implications of this "regnocentric" breakthrough in theology and church life and mission. If Christians take seriously the role of the church as *servant* of the Kingdom, if they affirm the "absolute" value of the Kingdom over the value of the church, if they live up to the church as a means to the end of the Kingdom, then they will have to be wary of traditional theological language about the Kingdom being "fulfilled" in the church or about all other manifestations of the Kingdom in the world being "ordered" toward the Christian church, or about the church being "necessary" for the Kingdom. In a sense, there is validity to all such assertions, for if what we examined in the previous chapter is true about Jesus being the bearer of a "universal, decisive, and indispensable" revelation, then the church indeed has a necessary, urgent, yes fulfilling contribution to make to the gradual formation of the Reign of God on Earth.

But in the way terms such as "fulfillment" or "necessary for salvation" have been—and as we shall see, still are—used by both theologians and church officials, the servant ends up telling the master what
to do and what is allowed. To insist that the Kingdom taking shape
beyond the church has to be fitted neatly and so fulfilled *in* the church
is to impose the church on, rather than adapt it to, what God is doing
in the broader Kingdom. It is to forget that "the important thing is for
the Kingdom to become reality, not for it [the church] to monopolize
the understanding and the praxis of the Kingdom" (Sobrino 1987,
139). I fear that many theologians and missioners who use Kingdom-
centered language have not yet taken seriously and consequentially
what they are saying. In order to avoid turning the "necessary" or the
"fulfilling" role of the church into an idol, Christians have to admit
clearly to themselves and to others that the Christian church is *a* necessary, unique, fulfilling means for realizing God's Reign on Earth,
but that the church is not *the* means. There can be, there most likely
are, other very different and very fulfilling ways of appropriating the
universal activity of God's Spirit and Kingdom.

THE SPIRIT AND THE CHURCH—ECCLESIOLOGY AND PNEUMATOLOGY

This conversion, as it were, in ecclesiology from a centering on the
church to a centering on the Reign of God is reflected in and given
deeper roots by another refocusing move in recent missiology: the
placing of the mission of the church within and as part of the *missio
Dei*—the mission of God. The church's purpose and task do not have
an identity in themselves; rather, they are part of something much
larger. The mission of the church is not its own; it is "sent" in order to
be part of, and to serve, something larger than itself.

> In the new image mission is not primarily an activity of the church,
> but an attribute of God. God is a missionary God . . . Mission is
> thereby seen as a movement from God to the world; the church
> is viewed as an instrument for that mission. There is church be-
> cause there is mission, not vice versa. To participate in mission is
> to participate in the movement of God's love toward people,
> since God is a fountain of sending love (Bosch 1991, 390).

And what God is up to in this divine going forth is an eternal,
dynamic, mysterious movement and presence that could never be contained in the Christian church. Just as we recognized that the Kingdom is larger than the church, so we now hear "God's own mission is
larger than the mission of the Church" (Bosch 1991, 391). "Kingdom" and "God's own mission" are synonyms. Both affirm the value
and necessity of the church's mission, but also put limits on it.

This necessary yet subordinate role of the church as part of and servant to the *missio Dei* can be more clearly and persuasively grasped by exploring Christianity's traditional trinitarian understanding of God and divine mission. In realizing, already in the early centuries of church history, that the God they had experienced through Jesus was "triune," Christians had to speak of different "persons" or "missions" of God. (The technical terminology was *relationes subsistentes*—subsistent relations within the Godhead.) Insofar as those persons or missions expressed themselves outside the Godhead (*ad extra*), they could be symbolized as God's creative movement (the Father or Parent), God's communicating mission (the Word), and God's sanctifying-animating mission (the Spirit). One has to be careful in making these distinctions too neatly; later trinitarian theology did add that "all the outward-moving actions of the Trinity are common to all the divine persons." Still, Christian experience and reflection were trying to recognize that there were genuine differences in the relations or movements or missions of the one God and within the one God.

Now, in exploring further the link between what we're saying about the church as part of the *mission of God* and what we said about the church as servant of the *Reign of God*, I would want to point out, along with other theologians, that our understanding of the church and its mission has been based almost exclusively on the mission of the Second Person of the Trinity, the Word, and that it now needs to be expanded and balanced by taking into consideration the mission of the Third Person, or Spirit. In theological terms, our ecclesiology and missiology have been developed too much within the framework of christology and now have to be re-visioned also within the framework of pneumatology. If it is true that Christians cannot make sense of the church without Jesus the incarnate Word, neither can they really understand the church and its mission without the Spirit.

The deeper, expansive content of that last sentence can be missed if we understand the Spirit only as "the Spirit of Christ"—the Spirit who is essentially related to the Word incarnate in Jesus and who enables Jesus as the Christ to live on in the church. We must also recognize the Spirit as genuinely *different* from the Word—as the Spirit who "fills and renews the Earth" and who works beyond the church. Or, to say the same thing differently, the Kingdom of God is alive and active in the world through *both* the Word incarnate in Jesus and the Spirit filling the Earth—the same Kingdom, indeed, but two genuinely different ways in which it can be felt and lived by humankind.

The startling implications of a pneumatological or Spirit-based understanding of the church first touched me in a presentation by Orthodox theologian George Khodr (Khodr 1991; see Knitter 1991). Khodr laid out the possibilities of a pneumatological ecclesiology and theology of religions mainly through his creative reflections on traditional trinitarian theology. The crux of these reflections was contained in the way he described the relationship between Word and Spirit and then applied that relationship to the church's mission to other religions:

> The economy of Christ is not understandable without the economy of the Spirit. The Spirit fills everything *in an economy distinct from the Son.* The Word and the Spirit are called the "two hands of the Father." We must here affirm their *hypostatic independence* and visualize in the religions an all-comprehensive phenomenon of grace. Pentecost . . . is not a continuation of the Incarnation but its consequence . . . Between these two economies there is *reciprocity* and *mutual service* (Khodr 1991, 27, emphasis mine).

In line with traditional trinitarian theology, Khodr affirms real difference and yet essential relatedness and reciprocity between Word and Spirit. This means that while the Spirit can never be understood and experienced without reference to the Word, neither can the Spirit, explicitly or implicitly, be reduced to the Word, subordinated to the Word, or understood as merely a different "mode" of the Word. There is "hypostatic independence," that is, real, effective difference. This is why Pentecost and the energy that it embodies and unleashes throughout history are to be understood not as a mere "continuation of the Incarnation"; that would make for subordination of the Spirit to the Word—or a form of modalism.[3] Rather, the economy of the Spirit is a consequence of the incarnation, originating from it (*Filioque*[4]) but living out its own identity (its own *hypostasis*). And yet, such "independence" is qualified, for both the economy of the Word and that of the Spirit are essentially bonded to each other, in a relationship that is complete within the Deity (*ad intra*) but still in process of realizing itself and being discovered by humans in the history of creation (*ad extra*).

When such a trinitarian theology is applied to missiology and a theology of religions, we are enabled and required, it seems to me, to admit that what the Spirit may be doing beyond the church, within other religions, can be different from what the incarnate Word has revealed in the church. The Reign of God, as it may be taking shape under the breath of the Spirit, can be seen as "an all-comprehensive phenomenon of grace"; that is, an economy of grace genuinely different from the one made known through the Word incarnate in Jesus (in whom, of course, the Spirit was also active). And in that sense, the Kingdom of God beyond the church is independent; that is, not to be submerged or engulfed or incorporated into the economy of the Word represented in the Christian churches.

Khodr can therefore boldly declare that it would be "too facile" to "comprehend rapidly all religions in Christianity. That would be a refusal of their genuineness"—or, it would be a refusal of the genuineness of the economy of the Spirit and the broader Kingdom. Christianity, he reminds us, should not be understood as "the last and final economy which destroys all others." Christianity understands itself as "the little flock, a leaven amidst the dough but never all the pastry, the salt for food but never all the food" (Khodr 1991, 26). And yet, at the same time, the independence of the economy of the religions is qualified, for there is an essential *relatio* between Word and Spirit, between the Kingdom as it forms within the church and as it takes shape beyond it. Though truly different, the Spirit exists within the Word, just as the Word exists also in the Spirit. Thus the genuine difference of the Kingdom in other religions must be related, understood, and clarified within the Word incarnate in Christ and living in the church. As the Word and Spirit have their existence in each other, so does the Kingdom within the church and the Kingdom beyond it.

Khodr's proposal finds an echo among theologians seeking ways to maintain the "necessity" of the church as well as the "necessity" of other religious ways. Such a pneumatological missiology "offers us the key to grasp the universality of God's saving purpose without dissolving the uniqueness of the Incarnation" (O'Donnell 1989, 45). To base our understanding of the church and its mission on christology *and* on pneumatology enables us to understand that our Christian mission is one of bringing the uniqueness of how the Kingdom is present in the Word incarnate in Jesus into a dynamic, open-ended conversation with the uniqueness of how the Spirit is fostering the Kingdom throughout the world (Bingemer 1990). But that conversation can be authentic and life-giving only if both sides are equally respected. "The work of the Spirit cannot be subordinated to the Logos" (Panikkar 1990b, 121). Christian missionaries should not "reduce the action of the Spirit to that of Jesus Christ" (Amaladoss 1989, 413).

If the Western, Latin church could take more seriously than it has the pneumatological or Spirit-focused perspective on Christian life and mission that is more alive in the Eastern churches, it could achieve a better-balanced understanding of its relationship to the broader Reign of God. There is an urgent truth in Samuel Rayan's admonition: "The Western Church has concentrated on the middle portion of the creed and elaborated a christomonistic theology [and ecclesiology], but failed to develop reflection on the Creator God and on the Holy Spirit, Lord or Lady and Life-giver and Father-Mother of the poor" (Rayan 1990, 129).

SEEK FIRST THE KINGDOM OF GOD

In what we are calling a "regnocentric" understanding of the church and its mission, there is the confidence that if Christians "seek first the Kingdom of God," rather than seeking first the welfare of the church, then "all else will be added" (Mt 6:33) and the church will prosper. But what does it mean to "seek first the Kingdom"? To use terms that are familiar to corporate board rooms and course syllabi, I think it means a rearranging of priorities in the church's *objective* and in its *goals*—in its general orientation and in its practical programs.

As regards *objective* or orientation, to seek first the Kingdom of God means that the primary energy flow in the church is *centrifugal rather than centripetal*. If the church is part of the *missio Dei*, then its very nature, its purpose for being (its *ratio sufficiens*) is to be sent, to "go forth," to move out of, beyond itself, into the world that is not church. As has been said, the church doesn't have a mission; the church *is* mission (Hoekendijk 1960). It realizes what it is by going outside of itself in service to the Kingdom of God. If the church community is not centrifugal, if it is closed in on itself in caring for only its own members, it can perhaps be called a religion but not a Christian church, for it is not "seeking first the Kingdom of God" (see Haight 1988).

But to prioritize the centrifugal movement of the church is not to deny the necessity of a corresponding centripetal flow of energy. Indeed, in order to go beyond itself, the community must form and care for itself. Energy must be generated before it can be dispensed. Thus, in a Kingdom-centered church, pastoral concerns such as liturgy, catechesis, piety, church groups, and retreats are all essential ingredients of being church. Unless the Christian community realizes and embodies and exemplifies the Kingdom within itself, its witness to this Kingdom before the larger society will not be very convincing. Christians must first *be* the Kingdom in their own community before they can *contribute* to the Kingdom in the world. Others will know they are Christian and that they are Kingdom by their love, by the loving, praying, struggling community they have formed. Therefore, the inward-directed, pastoral activities of parish life are absolutely necessary.

But they are also absolutely secondary. The ultimate purpose of coming together is to go forth together. The real reason Christians come together to feel and enjoy the love of God and of each other is to share that love with those outside the community, especially those who have been refused love and pushed to the sides of society. Christians gather to break the eucharistic bread in order to share bread with those who have none; if the Eucharist becomes only an "in thing," a primer for personal piety, it no longer can be called the Body of Christ found also in the least of our brothers and sisters (Hellwig 1992).

We're getting back to what was presented in the previous chapter as the uniqueness of Jesus and his message. For Jesus the Jew, God is a historical God who acts, and calls to action, within history. Therefore, the "Jewish" God of Jesus loves us individually not only because of our individual worth, not only to fill our hearts with purpose and peace, but so that God may love others in and through us. And we are to love and worship this God not only because it brings us joy and peace and personal fulfillment, but also in order to allow that love to do what it naturally tends to do—spill over into the lives of other beings. Love of God and love of neighbor are two commandments that are so close together as to be inseparable; they are two movements of the same energy. Even when the church community is turned inward in centripetal concern for itself, it is really moving in a direction that will reverse itself and centrifugally move into the world to seek first the Kingdom of God.

But if this is the objective, the basic orientation of the church, how is this orientation to be carried out? What are the church's goals in seeking first the Kingdom of God? As we saw in the previous chapter, the Reign of God was for Jesus, and remains for his community, a dynamic symbol that can never be pinned down in a precise definition. To declare that we know precisely and definitively just what the Kingdom of God means and demands is most likely to be using it for our own self-serving purposes. Still, as we saw in the previous chapter, there is a growing consensus among scripture scholars that one of the essential characteristics of the Kingdom preached by Jesus was its this-worldly quality.

For Jesus and for the church today, to seek the Kingdom of God is to seek the well-being of humankind in this finite world. On the basis of his extensive study of the New Testament witness and of recent New Testament exegesis, Edward Schillebeeckx concludes that when we say that the purpose of Jesus' preaching was the Kingdom of God, we mean that Jesus' primary concern was "the well-being of humankind" (Schillebeeckx 1980, Part 4). *Gloria Dei vivens homo*—the glory of God is the well-being of God's creatures (Irenaeus). Thus, in Jon Sobrino's more biblical terms, the Kingdom of God means life—God's intent that there be life, that *all* peoples (and we can add, all creatures) may have life and have it more abundantly (Sobrino 1984; 1987).

But what was clear to Jesus in his day is just as clear to us today: in order to foster the well-being of persons in *this world,* we will have *to change* this world. If the well-being of humanity is to be promoted, if there is to be ever more abundant life, clearly this world must be transformed, for as is painfully evident, so many of the practices and structures of nations and of the international community are death-dealing rather than life-giving for millions of people. The well-being of humanity and of the Earth demands social transformation, development, political liberation, yes, in some instances, revolution. Schillebeeckx states simply and starkly what must be counted among the essential goals of the church's missionary outreach: "Mission is therefore connected with questions of justice and peace, of the distribution of material and spiritual values, of the distribution of work and more just conditions of trade" (Schillebeeckx 1990, 185).

Vatican statements about the same goal are even more lucid and demanding: the International Bishops Synod of 1971 was unambiguous: "Action on behalf of justice and participation in the *transformation of the world* appear to us as a *constitutive dimension* of the preaching of the gospel, or, in other words, of the Church's mission for the redemption of the human race and its liberation from every oppressive situation" (in Gremillion 1976, 514). More recently, the Vatican Secretariat for Interreligious Dialogue reaffirmed that "the commitment to humankind, to social justice, to liberty and the rights of people, and the reform of unjust social structures" makes up "an essential mission of the Church and is indissolubly connected with it" (DP 12; see Fiorenza 1984, 207-12).

But to announce transformation of worldly structures as an essential goal of church mission is not enough. External structures will never be changed if internal structures are not also transformed. To change the world, we must also change the human heart. We are speaking about two different aspects of the same transformative process; political and spiritual conversion must be distinguished but they can never be separated (see Knitter 1995, chap. 5). The Bishops Synod of 1985 warned against separating or opposing what God has joined together for the mission of the church: "The saving mission of the Church with respect to the world must be understood as integral. For, while spiritual, the Church's mission implies the promotion of the human in the temporal domain as well . . . It is necessary, therefore, to set aside and to go beyond false and useless polarities, such as that between spiritual mission and service for the world" (in Geffré 1990, 66-67).

Jesus was a Spirit-filled prophet, not just a prophet. Only prophets who are Spirit-filled can come close to achieving their impossible dreams. While it is not sufficient to change individual human hearts in order that the Reign of well-being be realized, still, unless hearts *are* changed and unless people recognize and experience a power of transformation that is as much beyond them as within them and without which they cannot create new structures of justice and love—unless such internal conversion takes place, we build the Kingdom of God on foundations of sand.

The Kingdom of God therefore might be defined as the utopian vision of a society of love, justice, equality, based on the inner transformation or empowerment of human beings. It is a society in which people will *act* and *live together* differently because they will *be* and *feel* themselves differently. Such a Kingdom is both sociopolitical and spiritual. Its realization demands both development and evangelization.

THE RELIGIONS: AGENTS OF THE KINGDOM

With the Reign of God as the primary objective of missionary outreach, and with the well-being of all creatures as mission's foremost particular goal, Christian missioners will find that their way of seeing other religions will have to be refocused. This refocusing will be more than the visionary shift that took place especially in Roman Catholic theology since Vatican II—from viewing other religions as "works of the devil," which had to be abolished, to approaching them as probable "ways of salvation" (*viae salutis*), which can be affirmed as "legitimate" vehicles of saving grace. In a Kingdom-centered orientation of the church and mission, other religions are not only "ways of salvation," they are, more precisely and more engagingly, "ways of the Kingdom" (*viae Regni*).

Such a theology of religions, which enables Christians to look upon other religions as "positively willed by God" (Rahner 1966a) and as "sacraments" for their followers just as the church is a sacrament for Christians, has recently received a powerful affirmation from the official teaching body of the Roman church. Even though such a positive theology of religions has become the common opinion of mainline Catholic and Protestant theology since the '70s, there has been a good deal of theological bickering (see Ruokanen 1990 and Knitter 1990b) about whether the Second Vatican Council would go so far as to support a theology that affirmed other religions as sacraments of salvation. Those who argued that such an affirmation was implicit in what the Council had to say about other religious traditions (Knitter 1985, 121-24) had to admit that the conciliar statements were indeed ambiguous. Although it announced clearly that salvation was available to all people outside the church, the Council could not bring itself to say that such salvation was present in the conduits of other religions; at the most, the "Declaration on the Church's Attitude toward Other Religions" could venture the recognition that there were "rays of truth" in these other traditions.

Recently, the Vatican Council for Interreligious Dialogue and the Congregation for the Evangelization of Peoples have taken the further step of explicitly affirming other religions as bearers of the saving and enlightening Divine Spirit. This step was taken in *Dialogue and Proclamation*, a declaration issued jointly by both Vatican offices in May 1991. In what the document has to say about the value and role of other religions, we have "a weighty statement, not found before in official documents of the central teaching authority, and whose theological import must not be underestimated" (Dupuis 1994, 137). Abandoning the timidity of the Vatican II observations about other faiths, *Dialogue and Proclamation* (DP) states forthrightly that there are "positive values not only in the religious life of individual believers of other religious traditions, but also *in the religious traditions* to which they belong." And these positive values are not just the result of human efforts but are due to "the active presence of God through His Word" and to "the universal presence of the Spirit." Using jargon familiar to theologians, DP states more explicitly that the religions, therefore, play a "providential role in the *divine economy of salvation*" (DP 17, emphasis mine). Even more unambiguously DP announces: "Concretely, it will be *in the sincere practice* of what is good in *their own religious traditions* and by following the dictates of their conscience that the members of other religions correspond positively to God's invitation and receive salvation" (DP 29, emphasis mine).[5] This is indeed an example of how official Roman Catholic teaching evolves.

But in a Kingdom-centered ecclesiology, to affirm the religions as possible agents of saving grace is to affirm them as possible agents of the Reign of well-being. This is contained in the theology that undergirds the Vatican statements and contemporary Christian views of other religions—mainly the theology of Karl Rahner. To accept Rahner's persuasive argument that God's salvific will and saving grace operate not despite but by means of the religions, not outside but within their beliefs and practices, is also to recognize—perhaps more clearly today than Rahner did in the 1960s—that grace is a force that transforms not only the human heart but also human society. Liberation theologians and Christian communities of the Third World have helped Christians worldwide to recognize that grace is present in its full potency only when it is creating a new world of love and justice out of the present world of injustice and oppression. Therefore, wherever there is grace, there is the borning of the Kingdom. If Christians are to look upon other religions as vehicles of grace, they must also consider them co-workers for the Kingdom.

This, of course, is not to deny the all-too-evident and ugly reality that the religions often have been and still are obstacles to the well-being of humanity; they have served as opium for the oppressed or as ideological tools for the oppressors. But this is as true of Christianity as of other faiths. To recognize the reality of sin is not to cancel the possibility of grace. As Augustine argued against the Donatists, grace can also flow through sinful conduits. The Kingdom can be built with imperfect instruments. Like the Christian church, the religions of the world can be *simul justus et peccator*, both sinful and justified, both impediment to and instrument of the Kingdom.

But we must be careful here. To many, it may look as if this Christian move to view and interact with other religious persons as "agents of the Kingdom" is an up-dated version of the theory of anonymous Christians. In the '60s and '70s, Christians, out of good will and as an attempt at a kinder, gentler approach to other religious persons, declared Hindus and Buddhists to be Christians without a name, without knowing it, every time they followed their conscience or performed a good act; now, it seems, we're announcing that persons of other paths are "anonymous agents of the Kingdom" every time they perform an act of kindness or work for social justice.

Yes, there are clear similarities, but there are even clearer, qualitative differences between the two theological perspectives. In calling Muslims or Hindus anonymous Christians and hidden members of the Christian church, we know very much what we're talking about— Christianity and the Christian churches, in which these people are eventually to be incorporated if they are to find the fullness of grace and truth. With the Kingdom of God, on the other hand, things aren't that clear. In hoping for the Kingdom and in working toward it, we don't really know, fully and definitively, what we're talking about. This is the meaning, as laid out earlier, of the Reign of God as an eschatological reality, which is always still to come in ever greater fullness and as an open-ended symbol indicating a reality that is as real as it is beyond our full comprehension. So when we say that in the Kingdom of God we will realize the "well-being" of humans and the Earth, we don't know fully right now just what that well-being will include and how we are to work toward it. There's always more to realize and to learn.

And this means that in looking upon other religious men and women as potential agents of the Kingdom, Christians are not trying to "include" them neatly in an already clearly and definitively defined project and vision. While Christians feel that they have a universally meaningful and decisive grasp of what the Kingdom is to include, they also admit that there can be other meaningful, urgent, decisive contributions to the ever greater realization of a new way of being human and living together. Therefore, when Christians look upon others as agents of the Kingdom, they do not view the others as assistants but as co-workers. It's not just that Christians may have the *name* for what the others are searching for, but also, just as likely, the others may have the *name* for what Christians are searching for. To hold up the Kingdom of God as the Christian name for the common ground for inter-religious dialogue is to call for a level playing field where everyone is ready and expected both to learn and teach.

Christian churches of the south, the Two-thirds World, are reminding their brothers and sisters of the north, the One-third World, that in such a Kingdom-centered mission, there is much for Christians to both contribute *and* receive. Asian theologians like Aloysius Pieris (1988a), Samuel Rayan (1989, 1990), Michael Amaladoss (1992a),

Stanley Samartha (1991), Felix Wilfred (1994), Tissa Balasuriya (1980), Abraham Ayrookuzhiel (1994) are alerting especially their Latin American colleagues that the confrontation with suffering and injustice that has given rise to the theology of liberation within Latin American Christianity is having similar effects among Asian religions. Ordinary believers and religious leaders are reexamining their traditions and sacred scriptures and are performing what Christian theologians have called a "hermeneutics of suspicion," by which they lay bare the ideological and oppressive abuse of their religions, and then a "hermeneutics of retrieval," by which they seek to rediscover and reactivate the liberative content of their scriptures and central beliefs. What they are discovering and attempting can help Christians understand and realize what they envision as the Kingdom of God. Indeed, especially in Asia, Christians are realizing, painfully and happily, that building the Kingdom is too big and too complex a job for any one religion (see Knitter 1995, chap. 9).

WHAT ABOUT CONVERSIONS?

Can this *revised*, Kingdom-centered understanding of mission also *reaffirm* what has long been the fuel of missionary zeal down through the ages: conversions? Part of the motivation the disciples of Jesus felt in leaving their boats, nets, and all to follow him was the challenge of becoming "fishers of human beings" (Mk 1:17). They had something they felt others needed. They wanted others to "buy into it," to be better off for it. In a Kingdom-centered notion of mission, can Christians be fired by the zeal to convert?

Indeed, they can. Conversion remains a top priority for every missionary. But it is, first of all, *conversion to the Kingdom*. To enable all people to become members of the Kingdom of God is more important than to make them members of the church. "Mission is no longer seen narrowly as church extension, but as bringing the power of the Word to bear on any human situation to which it has a relevant message (Amaladoss 1992b, 2). The *foremost* intent of the power of the Word is to fashion human life and society according to the patterns of God's Reign—not to fill the pews for Sunday Mass. Just as, in a sense, it would be idolatry to make the church more important than the Reign of God, so it would be equally idolatrous to hold up conversions to the church through baptism as the most urgent goal of missionary work.

Such an understanding of mission can be not only sobering but consoling. A missionary who has no baptisms to report, but who has helped Hindus, Buddhists, and Christians to live together lovingly and justly is a successful disciple of Christ; a missionary who has filled the church with converts without seeking to change a society that condones dowry deaths or bonded labor is a failure.

This means that the understanding of conversion and the way it stands as a goal of missionary endeavor must be clarified and expanded. The assimilation of Jesus' message by another religious community may result in conversions that are real but that do not make for new members of the church. The Vatican document *Dialogue and Proclamation* clearly recognizes and approves the two meanings and the two goals that the word "conversion" carries: fundamentally, conversion is realized in "the humble and penitent return of the heart to God" (DP 37), but "more specifically, conversion may refer to a change of religious adherence, and particularly to embracing the Christian faith" (DP 11). Both types of change or transformation, in an individual or in a community, fulfill the nature and the goal of what the missionary intends by "conversion."

In the broader meaning of conversion as a return of the heart to God and God's truth, we are talking about a genuine, personal conversion by which the Hindu, for example, is really different, changed, transformed through her encounter with the God that is present in the gospel and the Christian community; yet, she remains a Hindu—perhaps a different kind of Hindu, a better Hindu, but still a Hindu. Such conversions are real. And they satisfy the purpose of "being sent." Gandhi is perhaps the most notable instance of someone whose Hindu-religious identity was deeply changed but at the same time confirmed by his encounter with the gospel. A more recent example of such a "convert" might be the Zen Buddhist scholar Masao Abe, who has admitted how much his understanding of Buddhism has been affected by his encounter with Christians, especially in the area of the meaning of history and social ethics (Knitter 1987).

But to distinguish and to prioritize is not to oppose. Conversions to the Kingdom and conversions to the church are very different, and sometimes there can be tensions between the two, but they do not contradict each other. Generally, the missionary does not have to choose one over the other. For, as we have seen, if enabling the Kingdom of God to come on Earth as it is in heaven is *the central end* of mission, planting and nourishing the community called church is *a necessary means* to that end. Therefore, missioners will seek after conversions not just to the Kingdom but also to the Christian community! As disciples of Jesus Christ, Christians are convinced that the Kingdom of God or the well-being of humanity cannot be realized to its full potential unless the vision and the empowerment of Jesus and his Spirit become part of the human project; therefore, they go forth to preach the gospel. And to make the gospel genuinely present in a new culture, they will have to seek to establish communities of gospel followers and preachers.

In this sense, then, we can say that the "church is necessary for salvation": the Christian community must make its necessary, universally meaningful contribution to the task of building God's Kingdom. Where this contribution is lacking, the formation of the Kingdom will be, in Christian convictions, incomplete. And so the missioner will be eager to increase the numbers of those who are committed to making the Christian vision of the Kingdom known to their neighbors, both across the street or across the seas. True, Christians will never try to force conversions to the church; nor will they measure their success in terms of the number of such conversions. Still, they will seek after, not just welcome, persons who freely decide to join the community of disciples responsible for embodying Jesus' vision of society.

In general, in seeking conversions to the Christian community missionaries will not be impelled by concerns that "eternal salvation" is hanging in the balance. For Roman Catholics, it is standard, "official" teaching that salvation is available through many other means besides the church; most mainline Protestants would share this conviction about God's unbounded love. Thus, while missionaries will certainly seek such conversions by baptism and will nurture persons who express interest in membership in the Christian community, they will be careful not to press or proselytize for such conversions. Better to allow the wisdom and promptings of the Holy Spirit to take the lead in such matters and be the deciding factor determining when conversion to the Kingdom (always intended) will include conversion to the church (hoped for).

In some particular situations, however, missioners may have to seek after conversions to the church community with special urgency, maybe with necessity. When in their efforts to proclaim the values of God's Reign as Jesus saw them, they encounter dominant values in a culture or religion that are not only different from, but clearly and certainly opposed to, those values—when they honestly and sadly confront what Jon Sobrino has experienced in El Salvador as the "anti-Kingdom" (Sobrino 1994, 16-79)—then to proclaim the gospel will mean to disclaim cultural or religious attitudes or practices. To announce will mean to denounce. Where cooperation had been the hope, resistance becomes the choice. In such situations, the missioner will consciously and urgently seek to convert to the church community. If it is impossible for persons to integrate Kingdom values of justice, love, and concern for the poor into their own religious community, the missioner will seek, carefully but resolutely, a conversion of these persons to a community where such values can be affirmed and practiced. The missioner will invite these persons to join the community of disciples of Jesus. Though I have said that conversion to the Christian church is not a necessary goal of mission, it sometimes can be.

But if conversion is still a valid and necessary goal of missionary activity, it becomes, in a Kingdom-centered ecclesiology, a beneficial two-edged sword. The Kingdom-centered missioner will also recognize that the purpose of mission is to bring about not only the conversion of the other but also the conversion of the missionary and of the church. Missioners go forth to expand the church not only through the increase of members but also through the increase of new truth, new cultural identity, new challenges within the church. The church, in other words, needs missionaries not just to change others but to change itself; without missionary activity the church would not be able to carry out the vital principle of its well-being: *ecclesia semper reformanda*—the church must always be reformed.

So in proclaiming the good news, missionaries realize that others may have good news to proclaim to them. And they know this not simply on the basis of some philosophical truth, but because of what they have discovered in Jesus Christ—that this God of Jesus, in God's love and wisdom, is always more than what they already know through Jesus. And because of Jesus, they can search for and receive the truth wherever it may present itself. More concretely, because missioners are so committed to the Kingdom revealed in Jesus they are ready to have their knowledge of that Kingdom clarified, perhaps corrected, through their encounters with others. The most effective missionaries are those who have also been converted by their converts.

A ROMAN CATHOLIC INTER-MISSION

Dialoguing with Vatican Views of Mission

Those Catholics, lay people and theologians, who find themselves at home with the basic features of a Kingdom-centered ecclesiology have something to be worried about. In official, public statements, the central teaching body of the Roman Catholic Church has expressed grave concern, even an explicit rejection of "Kingdom-centered" models for the church and its mission. This was mainly in the 1990 papal encyclical, *Redemptoris Missio* (RM), but also in *Dialogue and Proclamation* (1991), the already mentioned joint document of the Vatican Council for Interreligious Dialogue and the Congregation for the Evangelization of Peoples. Such concerns, of course, are not just "Catholic"; indeed, they are often expressed more broadly and more passionately by Protestant Christians and missioners (see Mojzes and Swidler 1990; Braaten 1985; Tippit 1987; for an overview, see Yates 1994). In taking seriously these warnings, in their official Vatican articulation—that is, in trying to respond to their authentic concerns and in pointing out what seem to be their inconsistencies—we can, I trust, clarify both the promise and the pitfalls of a Kingdom-centered mission within a globally responsible dialogue. At the same time, perhaps we can reduce what appears to be a cause of dissension both *among* the ranks of theologians and *between* the ranks of theologians and hierarchy within the Roman Church.

From one perspective, both RM and DP stand as milestones in official Catholic teaching on the relation between church and Kingdom. For most of the history of ecclesiology, if there was ever any talk about the Kingdom of God, not only was it taken for granted that this Kingdom and the church were identical, but there was also a strict identity between "church" and "Roman Catholic Church." Pope Pius XII in his 1943 encyclical, *Mystici Corporis,* left no doubt about this. The documents of the Second Vatican Council, for the most part, offered rather clear distinctions between the church and the Kingdom of God, adding further distinctions between the Kingdom as it exists on this earth and in its eschatological fulfillment.

But it seems that especially in *Lumen Gentium* (*The Constitution on the Church*) the two realities that were distinguished were still held tightly together. The church "is, on earth, the seed and the beginning of that Kingdom" (LG 5). The divine reality that will take its future form in the world to come is now, here on earth, present in the Christian church as "seed and beginning." So "the Church—that is, the Kingdom of Christ already present in mystery—grows visibly through the power of God in the world" (LG 3). The church here is identified as that *locus*—the construction site, as it were—where the Kingdom of God in Christ assumes shape in the world. Jacques Dupuis observes: "It would be right to conclude that in the Dogmatic Constitution *Lumen Gentium* the Church and the Reign of God are still identified, both in their historical realization and in their eschatological fulfillment" (Dupuis 1993, 7; see also LG 9, 48).[1]

This is the theological context in which the two Vatican documents *Redemptoris Missio* and *Dialogue and Proclamation* take up their milestone function, clearly moving official Catholic teaching in the direction it was bending toward since Vatican II. Not only is the Christian church no longer able to be identified with the Catholic church (that Vatican II confessed clearly, if not humbly, in the "Decree on Ecumenism"), but the Kingdom of God is no longer able to be identified with the Christian church. "RM and DP appear to be the first two documents of the recent central doctrinal authority to distinguish the pilgrim church from the reality of the reign of God in history; both documents profess that the reign of God is a broader reality than the Church" (Dupuis 1994, 148-50). But even more significantly, not only do these statements clearly distinguish church and Kingdom so as to recognize that the one larger reality of Kingdom *cannot* be encompassed and contained within the church, but also the documents unambiguously *subordinate* the church to the Kingdom by affirming that the church is meant to be a *servant* of the broader and more important Reign of God.

- It is true that the church is not an end unto herself, since she is ordered toward the Kingdom of God of which she is the seed, sign, and instrument (RM 18).
- The church is effectively and concretely at the service of the Kingdom (RM 20).
- The church's mission is to foster the "Kingdom of our Lord and his Christ" (Rev. 11:15) at whose service she is placed (DP 35; see also 59).

From all appearances, we have here an official, papal endorsement of what has been called a Kingdom-centered ecclesiology.

VATICAN OBJECTIONS

But we don't. In the very same document, Pope John Paul II expressly sounds a warning against "kingdom-centered" views of church and mission. In a description that sounds like a further development of the citations just given, the pope identifies a picture of the church he feels has to be rejected:

> They [proponents of a Kingdom-centered mission] stress the image of a church which is not concerned about herself, but which is totally concerned with bearing witness to and serving the kingdom. It is a "church for others" just as Christ is the "man for others." The church's task is described as though it had to proceed in two directions: on the one hand promoting such "values of the kingdom" as peace, justice, freedom, brotherhood, etc., while on the other hand fostering dialogue between peoples, cultures, and religions so that through a mutual enrichment they might help the world to be renewed and to journey ever closer toward the kingdom (RM 17).

The pope admits that there are "positive aspects" in such a Kingdom-centered picture of church, but in his judgment they are outweighed by "negative aspects." The negatives are primarily two. First, to place human well-being in this world center-stage in missionary practice is to fall into the temptation of "reducing" the role of the church to an "anthropocentric" agenda. In making "man's earthly needs" the focus of mission, "the Kingdom tends to become something completely human and secularized; what counts are programs and struggles for liberation which is socioeconomic, political, and even cultural, but within a horizon that is closed to the transcendent." This "easily translates into one more ideology of purely earthly progress" (RM 17).

Second, such Kingdom-centered models for mission are so concerned about avoiding "ecclesiocentrism" that they end up remaining "silent about Christ." "The Kingdom of which they [proponents of regnocentrism] speak is 'theocentrically' based." The pope fears that in seeking to be so centered on the Kingdom and on God, Christians lose their centering in Christ. There is much talk in these Kingdom-centered views of "the mystery of creation" and the need to preserve the environment, "but they keep silent about the mystery of redemption" and about the role that Christ plays in redeeming the mess we have made of creation and the human situation (RM 17).

So the pope issues his bottom-line evaluation of these Kingdom-centered approaches to the church's mission: "This is not the Kingdom of God as we know it from Revelation." And in the very next sentence, he gives the reason why this is so and why such Kingdom-focused views must be rejected: "*The Kingdom cannot be detached either from the Christ or from the Church*" (RM 18).

Trying to sort out and connect the milestone statements about the Kingdom and church being so genuinely different that they cannot be identified with these assertions that the Kingdom cannot be "detached" from the church and Christ, we can surmise that for the Vatican, although Kingdom and church can be distinguished, they *can't be separated*. They are different, but you can't have one without the other; you can't promote the Kingdom unless you are promoting the church. Like hydrogen and oxygen in water, if you separate them, you no longer have the reality of water. This is not identification, but inseparability. Yet it's an inseparability in which it is difficult to claim that one element is subordinate and the "servant" of the other.

The fundamental reason why the pope refuses to detach Kingdom and church is because of the *identification* he sees between the Kingdom and Jesus. In affirming such an identification, he argues that he is merely following the witness of the New Testament: "The preaching of the early church was centered on the proclamation of Jesus Christ, with whom the Kingdom was *identified*" (RM 16, emphasis mine). He takes this identification in an almost literal sense: "The Kingdom of God is not a concept, a doctrine, or a program subject to free interpretation, but is before all else a person with the face and name of Jesus of Nazareth, the image of the invisible God. If the Kingdom is separated from Jesus, it is no longer the Kingdom of God which he revealed" (RM 18). It is because of this tip-to-toe identification of the Kingdom with Jesus that the pope insists on an inseparability between the church and the Kingdom that for all practical purposes seems to be an identification: "One may not separate the Kingdom from the church . . . While remaining distinct from Christ and the Kingdom, the church is *indissolubly united* to both" (RM 18, emphasis mine).

It seems that *Dialogue and Proclamation* attempted, at least in its earlier stages of composition, to stretch beyond this identification or inseparability between the church and the Kingdom. But a history of the text's genesis reveals that every time DP attempted to do this, a later addition was made to the text that would qualify such "stretching" and bring it back in line with the views of the pope in *Redemptoris Missio*. In paragraph 34 DP humbly admits that "the relationship between the Church and the Kingdom of God is mysterious and complex." The implication, it seems, is that one should be careful of making statements that would pin this relationship down to one mode. But even after the fifth draft of DP had been approved by the Plenary Assembly of the Council for Interreligious Dialogue in April 1990, the following statement (drawn from John Paul II's 1989 talk to the Indian Bishops) was added, evidently at the urging of the Congregation for the Doctrine of the Faith, to paragraph 34: "The Kingdom is inseparable from the Church, because both are inseparable from the person and work of Jesus himself."

When the earlier drafts of DP went on, in paragraph 35, to make the qualified but still bold statement that "the inchoate reality of the Kingdom can be found *also beyond the confines of the Church*, for example in the hearts of the followers of other religious traditions," another cautionary statement was added before final publication: "It must be remembered nevertheless that this is indeed an inchoate reality, which needs to find completion through being related to the Kingdom of Christ already present in the Church." The glimmers of the Kingdom found "beyond the confines of the Church" are so "inchoate," in other words, that they "need" to be fulfilled by inclusion in the church.

Because of this *necessary* fulfillment or completion, the pope in RM has to point an admonishing finger at those who suggest that conversion can be understood in two different ways—to the Kingdom or to the church; above I indicated how DP endorsed both types of conversion and I suggested that *either* could fulfill the goal of missionary outreach (see pp. 121-22). Even though John Paul recognizes that the gospel of Jesus requires his followers to promote the well-being of society and that "building the Kingdom means working for liberation from evil in all its forms" (RM 15), he still declares that such endeavors, though necessary, are insufficient in themselves to fulfill the purpose of missionary work. Unless missionaries are seeking to baptize and fill their churches with new members, they are not missionaries. "The mission *ad gentes* [to the nations] has this *objective:* to found Christian communities and develop churches to their full maturity. This is a *central and determining goal* of missionary activity, so much so that the mission is not completed until it succeeds in building a new particular church which functions normally in its own setting" (RM 48, emphasis mine).

In this statement, the pope is not just saying that making converts to the church is a project the missioner cannot forget as he or she seeks to promote the broader Kingdom. The pope insists that converts through baptism must remain the missionary's top priority. "It is necessary *first and foremost* to strive to establish Christian communities everywhere" (RM 49, emphasis mine). And he reprimands anyone who would "separate conversion to Christ from baptism, regarding baptism as unnecessary" (RM 47). To make sure that such priorities are perfectly clear, the pope expressly rejects those Kingdom-centered conclusions that were advanced earlier in this chapter—which claim that the purpose of mission has been achieved when missioners "help people to become more human and more faithful to their own religion" or when they "build communities capable of working for justice, freedom, peace, and solidarity" (RM 47). For the pope, such noble, necessary goals may be enough for a social worker but not for a Christian missionary.

VATICAN CONCERNS AND AMBIGUITIES

Clearly there are brittle tensions, if not downright disagreements, between the Kingdom-centered, globally responsible paradigm for church and mission that I have presented in this chapter and aspects of the ecclesiology and missiology presumed and proffered in these Vatican teachings, especially in *Redemptoris Missio.* In the Catholic context, such dissonance between theologians and the magisterium cannot be made light of or swept under the rug of scholarly journals. These differences have to be discussed openly and charitably within the community, in the knowledge that this is part of the life of the church. As Karl Rahner reminded us: In the stark but caring clash of differing views, the breath and dynamism of the Spirit are felt (Rahner 1964).

In trying to carry on a conversation about these differences, I want to distinguish between the content of the pope's concerns and the adequacy of the theology he uses to meet those concerns. I trust that most Christians, not only Catholics, will affirm the validity of what the pope is concerned about: that the authentic gospel be preached, that the "grace and truth" made flesh in Jesus be made available to all, that new communities of disciples be formed throughout the world to embody the Kingdom. As a so-called pluralist or correlational Christian, as a proponent of a globally responsible mission of the church, I deeply share these concerns with the pope. I would like to review some of the main ingredients of the correlational christology and the Kingdom-centered ecclesiology proposed in this and the previous chapter to try to make clear that the pope's concerns can be respected and met.

First, to place global responsibility for the *soteria* or well-being of this world on the top of the missionary agenda *does not*—indeed, it *should not*—necessarily lead to what the pope presents as a "reduction" of mission praxis to purely social or political or economic concerns. Even though the missionary and the social worker may share the very same goals, even though they may work shoulder to shoulder in trying to bring about land reform or the prosecution of dowry deaths, the Christian missioner, by self-definition and self-understanding, will bring something unique to the effort: the vision and values of the gospel. Yes, such vision and values dovetail with what many hold up as human or social or political values; they are, to use an often misused word, humanistic. But it is a humanism that is transfused and ani-

mated by the Spirit—a humanism convinced that the goals of the social worker or the platform of the politician can truly and firmly be
achieved only if such human works are also spiritual works, only if
the Spirit is embodied in such efforts at organizing cooperatives or
saving rain forests.

True, the missioner will rejoice when such human efforts for eco-
human justice bear fruit, whether the Spirit is acknowledged or not,
for in the Kingdom-centered theology we are endorsing the Spirit moves
as she will, in often hidden ways; such a theology acknowledges the
presence of the Spirit in every human act of love, or struggle for justice, or giving one's energies and life for others. Yet, the Kingdom-
centered missioner also insists that where this Spirit is explicitly acknowledged and nurtured, the this-worldly work of the social worker
or politician can be made all the stronger, more persevering, and hope-
filled.

In other words, in trying to respond to the pope's legitimate concerns, I can say more clearly and more carefully that to place work for
the this-worldly realization of the Kingdom *first* does not mean to
place concern for the Spirit *second*. When missionaries announce that
our most pressing order of business is to address the cries of the poor
or of the suffering earth, they will also announce—and will experience personally in taking up their work—that such business is precisely where the presence and the need for the Spirit's animating power
is experienced. This nondual, co-inhering relation between working
for the Kingdom and experiencing the Spirit can be spelled out more
precisely in two convictions that I tried to express in earlier chapters.
First, essential to the globally responsible dialogue and the Kingdom-
centered mission that we have been exploring is the foundational conviction that *social* transformation requires *personal* transformation.
As Jesus can best be understood as a Spirit-filled prophet, as a prophet
who was also a mystic, so Christian missionaries must be Spirit-filled
activists who see social-political transformation and personal-spiri-
tual transformation as two blades on the same propeller. As Latin
American liberation theologians have always insisted, and are insisting even more forcefully of late, in order to "raise consciousness" as
to social evils and rights, they must also "deepen consciousness" as to
the inner, spiritual depths of human beings and society (Gutiérrez 1984;
Sobrino 1988). To reduce the mission of the church to either one or
the other—to either the material or the spiritual—is to do violence to
the gospel.[2]

Second, for the Christian, essential to the "deepening of consciousness" is the discovery and celebration of that which cannot be reduced to the human or finite—in the pope's terms, the *Transcendent*.
A Kingdom-centered model for mission understands this goal as the
Kingdom *of* God. Working for and within this Kingdom can never be

a purely human affair. To attempt to construct a society of Kingdom values on purely human efforts is like laying cement without mixing it with water. The Transcendent, the more-than-human, is an essential part of the Christian witness and effort to Kingdom-building. Whether that Transcendent is called Spirit or Parent or the "religious dimension," Christians will gently insist, as they roll up their sleeves and work alongside the atheist social worker, that openness to some such "More" is crucial for the effective and enduring transformation of this world. There is an Energy or a "Grace" available to, and necessary for, the incredibly complex and often frustrating task of being a human being and fashioning a human society. Granting that Christians have much to learn from others as to just what this Reality is (and is not), they still will understand a witness to this Reality as an essential part of their contribution to the Kingdom.

So in the understanding of the regnocentric missionary program that I have tried to formulate, I would fully agree that an "anthropocentric" reduction of this program to "purely human" ends by way of purely human means would be not only dangerous but destructive of what the church is all about. But I have less fear that such a reduction will take place.

A second papal concern has to do with conversions—conversions to the church. Again, in referring back to the outline of a Kingdom-centered missiology presented above, I can share and respond to the pope's concern. To assert that "conversions to the Kingdom" should be more important for the missioner than conversions to the church is not to assert that conversions to the Christian community are *unimportant*. Because the gospel must be announced to all peoples and because announcing requires an announcing community, the "planting" of new local churches remains not only important but necessary. If a Kingdom-centered mission does not affirm this, it will soon lose its center. Therefore, to prioritize A over B is not to exclude or even belittle B. *My* concern is that the pope in RM, by holding up church conversions as more important than Kingdom-conversions, ends up, contrary to his own intentions, making the church more important than the Kingdom. But to address this issue, we have to take up the pope's last, and central, problem with a Reign-centered mission.

For John Paul, the new views of mission and other religions seem to "remain silent about Christ" and about "the mystery of redemption" (RM 17). Or, by being so Kingdom or God-centered, they lose their central rootedness in Christ. I would hope that the description of a correlational christology presented in the previous chapters might serve to assuage the pope's fears. Again, distinctions are the axle of what is being asserted: to question Jesus as God's "only" message of well-being is not to deny that he "truly" bears such a message. While Christians need not insist that Jesus is God's "full, definitive, unsurpassable" statement, they can and must continue to show others why they feel that Jesus is indeed a "universal, decisive, and even indispensable" revelation of God's hopes for the world. And they owe it to themselves and to others to show what it is, for this day and age, that makes Jesus *unique*—that is, what is the universally pressing, indispensable, and decision-provoking meaning in his message. To so clarify how a Kingdom-centered mission remains christocentric will, I expect, elicit a papal nod of approval.

But I'm afraid that that is as far as nodding approval will go. For neither *Redemptoris Missio* nor *Dialogue and Proclamation* shows itself ready to even consider a revision of the exclusive claims of traditional christology. Official Roman Catholic Church teaching has in no way opened itself to the possibility of a *representational christology* that holds up Jesus as a decisive representation or embodiment or revelation of God's saving love—a love that "pre-dates" Jesus and is "unbounded" and universally active by the very nature of God and of creation (Ogden 1994, 9-10). Rather, the official Magisterium has adhered to a *constitutive christology*, according to which Jesus, especially in his death and resurrection, causes or constitutes the universal availability of God's salvific love. Without Jesus such love would not be active in the world; whatever experience of Divine Presence is realized in the world has to be seen as caused by Jesus and necessarily in need of fulfillment through membership in the church. Because Jesus *constitutes* and not just *represents* God's saving activity, Jesus has to be proclaimed as "full, definitive, unsurpassable."

Such claims for Jesus Christ are foundational and determinative for everything the pope has to say in RM. In fact, sometimes his christological claims seem to be so strong that it is difficult to reconcile them with the pope's express recognition that salvation is possible through other "forms of mediation" besides Jesus and the church (RM 5). He affirms that "Christ is the one savior of all, the *only one able to reveal God and lead to God* . . . salvation can *only* come from Jesus Christ" (RM 5, emphasis mine). This means that no one else can reveal and lead to salvation. "In him, and *only in him*, are we set free from all alienation and doubt" (RM 11, emphasis mine). Therefore, to claim uniqueness for Jesus is to insist that he has a place in history that surpasses all others: "It is precisely this uniqueness of Christ which gives him an absolute and universal significance whereby, while belonging to history, he remains history's center and goal" (RM 6). Stressing the absolute superiority of Jesus, the pope clarifies further that whatever other "mediations" of God's love there may be in other religions, "they cannot be understood as parallel or complementary to his" (RM 5). The pope here rejects not just parallel revelations that would all be equalized, but he also rejects complementary revelations that could learn from each other.

Dialogue and Proclamation, though not as insistent and extensive in its christological statements as RM, is in fundamental agreement: Jesus is the "new and definitive Covenant for all peoples" (DP
19); "In Jesus Christ, the Son of God made man, we have the fullness of revelation and salvation" (DP 22). And so there is "one plan
of salvation for humankind, with its center in Jesus Christ" (DP 28)
(see also the New Universal Catechism, 66-67, 843, 845).

This constitutive, definitive *quality* of Jesus Christ as the only source
and reason for God's saving love in the world seems to be for the pope
the reason why the church is missionary. The following statement is,
for me, as surprising as it is lucid: "This *definitive* self-revelation of
God [in Christ] is the *fundamental reason* why the church is missionary by her very nature" (RM 5, emphasis mine). The "fundamental
reason," therefore, why Christians go forth is because they have something "better" than anyone else, rather than simply because they have
something they want to share with everyone else.

As we shall see in the next chapter, such a constitutive, exclusive
understanding of Christ's saving role makes it very difficult, if not
impossible, for the pope and the authors of DP to practice all the
things they preach about *dialogue*. But this same christology, and the
pivotal place it holds in the pope's understanding of church and mission, also makes it difficult for the pope to coherently maintain the
distinction he and DP make between the Kingdom and the church,
especially regarding the *servant role* the church is to carry out for the
sake of the Kingdom. It is because the pope insists that Jesus is the
only savior, the "only one able to reveal God and lead to God," that
he *identifies*, as was pointed out above, Jesus and the Kingdom. Every
expression of the Kingdom is affected by, and oriented to, the Christ
event. And this christological identification of Jesus and Kingdom
becomes the reason why the pope also insists on the *ecclesiological
inseparability* between the church and the Kingdom. If the Kingdom
can be found only in Jesus, and if the church is the continuation of
Jesus' presence through the ages, then the Kingdom can really be found
only in the church. Essentially, that's what both the pope and DP end up
saying: "The Kingdom is inseparable from the Church because both are
inseparable from the person and work of Jesus himself" (DP 34, quot-
ing John Paul).

But that would seem to contradict other statements in the two documents that indicate, as Jacques Dupuis points out, "that the Reign of
God is a broader reality than the Church" (Dupuis 1994, 150). To
speak about "inseparability" means that the Kingdom cannot be anywhere other than where the church is; that is to confine the Kingdom
to the parameters, or at least the definitions, of the church. But then,
how can we speak about the church as the servant of the Kingdom,
for now we have the servant telling the master what can or cannot be.

If the church is genuinely the servant of the Kingdom, then it cannot predetermine what the Kingdom can be or require that whatever the Kingdom might be has to be "fulfilled" and "perfected" in the church. To take seriously this rather antiquated imagery, masters are not fulfilled and perfected in servants.

I have to agree, therefore, with those critics who declare that the pope's reassurance that "one need not fear falling . . . into a form of 'ecclesiocentrism'" (RM 19) is not very reassuring. Given the way the pope presses the inseparability of church and Kingdom and the need for the Kingdom to be fulfilled *in* the church, "one can hardly avoid the impression that ecclesiocentrism is the model underlying papal thinking in *Redemptoris Missio* . . . *Redemptoris Missio* fails to convince one that its spirit is truly at the service of the kingdom" (Gittens 1994, 218-19). Or, the same concern spelled out in particulars: In RM, "the institution seems to prevail, the juridical system seems more important than the living person of Christ—despite many affirmations that this is not the case" (Hearne 1993, 93).

I suggest that the deeper, clandestine reason for the critics' reservations about papal inconsistencies has to do with the tension or contradiction between the constitutive-exclusive christology that the Vatican holds to and the Kingdom-oriented ecclesiology and missiology that it is trying to plot in RM and DP. Simply stated, it is impossible to develop a Kingdom-centered understanding of church that will coherently and persuasively present the church as the servant of the Kingdom on the basis of a christology that insists that Jesus is the only cause of and the unsurpassable criterion for the salvation to be realized in the Kingdom. With such an understanding of Jesus, the universality of the Kingdom is continually reduced to the particularity of the church.

It is therefore my hope that future conversations between missiologists and theologians in general, and especially between Catholic theologians and the papal Magisterium, will take up this issue of whether the new and generally accepted ecclesiological developments that present the church as the servant of the Kingdom can be reconciled with dominant christologies that identify the Kingdom with Jesus. My hope is that the pope and Vatican experts, as well as theologians and missiologists in general, will respond positively, or at least more explicitly, to the suggestions that a correlational, global christology, even though it no longer insists on Jesus as the total or definitive revelation of God, can still affirm him as God's universal, decisive, and indispensable Word—and that such an understanding of Jesus would truly allow and enable the church to be servant of the Kingdom.

7

MISSION REAFFIRMED

Mission as Dialogue

Integral to the new paradigm for understanding the mission of the church as service to the Kingdom is the necessity of integrating dialogue into that mission-as-service. If, in this new regnocentric paradigm, the religious traditions of humankind are looked up as potential "agents of the Kingdom" (see chapter 6, pp. 118-21), then clearly, cooperation and dialogue with them are essential elements in a missioner's job description. Dialogue, long looked upon by preachers of the gospel as someone else's job or as a dangerous or distracting pastime, is now viewed as a necessary ingredient in any missionary recipe.

A DIALOGICAL CHURCH AND MISSION

In order to carry out the great commission and "teach all nations," Christians are coming to understand that they will have to dialogue with all nations. Somehow, mission has to include dialogue. As Roger Haight puts it, "dialogue defines the framework for the unfolding of the church's mission" (Haight 1995, 14); or "dialogue can be seen as a metaphor for the distinctive change in the concrete conception of the church's mission" (ibid., 20). One of the most widely known male missionary orders in the Roman Catholic Church, the Society of the Divine Word, reflected the declarations of other missionary groups when it officially announced to all its members: "Dialogue is at the core of the missionary activity of the Society."[1]

ANOTHER VATICAN MILESTONE

The two Vatican documents that we have been analyzing, *Redemptoris Missio* and *Dialogue and Proclamation,* not only confirm but

136

push forward the recognition on the part of theologians and missiologists that mission and dialogue are essentially linked. In fact, once again these Vatican statements—especially DP—set up another milestone in official Roman Catholic teaching on the nature of the church and its mission. This is the first time that those charged with coordinating the pastoral and teaching responsibilities in the Roman Catholic Church have stated so expressly and unambiguously that dialogue constitutes an integral and essential part of the church's mission.

Since the Second Vatican Council, dialogue with persons of other religious traditions has certainly been encouraged. But never was it said that the church *must* dialogue with other religions in order to carry out its mission and identity. Even Pope Paul VI, often called "the pope of dialogue" because of his encyclical *Ecclesiam Suam* (1964), in which he depicted the history of salvation as a dialogue of God with humankind, did not place dialogue within the fundamental mission of the church. In fact, in his mission encyclical, *Evangelii Nuntiandi* (1975), even though he urged a positive attitude toward other religions, Paul VI affirmed such a radical difference between Christianity and other traditions that one must ask what kind of conversation between them is really possible. As the one "supernatural religion" in a world of "natural religions" (EN 53), Christianity must be considered, according to the pope, "the one true religion" (EN 56).

A clear step beyond this attitude was taken in 1984 when the Vatican Secretariat for Non-Christian Religions issued "The Attitude of the Church toward the Followers of Other Religions (Reflections and Orientations on Dialogue and Mission)" (D&M). Here, for the first time in an official Vatican document, dialogue "with the followers of other religious traditions in order to walk together toward truth and to work together in projects of common concern" was listed as one of the principal elements of the church's mission (D&M 13). Furthermore, it reminded Christians that a "dialogical spirit" must infuse every aspect of the church's interaction with the world (D&M 29). But such radical, inspiring announcements were simply delivered by the 1984 document and left on the table; nothing was said about how such a dialogical attitude, in which both sides really "walk together toward truth" was to be integrated and balanced with other aspects of the church's mission, especially its duty to proclaim. Further reflections on how to achieve such balancing were offered in *Dialogue and Proclamation* and, less so, in *Redemptoris Missio*.

While RM basically, but more authoritatively, repeats the 1984 pioneering announcement that "interreligious dialogue is a part of the church's evangelizing mission" and that there is "no conflict between proclaiming Christ and engaging in interreligious dialogue" (RM 55), DP takes as its task to lay out the distinctive "characteristics of these two elements" (dialogue and proclamation) and to show how these characteristics make for a "mutual relationship" (DP 3). With this document, the Vatican Council for Interreligious Dialogue hopes to help, and realign both those who have not yet admitted that dialogue is now a vital piece of the church's mission and those who think that dialogue can take the place of proclamation (DP 4/c).

The milestone claim of DP is tightly contained in one sentence: "Proclamation and dialogue are . . . both viewed, each in its own place, as component elements and authentic forms of the one evangelizing mission of the Church" (DP 2). Attempting to explain how both "component elements" play their role in the "single but complex . . . reality" of the church's mission (DP 2), the document first clarifies its terminology. The expression "evangelizing mission," long used in ecclesiastical idiom, may be rather misleading in this context. It does not mean the mission of preaching; for that, the document uses the word "proclamation." Rather, "evangelizing mission" is an umbrella image for all that the church is about in order to do its main job; that job consists of two intertwined ideals: a) to let all humanity hear and feel the values of the *good news*, in order b) "to *transform* that *humanity* from within, making it new" (DP 8). The evangelizing mission of the church is to communicate its vision in such a way that humankind will be transformed. Such a broad goal will call for a variety of activities: "presence and witness, commitment to social development and human liberation, liturgical life, prayer and contemplation, interreligious dialogue, and finally, proclamation and catechesis" (DP 2).

So dialogue and proclamation are "component elements" and "authentic forms"—among many others elements and forms—that make up the general mission of the church. DP makes clear that "they are both oriented towards the communication of salvific truth" (DP 2). So the good news, the saving truth of God, is being communicated not just when Christians are proclaiming, but also when they are listening. In doing both, the saving mission of the church is being realized. DP is exceptionally clear and insistent in pointing out that both elements, in their real difference, are essential. "There can be no question of choosing one and ignoring or rejecting the other" (DP 6). "Both are legitimate and necessary. They are intimately related, but not interchangeable" (DP 77).

To say such things about proclamation will surprise no one familiar with the way the church has traditionally talked about its mission; of course preaching the gospel is "necessary," "essential," never to be interchanged with anything else. But to say the very same thing about dialogue? This is a breathtakingly new statement. The document seems to press the novelty of what it is saying to make sure people get the message: Proclamation, Christians should remember, is "only one aspect of evangelization" (DP 8); it needs to be balanced with other aspects and can never be interchanged with other aspects. Thus, preaching the good news to Hindus, Buddhists, or Native Americans is only a part of the job; the missionary must also listen in dialogue. Like proclamation, "interreligious dialogue possesses its own validity" within the mission of the church (DP 41).

The genuinely new import of what DP is saying is made all the more surprising when the document goes on to clarify its two principal terms. The description of *proclamation* is nothing new: "the communication of the gospel message . . . an invitation to a commitment of faith in Jesus Christ and to entry through baptism into the community of believers which is the Church" (DP 10). What is surprising, even astounding, is the document's understanding of *dialogue*. Dialogue with other believers is in no way understood as a mere "softening up" tactic to make the proclamation of Christian truth all the more acceptable; it is not merely a patient, courteous letting the other side have its say so that we can deliver our message. Rather, the Vatican document affirms dialogue as a genuine two-way process in which both sides are called upon to speak and to listen with the same degree of intensity and sincerity. The following is a snapshot of some of the bold brush-strokes with which both RM and DP paint the kind of dialogue that they understand to be essential to the church's mission:

- Dialogue calls both sides to the possibility of *mutual enrichment*:
  — "Dialogue means all positive and constructive interreligious relations with individuals and communities of other faiths which are directed at mutual understanding and enrichment, in obedience to truth and respect for freedom" (DP 9).
  — Dialogue is "a method and means of mutual knowledge and enrichment" (RM 55).

- To make this mutual enrichment possible, dialogue will require from all participants both an honest, forthright *witnessing* of one's own convictions and an honest, sincere *exploration* of the other's convictions.
  — Dialogue requires "a mutual witness to one's beliefs and a common exploration of one's respective religious convictions" (DP 40, 9).
  — "Dialogue can enrich both sides. There must be no abandonment of principles or false irenicism, but instead a witness given and received for mutual advancement on the road to religious inquiry and experience, and at the same time for the elimination of prejudice, intolerance, and misunderstanding" (RM 56).

- In this exploration of the truth proposed by the others, Christians have to recognize that they may have something to *learn* and that they may have to be *corrected*.

— "Christians too must allow themselves to be questioned . . . The way Christians sometimes understand their religion and practice may be in need of purification" (DP 32).

— Christians "do not have the guarantee that they have grasped the truth fully . . . While keeping their identity intact, Christians must be prepared to learn and to receive from and through others the positive values of their traditions. Through dialogue, they may be moved to give up ingrained prejudices, to revise preconceived ideas, and even sometimes to allow the understanding of their faith to be purified" (DP 49).

— Even the pope admits that "other religions constitute a positive challenge to the church" (RM 56).

• In the dialogue DP recognizes, indirectly, that Christians may not always "keep their identity intact" as comfortably as has been thought in the past. To dialogue authentically, one must be ready to *change*, even to *transform* one's previous religious identity.

— Among the "dispositions required" for real dialogue are "the will to engage together in commitment to the truth and the readiness to allow oneself to be transformed by the encounter" (DP 47).

— If, as was indicated above, the goal of "proclamation" is conversion to the church, the goal of dialogue is "a deeper conversion of all toward God." And then DP spells out what one would have thought it would have left only implied: "In this process of conversion, the decision may be made to leave one's previous spiritual or religious situation in order to direct oneself toward another" (DP 41). The document here is addressing all participants in the dialogue, not just the non-Christians.

In what both these Vatican documents have to say about the essential place that dialogue plays in the mission of the church *and* in the way they describe such dialogue, they constitute, I think, a paradigm shift—or at least a readjustment—in how the Catholic Magisterium understands mission.

AN UNCLEAR MILESTONE—A WOBBLY PARADIGM SHIFT

Unfortunately, ambiguities in the Vatican documents about the relationship between the Kingdom and church reappear and overshadow the statements we have just reviewed about the relationship between dialogue and proclamation. It's as if the ecclesiastical teachers make bold advances in their efforts to understand the church's mission according to the signs of the times, and then, having made the move, call for a retreat. Both movements—advance and retreat—are present in these documents.[2]

While the pope advances with his call to include dialogue in the church's mission and to foster cooperation rather than conflict between proclamation and dialogue (RM 55), he then steps back to remind us that proclamation must always hold a "permanent priority" over dialogue (RM 44) and that it, and it alone, gives substance to "missionary activity proper" (RM 34). What is "prior" is evidently more important; what is "proper" must be present to avoid impropriety. DP, after its rousing calls to place dialogue alongside proclamation in the line-up of authentic missionary obligations, follows the pope's retreat, but adds even more ambiguity when it declares that dialogue and proclamation may both be necessary but they are "not on the same level" (DP 77). Dialogue "remains oriented toward proclamation," which means that dialogue is at the service of proclamation, and not the other way around. Why this is so is stated: proclamation (not dialogue) "remains central" (DP 75); it makes up the "climax and fullness" of the church's mission (DP 82). What started out as a relationship of mutuality ends up as one of subordination.

What Jacques Dupuis calls "ambiguity" and a "certain tension" between these different statements on dialogue and proclamation appears to some as inconsistency, if not contradiction. Theologian A. Pushparajan, heading the Indian Bishops' Committee on Dialogue and experiencing the reservations and resistance that these documents have raised in India, is more precise, though circumspect, in identifying this tension or inconsistency:

> The overall impression one gets from the document [DP] is that it makes proclamation more important and makes dialogue subordinate to proclamation, though it also states that both dialogue and proclamation are absolutely necessary. Here arises a question: Can we make dialogue subsidiary to proclamation and yet carry it out really as absolutely necessary?
>
> If one is really subsidiary to the other, can they *both be absolutely* necessary? Or to put it in another way: if both are really taken to be absolutely necessary, can one of them be considered to be subsidiary to the other? Thus there is some lack of clarity regarding the proper relationship between the two "absolutely necessary activities" (Pushparajan 1992, 231-32).

Such ambiguity explains the fears or mistrust that these Vatican statements have encountered in India (see Puthiadam 1992, 302). To many, especially those in countries that have experienced the degradation and cultural violence of some forms of missionary proselytizing of the past, all this language about dialogue would seem to be a Trojan horse to smuggle in an army of proselytizers. If dialogue is "oriented toward" proclamation as its "climax and fullness," it looks as if dialogue is but a means to the end of proclamation. In the final analysis, it seems that Christians still feel they have a lot more to teach than they have to learn, and that they are much more intent on converting than on being converted. Such suspicions are not assuaged when the pope adds his reminder on how Christians are to dialogue: "Dialogue should be conducted and implemented with the conviction that the church is the ordinary means of salvation and that she alone possesses the fullness of the means of salvation" (RM 55; see also DP 19, 22, 58). When one already has the fullness of truth, there can't be too much still to learn.

MISSION IS DIALOGUE

I would like to propose what I think is a solution for the ambiguity and tension in these Vatican statements about dialogue and proclamation—the same tension I frequently find in the efforts of Christian missionaries to reconcile their commitments to dialogue and respect for other religions with their commitment to the gospel and their obligation to proclaim. This solution is, I trust, consistent with, and in a sense, carries out the logical content of these recent milestone efforts of the Vatican to achieve a better balance between church and Kingdom and between dialogue and proclamation; I hope this solution will also get at what the pope is rightly concerned about in that last citation from RM when he reminds missionaries to carry on dialogue without abandoning the "fullness of salvation" that the church bears.

What I'm trying to propose may sound like playing with words or an excessive concern with definitions. To an extent, that's true. I want to get our language straight—in the conviction that if we can clarify for ourselves and others just what we are doing as church, if we can translate that clarity into words, and then if we take these words seriously and faithfully, we can move beyond the confusion in these recent papal statements without denigrating the concerns that are the seed of the confusion.

After that lengthy introduction, I suggest that what these Vatican documents, and much recent missiology and ecclesiology, are trying to achieve when they include dialogue as part of the church's mission and then go on to balance dialogue with proclamation could be more coherently and engagingly achieved by simply announcing that mission *is* dialogue. Rather than trying to include dialogue in mission, it would make more sense to include mission in dialogue—or to see mission *as* dialogue. Mission can best be understood and practiced today as dialogue. Or, the best way for the church to serve the Kingdom of

God in today's religiously plural and globally threatened world is *through* dialogue.

If we go by the common-sense picture of dialogue, as well as the understanding of dialogue that is generally affirmed or presumed by participants in interreligious encounters, then it appears that what is supposed to take place in the full process of dialogue essentially dovetails with what the church understands to be its "evangelizing mission." Simply put, we can't have a real conversation unless both sides are both *listening* and *speaking*. Dialogue, as the Vatican documents recognize, is not just listening authentically; it also requires speaking honestly. In interreligious dialogue we confront the other as someone we want not only to embrace but also to address.

Ideally, we come to the conversation from a position of richness, not impoverishment; that is, we speak to each other out of our own religious experience. We speak because we have discovered something of value, the pearl of great price. As Raimon Panikkar has continuously insisted, in order to have religious encounter, we must speak from religious experience, or at least from religious quest. Such subjective contents and perspectives are not to be cut out and packed in some kind of deep-freeze "epoché" but rather are to be poured, warm and bubbling, into the conversation (Panikkar 1978, 39-52). The object of dialogue is approached through a meeting of subjects.

In dialogue, I not only want to understand you and possibly be changed through that understanding, but I also want you to understand me and be changed by the truth that I feel has enriched my life. To experience truth is to want to share it. And sharing means wanting others not only to understand it but to affirm it. But if I want you to affirm my truth, that means I want to "convert" you to it. In dialogue, both sides seek to witness and proclaim, and also to persuade or convert each other to the truth as they see it, always, as DP adds, "with respect for freedom."

Therefore, "to proclaim" and "to dialogue" are not two aspects of a broader, distinct activity; rather, dialogue is the broader activity that includes and is made up of proclaiming and listening. Both undertakings—witnessing and listening—have to be carried out in a "dialogical manner." As Ignatius Puthiadam has learned from his long-standing and successful experience of dialogue in Varanasi, the holy city of Hinduism:

> If proclamation is not dialogical it degenerates into a meaningless monologue where no response is expected. Dialogue is not the denial of proclamation but its affirmation in a genuine Christian sense . . .
>
> Dialogue is by its nature an "announcing," a "proclamation," a "witnessing," a "giving the reason for our hope." From our

Christian angle, every Christian dialogue partner is invited and invites the other to be converted . . . Dialogue is a "mutual proclamation"—it is a "mutual witnessing." It is a mutual call to conversion (Puthiadam 1992, 306, 307).

The two Vatican documents we have been considering clearly affirm that for dialogue to work, it must be this two-way flow of traffic—listening *and* witnessing. Dialogue is "a witness given and received for mutual advancement" (RM 56); it must include "both witness and the exploration of respective religious convictions" (DP 9). In real dialogue, one is just as eager to proclaim as to listen. Both endeavors are absolutely necessary. So it is not required to stretch logic in trying to connect or balance dialogue and proclamation, for both of them, to the same degree, are *integral parts of dialogue*. To speak about a permanent priority of one over the other or to maintain that one makes up the "climax" of the other, is like trying to walk on crutches that are not the same size.[3]

To define the church's mission as dialogue is not to reduce that mission to any one particular activity, but rather, to broaden this mission beyond traditional attitudes and practices and to better balance the various aspects of mission. To view and practice mission as dialogue is to see the church's mission essentially as one of *communication*. In fact, if one accepts this definition of mission-as-dialogue, then a more appropriate defining adjective for what the church is about is not the one used in these documents—*evangelizing* mission—but rather, and more clearly, the church's *communicating* mission. This calls for a communication in which Christians will speak as vigorously and persuasively as ever, but they will also know that in authentic communication one cannot speak clearly and hope to be heard unless one is just as vigorously and openly listening. "Now this is mission! Openness to the other, saying welcome to the other, unlocking my closed world to let the other in, this is *missio* . . . Mission . . . is a call to communicate with people who share different world views and value systems" (Hearne 1993, 97).

Earlier in this chapter, we noted that a common opinion among missiologists is to present the mission of the church as a part—a vitally important part—of the *missio Dei*, the very mission of God. This is a further reason and clarification for describing the mission of the church as dialogue. The mission of God, as Karl Rahner experienced and described it, is essentially one of *self-communication;* this is what revelation and salvation consist of—God's communicating God's self and life. But this divine communication, according to Christian belief, is never a monologue; it never takes place as a one-sided activity that would minimize or absorb the identity and responsiveness of the recipient of this communication. Which means: God's mission of self-communication is *dialogical*. Both within the very divine life (*ad intra*) (as much as that has been revealed to Christians through Jesus), as well as in God's activity in and throughout creation (*ad extra*), there is communication, and it is never-one sided. The "other" is always important, yes, essential.

Within God's very being there is communication, communication that is not one-sided but *relational*. Therefore, God is "more than one"; in order for communication to be relational, there must be difference within the Godhead. Christians speak of this as the Trinity— threeness or manyness in God, within which there is communication *between* the "persons" or "relationships" that constitute God's life. The Divine Persons, in traditional theological language, are said therefore to speak with each other, to interact. To dialogue! To say that God is trinitarian is to say that God is dialogical.

And this same dialogical nature of God is carried out in God's *missio ad extra*—the divine going forth in self-communication to finite creatures. It is a communication that is never imposed on the recipients. Rather, creatures are affirmed, respected. They, too, must speak. And God's communication, in a real sense, is dependent on that speaking and response (otherwise free will would not be real). Creatures may not have the power to break off the conversation for good, but they certainly are part of determining its content, direction, and outcome. Therefore, in the self-communicating mission of God, the Divine not only speaks, but listens, waits, values, challenges, and—some Jewish and process theologians would add—learns from the response of creation. The *missio Dei* therefore is the *dialogus Dei*.

If the church's mission is a part of this divine mission, then it is a vast understatement, perhaps even a misunderstanding, to recognize merely that the church's mission must *include* dialogue. It *is* dialogue. Without dialogue, the nature and purpose of mission is lost.

So far, we have stressed that because the church's mission *is* one of dialogue, this mission will have to include proclamation. While the reason for that statement might sound novel to many Christians (mission is dialogue), the conclusion certainly does not (mission requires proclamation). But there's another conclusion that will not be so familiar and comfortable: to envision the church's mission as dialogue also means that such a mission will have to include *listening* and possibly *learning*. This is not something that one finds on the first page of recruitment literature of missionary orders—that missionaries go forth both to teach *and be taught*, that both activities are essential and integral parts of the missionary's job. As much as missioners try to be good preachers of the Word incarnate in Jesus, they will also have to make equal efforts to be good listeners of the Word that God may have cast like seeds among the nations (the *logoi spermatikoi*, Justin and Clement of Alexandria would say). In fact, by being good listeners, they will be better proclaimers. Needless to say, such a broader understanding of the missionary task will call for bold changes in the way missionaries are trained. Courses on crosscultural anthropology and how to listen to and understand a totally different culture will be as essential as courses on homiletics and Bible.

But to prepare for and carry out such a model of mission, in which one genuinely witnesses as much as one is witnessed to, will also require revisions in christology. On the basis of the constitutive or inclusivist christology that pervades the Vatican documents, one cannot honestly and consequentially describe the church's mission as dialogue. As we pointed out in our "Inter-mission," the pope and the authors of DP cannot live up to all the wonderful things they say about being fully open to the truth of others and ready to be transformed by it (DP 47) as long as they insist, to themselves if not to others, that they have God's "full, final, and unsurpassable" Word.

DP indirectly recognizes this contradiction. After announcing that "Christians, too, must allow themselves to be questioned [in the dialogue with others]," it adds immediately, "Notwithstanding the fullness of God's revelation in Jesus Christ, the way Christians sometimes understand their religion and practice it may be in need of purification" (DP 32). Given its understanding of the role of Christ, this, according to the Vatican viewpoint, is as far as Christians can go—to have their grasp of the fullness of truth "purified." Or as DP puts it elsewhere, even though Christians have received "the fullness of truth," they "have no guarantee that they have grasped the truth fully" (DP 49). At the most, dialogue can enable Christians to realize more fully what they already have but didn't know it; or it can "purify" what they already possess but perhaps misuse. But to be ready to learn something genuinely new; to be given truth that they didn't already have, that, given their christology, is impossible. I agree, therefore, with Anthony Gittens's conclusion that in light of DP's insistence on the finality and superiority of Jesus, it cannot really listen to and learn from the "real insight, real wisdom, and real elements of the revelation of God whom we say is present in all cultures" (Gittens 1994, 220).

To envision the church's mission along the lines we have just been exploring—*as dialogue*, as a two-way communication with the world in which Christians are as energetic in proclaiming as they are open to learning—such a picture of missionary activity will clarify and broaden, as well as make more meaningful and attractive, the missionary vocation. In embracing such a missionary vision, the pope need not fear that missionary zeal will "wane" or that such an understanding will foster a "lack of interest in missionary work" or lead to "widespread indifferentism" (RM 2, 35). To present missionary work as dialogue, to send forth missioners to the ends of the Earth not just to witness but to be witnessed to, not just to proclaim the good news in Christ Jesus but to embrace the good news that the Spirit has made known to others will be, I strongly suspect, to make the missionary vocation that is given to *every* Christian much more attractive for all Christians, including those young people who want to respond to the love of Christ and the needs of the world.

THE RESULT OF MISSION-AS-DIALOGUE: A WORLD CHURCH

Christians can tune in to the value, indeed the urgency, of viewing and practicing mission *as* dialogue from another perspective—a perspective provided by one of the most discomfiting and perplexing problems facing Christian communities throughout the world, especially in non-Western cultures. More or less since the end of World War II, as the European-American colonial empires began to be questioned and dismantled, Christians and non-Christians, especially in those colonial regions, came to see how *monocultural* Christianity really was. Although the Christian missionary enterprise cannot be simplistically reduced to the religious wing of imperialistic evil empires, and even though Christian missioners also contributed mightily if indirectly to the self-identity and resilience of cultural groups (see Sanneh, 1989), still it must also be confessed that for the most part missionaries did not produce Christian communities that were truly indigenous to, or inculturated in, the cultural ethos of the peoples to whom they were sent. If the "church was implanted," it was still a foreign import; it did not grow up out of the local soil.

In the imagery that spoke to Karl Rahner, as he looked back at the significance of the Second Vatican Council, the Christian church in general—and the Roman Catholic Church in particular—had not yet become the *world church* that it was intended to be. For Roman Catholics, Vatican II acknowledged the problem and provided some promise for its solution. From Rahner's historical bird's-eye view, Christianity had so far moved through two historical-cultural epochs and was poised promisingly but anxiously on a third: the Jesus-movement—the seedling that was to become the Christian tree—began as a thoroughly Jewish sect; basically, to be a disciple, one had to be Jewish and embrace the dietary, ritual practices of faithful Jews. That was phase one. As these communities of Jesus followers were forced or attracted to move beyond their Jewish borders, they entered the world of Roman-Greco culture and empire. Paul was the "Apostle to the Gentiles" and one of the crucial early agents in the transformation of the Jewish Jesus-movement into the community of *Cristianoi*. The New Testament is the documentary witness to the formation of phase two of Christian history, when Christians formed a religion clearly distinct from Judaism and took on a new cultural identity. From being a Jewish Christianity it became a Latin or European Christianity (Rahner 1979).

And that is what it has essentially remained for all these centuries: a monocultural religion, a monocultural expression of the vision of the gospel. Few people realize that when they say "Christianity," they are not talking about a "world religion" that is genuinely present in various world cultures; rather, they are speaking about a religious community that has lived most of its existence in one cultural garb—that of Europe. Christianity as a world religion or, in Rahner's terms, a "world church," has yet to be born. For Roman Catholics, the Catholic church is not yet the "catholic church." Though in its claims and in the dynamic of its origins Christianity is meant to be universal and to go to all nations, it has not yet found a truly indigenous home among those nations. Despite all the talk before Vatican Council II about the necessity of "adaptation" and "accommodation" to local cultures, that's all that usually took place—important but still superficial adaptations and adjustments. For the most part, in India, in Africa, in Japan, Christianity may speak the local language, but it still wears a European or Western face. Genuine *inculturation* is still to take place. That was Rahner's point and lament.

But it was also his hope that things could be different, that they had begun to show the first glimmers of change, especially in Vatican II. And thanks to the complaints and struggles of Christians in what were for the most part the colonized nations of the world, Christianity is waking up to the recognition that it has much to do and much to let go of if it is to shed its Eurocentric way of thinking and acting and truly become a world church. An essential piece of that new way of thinking and acting will be, I suggest, a more dialogical understanding of the church and its mission.

FROM SUPERCULTURAL TO SUPRACULTURAL TO CROSSCULTURAL MISSION

Much has recently been discussed and written on why the Christian church must, and how it can, incarnate itself—not just inject or implant itself—in cultural identities outside of the West. Calls for "contextual theology" or "local theologies" or "inculturation" are practical moves toward a world church (see Schreiter 1985; Bevans 1992; Schneller 1990; Hillman 1993). In an essay titled "Can Theology Be Transcultural?" Raimon Panikkar offers a series of lenses that provide a simple yet enlightening insight into why the "world church" has had such a slow and difficult birth and why "mission-as-dialogue" must serve as its midwife. Within Christian history and still in present-day church practice, Panikkar finds three very different sets of instructions for how the church is supposed to relate to culture: the *supercultural*, the *supracultural*, and the *crosscultural* approaches (Panikkar 1990a). Because the first two approaches have held sway, the "world church" has been caught in what has been called the "Latin Captivity" in the West (Robinson 1979, x).

THE SUPERCULTURAL APPROACH

In the *supercultural* perspective, the Christian church, consciously or unconsciously, holds to a tight bond between Christianity and culture. With contemporary postmodern consciousness, this approach recognizes that one cannot just be Christian, one has to be Christian in a specific way, in a concrete cultural form. Even more, according to this view, Christianity requires a certain cultural level; it cannot take shape in just any culture. Rather, before the gospel can assume cultural flesh, it must *civilize* that flesh! So cultures are distinguished between those that are civilized and those that are primitive. The primitives must first be elevated and educated before, or at least as part of, being evangelized. Thus, Augustine could write a book on "De catechizandis rudibus"—"Catechism for the Uncultivated." And for centuries, European and American Catholic missionaries did not dream of allowing African, Asian, or South American natives to become priests. They would first have to be brought to a minimal cultural level; they would have to "evolve." In fact, this model for inculturating Christianity resonated with a kind of popular Darwinism. "The human race is evolving and Christianity belongs to the superior strata of that evolution" (Panikkar 1990a, 9).

To find that superior strata, or the criteria for civilized culture, one had to go to—or better, study in—Rome or London or Paris, and eventually New York or Chicago, certainly not in Kyoto or Benares or Kinshasa. There were, however, some progressives through the centuries, like Mateo Ricci and Robert de Nobili, who recognized the too-narrow definitions of the required cultural level that the church was using; they urged, often in vain, that great thinkers like Confucius or Shankara be granted a hearing equal to that given to Plato and Aristotle. But hardly anyone ever dreamed of listening to a Siberian shaman or a Native American or African medicine man. In such a supercultural mind-set, Christians were often blinded both to the value and beauty within the so-called primitive, as well as to the danger and evil within the civilized. Such blindness endures to the present. "Today the same church considers African polygamy incompatible with Christian ethics—but it has no major problems with atomic weaponry" (Panikkar 1990a, 10-11).

It is evident how such a supercultural model for bringing the gospel to culture has kept the Christian church in its civilized Latin Captivity. Yet within this prison, Christianity has had the power to bring about the *destruction* of "primitive" or "unevolved" cultures as part of announcing the good news. Educating the natives usually meant stripping them of their culture.

THE SUPRACULTURAL APPROACH

The *supracultural* perspective recognizes the beast of cultural imperialism that is hiding within the noble intents of the supercultural model. It also is more attuned to the actual richness and achievements of non-Western history and ethos. And so it affirms a Christianity and a gospel that could and must be multicultural. The good news can be heard and take shape in a variety of cultures; there is no one "super-culture" that alone is able to receive and give historical form to the gospel. But in affirming, as it were, the possibility of "multiple cultural incarnations" of Christianity, this viewpoint works with a notion of the Christian message as being somehow *above* all cultures; the gospel is understood as a free-floating vision or a Platonic world of ideas which can descend and take shape in any cultural material precisely because it is "above it all." The gospel, in its purest form, is the heavenly Logos which, having descended and incarnated itself in Jesus the Jew, must now continue that process through the missionary work of the church.

This supracultural approach is exemplified clearly in the thought of Karl Barth—and, Panikkar holds, in Pope Pius XII. Christianity—or for Pius XII, the Roman Catholic Church—is not a religion like other religions or a church like other churches. Rather, its true nature, its inner essence, is *revelation* or *the mystical Christ*. Other religions are just that—religions. Christianity is first and foremost revelation, the truth of the Living Christ. In other religions, what dominates is the effort of humans to reach the Divine; in Christianity, the dominant reality is the divine reaching out to humans. And because the heart of Christianity is revelation rather than religion or culture, it can stand in judgment over all religions and cultures—and in judging, it can save and assume a variety of religious and cultural forms. "Per se, nothing stands in the way of its taking flesh in the most remote and, for the Western taste, most exotic cultures." (Panikkar 1990a, 6). As Vatican Council II put it, "The Church rejects nothing that is true and holy in these religions" (*Nostra Aetate*, 2).

So this supracultural model for outreach clearly affirms that there is much that is "valuable and good" in other cultures and religions; here Christians find the embryonic material, as it were, that can be infused with the life-giving spirit of the gospel and so give rise to new cultural embodiments of Christianity. Such a vision is grandiose and sincere in its hopes of conceiving and nurturing new forms of Christianity. But this approach, as it was applied in the '50s and '60s and still today, does not seem capable of moving beyond surface-level adaptation or accommodation to other cultures. From local churches in non-Western nations we still hear recurring complaints and pain that they have not been able to be their own cultural and very different selves. The problem lies in just how the valuable and the good in non-Christian cultures and religions is identified, and how it is adapted.

This is where a genuine inculturation process breaks down in the supracultural model. The deeper problem is embedded in the model itself—mainly in the presumption that Christianity or any religion or value system can have a culture-less essence, an internal identity that hovers *above* culture. As much as we can tell, there is no such thing as a revelation or a truth that can have a meaningful, human reality outside of a religion. The gospel is not like "the soul" in older theories of human conception in which it was thought that the parents provided the fetus into which God then infused the soul. The gospel is not something that can neatly be "infused" into this or that cultural body. Rather, like the human spirit or soul, it can exist and be itself only within, or in relationship with, a particular culture. The supracultural view of religion and culture evinces striking similarities to the dualism of matter and spirit that has long infused Western thinking.

Because of this dualism, when missionaries decide what is "valuable and good" in other cultures and religions, they generally are not using a disembodied gospel available above culture; rather, their criterion is the gospel *as it has been embodied* in Western, European forms. The standard they hold up to determine the valuable and the good may not have as much to do with the "heart of the gospel" or the "immutable content of faith" as it does with deeply rooted, never-questioned convictions or presumptions of European—or even earlier Jewish—cultural givens. When we said earlier that the word "Christianity" really means not a universal reality but the Western inculturation of Jesus' message, few of us can appreciate the far-reaching content of that statement. It means that right now, for the most part, in order to be a Christian, one must be a Westerner, just as in the early years of the church, in order to be a Jesus-follower one had to accept Judaism. By "being a Westerner" I mean that one must assume or accept elements of the Western mind-set that have become so integral to the interpretation of the gospel as to be identified with it. Panikkar offers some examples:

> I would argue that, until now, without a certain Semitic and Hellenic mind-set we are not even able to understand what Christianity is all about. The meaning of revelation, the notion of history, the idea of a personal God, and the like, are not even understandable without a particular *forma mentis* [mind-set]; such notions are not cultural invariants (Panikkar 1990a, 8).

In other words, there may be other, non-Western ways of understanding "God," or "history," or "revelation" that could provide new cultural embodiments of the gospel. But Christians have not had the eyes to see such other possibilities because they have not sufficiently recognized how intricately culture and religion are intertwined—how much they have read and lived the gospel through their own cultural glasses. And so, they have not allowed that gospel to be "born again" in other worlds and religions. If the *super*cultural approach leads to the destruction or rejection of other cultures in the name of Christianity, the *supra*cultural model leads—again without intending it—to the imposition upon or exploitation of other cultures.

THE CROSSCULTURAL APPROACH

Panikkar believes that something like a *crosscultural* understanding of gospel and culture is the most promising. In this approach, one affirms and works with the distinction *and* the bi-polar unity between body and spirit, between culture and religious experience. The gospel, therefore, is to be distinguished from culture, but it can never be found separated from it in a kind of disembodied state. Such a state doesn't exist. Therefore, the missionary approach to other non-Christian cultures will be one in which the Christian, consciously and cautiously, seeks to bring a culturally embodied and culturally limited understanding of the gospel into relationship with another culturally embodied and limited worldview or religion—in the hope that *out of the relationship* there will grow a new embodiment of Christianity. In this approach Christians do not operate with a notion of the gospel that is identified with one, superior culture or with a transcendental form that is to be found on a sphere above cultures; rather, Christians recognize, happily and humbly, that the gospel they announce is the one that was first incarnated in the Jewish world and then took on a new incarnation, for better and for worse, in the Greco-Roman-European-American world.

Just how this gospel is to be incarnated in other cultural worlds is a question which, in this crosscultural model, Christians admit they can't answer. Or better, they can't answer it before they begin the relationship with other cultures. They cannot determine what is "valuable and good" in other cultures by looking at them *from the outside*, or *from above*—from the mountaintop of a superior culture (the supercultural model) or of a Platonic world (the supracultural model). Such judgments can be made only from within, from a relationship between cultures—from dialogue.

The crosscultural understanding of the church's mission to the nations requires, necessarily and inherently, a dialogical model for mission. In this understanding, outreach or mission *is* dialogue. If the gospel, like all religious experience and vision, is always embodied in a culture, then there is no way to make contact between what is valuable and good in the gospel and what is valuable and good in another religion except through a crosscultural, intercultural conversation.

Panikkar draws the same direct and demanding conclusion: "Each culture has its proper *logos,* and every *logos* is housed in a culture. Each language is culturally bound. A possible *meta-logos* can only be a *dia-logos*, which creates a new language, a new culture, but it is not supracultural" (Panikkar 1990a, 11). The "new language" and the "new culture" would be, in our context, the new cultural embodiment of Christianity.

This crosscultural, dialogical understanding of mission is a lot messier and uncertain than the other two models. In the super- or supracultural outlooks, one has in advance the measuring stick by which to determine what in the new culture will or will not fit the gospel. In the crosscultural method, the measuring stick has to be constructed or discovered in and through dialogue with the other culture; only in this way can Christians come to the ad-hoc, and always to be remade, distinction between what belongs to the core of the gospel and what is an adjustment to Western ways—or between what must remain basically the same and what can take on a brand new form. More concretely, only in the actual, on-site conversation can European and African Christians determine whether the condemnation of polygamy is a demand of the gospel or a reflection of Western family structures (see Hillman 1975). Such a protracted, open-ended process can make Christians who have never known any other Christianity than the present one very uncomfortable and fearful.

This crosscultural, dialogical pattern for enabling Christianity both to respect and to take on new cultural forms is not only messy, but it can also be dangerous. We said that while the supercultural method almost always leads to the *domination* of other cultures, and the supracultural view facilitates an *exploitation* of other cultures, the crosscultural approach calls for *conversation.* Yet how can we be certain that in such conversations we are not unconsciously holding up Western interpretations of the gospel as superior, or imposing our cultural mores rather than Christian values on others? There are no absolute safeguards. All we can do is carry on this "mission to the nations" *as a dialogue* that is as authentic and honest as possible. This will require, as I stressed in our analysis of Vatican attitudes, that we do not subordinate dialogue to proclamation, that we go forth to other nations as desirous to listen and learn as we are eager to preach and proclaim. And in order to do this, we cannot converse with other religions and cultures with the conviction that we have final, unsurpassable answers. We need an authentically dialogical disposition if we are to avoid manipulating or degrading other cultures; then we need persistent human effort and even more persistent help from the Holy Spirit to hold to that disposition.

But can it work? Can such real crosscultural communication take place? Can there be a "spontaneous fecundation among cultures, a positive osmosis among beliefs, a crosscultural enrichment that does not need to be an invasion of foreign goods, ideas, or people for the sake of profits, material or spiritual"? (Panikkar 1990a, 15). Can Christianity take on new cultural identities in a way that will truly enrich, rather then impoverish, both Christianity and the new culture? To answer yes to those questions is a matter of both *trust* and *tactic*.

It is a matter of *trust* because to engage in such a dialogical encounter is to trust that what Christians have always professed is indeed true—that the grace and truth that have been revealed in Jesus Christ can enlighten all persons of all cultures. It is to trust, more generally, that truth is not just many but also one; and that God is not just one but many. Finally, from the perspective of our human experience, such crosscultural efforts are also based on the trust that our human family, though bewilderingly and happily diverse, is also one, that our human problems can have not just different but common solutions, and that the truth of each of us can somehow also be the truth for all of us (Panikkar 1990a, 11-12).

In articulating this kind of "cosmic trust," Panikkar also endorses the same dialogical *tactic* that many are proposing as a globally responsible starting point and foundation for mission-as-dialogue. If crosscultural communication requires some kind of common ground or shared experiences and needs in order to begin and guide the process of understanding, challenging, and learning from the stark differences between cultures and religions, Panikkar urges that there is a reality that is indeed common to all cultures. To make his point, he does a free-style interpretation of Mark 14:7: "The poor you will always have with you." "The poor are precisely those who have not 'made it' in any culture; they remain at the bottom line. They are undifferentiated, not culturally specialized. They are cross cultural, for they are found in all cultures" (Panikkar 1990a, 12). By hearing and responding to the cries of the poor (the poor of the Earth and the impoverished Earth itself), by making the poor the primary topic or the preferential option for mission-as-dialogue, by proclaiming how the gospel responds to the needs of the victims and listening to how other religious traditions are seeking similar responses—here we have the most reliable, the most urgent, and the most promising ground on which the Word can continue to become flesh and Christianity can be born again.

THEOLOGY AS DIALOGUE

In urging why and how the church should consider mission as dialogue, we have been primarily viewing mission as it extends outward, beyond the Christian community. But if we understand mission the way the Vatican documents *Redemptoris Missio* and *Dialogue and Proclamation* do—as embracing the many, diverse activities by which the church lives its life of practicing and proclaiming the good news about the Reign of God—then dialogue must inform and direct all these activities: the daily living of Christian life, social development and liberation, liturgy and spirituality, catechesis and theology (DP 2). According to the statement "Dialogue and Mission," issued by the Vatican Secretariat for Non-Christian Religions in 1984, all these expressions of the church's mission must be "permeated by . . . a dialogical spirit." Dialogue should be "an attitude and a spirit" and "the norm and necessary manner of every form of Christian mission, as well as every aspect of it, whether one speaks simply of presence and witness, service, or direct proclamation" (D&M 29).

One could profitably reflect on how much of the church's internal or pastoral mission would have to change if these Vatican directives were put into practice. All the pastoral activities of teaching, healing, celebrating would have to be carried out as a *conversation* with the recipients of these ministries. In teaching, or nurturing, or celebrating, church ministers could not allow themselves to be considered simply leaders or presiders or directors. Rather, they would have to act, first and foremost, as servants and friends engaged in a conversation by which they try to listen to the experience and respond to the needs and ideas of all. To minister is to dialogue.

I would like to single out one particular church ministry, or one expression of the church's mission, and explore what it means to carry it out in a truly dialogical manner. If we understand theology as dialogue, if theology is "permeated by . . . a dialogical spirit" (D&M 29), then the way one does theology will be different and more demanding than is presently the case in most high school and university theology departments and in most seminaries.

Although the current diversity of views on the nature or method of theology may look to some like the variety of cereals in an American supermarket, most of them do recognize, with Bernard Lonergan, that the theologian's job is to "mediate" between religion and culture (Lonergan 1973, xi). The theologian is the middle person between what's going on in the world and what's going on and has gone on in the Christian community. The theologian's task is to help Christians "reflect" on how to connect their "Christian identity" with their "existence and action in the world" (Farley 1988, 133). In carrying out this mediator's role, the theologian or religion teacher has to keep in touch with two poles, or two sources of data. Many, with David Tracy and Schubert Ogden, would describe these poles as, on the one hand, "human experience" broadly considered and, on the other, "Christian tradition" or "the Christian fact." Theologians carry out their job by trying to bring both these sources into a creative, fruitful conversation. Theology, we might say, is a mutually clarifying and mutually criticizing conversation between cultural experience and religious tradition. We try to make sense of our world in the light of Christian experience and tradition, and we try to make sense of Christian beliefs and practices in light of what the world is saying or suffering. As we said earlier, Barth put it more simply: A good theologian, like a good Christian, must read the Bible and the daily newspaper.

In this description, theology, by its very nature, is dialogical; it consists of a dialogue between our experience of involvement in the world and our experience of involvement in the Christian community. But in urging us to consider theology as dialogue, I'm pushing this point even further. I'm suggesting that dialogue is necessary not just to connect the two poles of experience and tradition but to properly understand the poles in themselves.

CHRISTIAN THEOLOGY CANNOT BE JUST CHRISTIAN

Regarding our understanding of human experience, liberation theologians have pointed out how narrow and non-dialogical the traditional approach to experience has been. They remind representatives of the so-called dominant theology (European-North American, white, male, middle-class) that in trying to work out a correlation between tradition and common human experience, the experience that has counted most, or been used most, is not at all that common. It has indeed excluded, or at least neglected, the majority of humankind who, caught in a variety of oppressive structures, have not had a voice in the assemblies of government, church, or academy.

So the voices and experience of the "wretched" of the Earth (who populate not only the so-called Third World), who because of class, gender, or race have been excluded, must also be given "authority" in the hermeneutical task of theology. In other words, to be able to "hear" what experience broadly conceived is saying and asking of Christian tradition, there must be a dialogue between the various sectors of experience, especially as that experience is divided according to classes—according to those who have and those who have not. Only in a dialogue in which the "have nots" finally *have* a voice in the common effort to understand the Bible and Christian tradition will the Christian churches be able to carry out, as adequately as possible, the task of theology. If human experience is an essential source of theology, then, we can get at that source only through inter-class dialogue.

Leaving it to liberation and third-world theologians to stress the necessity of dialogue for understanding human experience, I turn to the other pole or source of theology: the Christian fact or tradition. What was just said of experience can also be affirmed of Christian tradition: it can be properly understood only if it is understood dialogically. Or, we cannot adequately grasp the religious content of Christian tradition if we try to grasp it only by itself. Certainly, the Christian fact—the Bible, the teaching and practices of the Christian communities through the ages—is the primary and focal content of Christian theology, but it cannot be the *only* content. If it is, something essential is missing. Stated more dramatically, for Christian theology to competently do its job, it cannot be only Christian.

In making this claim, I think I am sharing a suspicion or a conviction lurking in the awareness of many colleagues in the Christian theological community that one of the reasons why Christian theological education is not adequately doing its job of mediating between culture and religion has to do with the *mono-religious* character of most Christian theology today. Theological educators are going about their job on the basis of an exclusive, or too restrictive, use of Christian tradition. They are religiously isolated. They have closed themselves to, or are not sufficiently open to, other religious traditions and identities.

So in recognizing that theology, like the church's entire mission, must be carried out "with a dialogical spirit" (D&M 29), one becomes aware that Christian theology can no longer be done mono-religiously, that theologians must not just recognize but embrace the reality of many religious facts besides the Christian fact. The reasons for such a dialogical understanding of theology are scattered throughout this book, especially in chapter 2 where we discussed the cultural supports for a correlational, globally responsible dialogue. Here I gather some of these reasons together in summary fashion in order to show that Christian tradition, by itself, is both *incomplete* and *inaccessible* for the work of theology.

Recent insights in what we might call the theory of conversational hermeneutics make a convincing case why Christian tradition, like any religious tradition, is incomplete if it refuses to converse with other traditions. If historical consciousness and postmodern awareness have persuaded many that every perception of truth is constructed and therefore limited, a growing dialogical consciousness would immediately add that all these diversified and limited perspectives can—not always, but usually—talk to each other. In fact, this is precisely the way in which each individual and constructed truth claim can, as it were, overcome its finitude—by linking up with, by speaking and listening to other finite perspectives. If for some people it is bad news to acknowledge the limitation of every perception of truth, they can be consoled by the good news that limited perceptions are related—better, relatable—to other such perceptions.

This is what is meant by a theory of conversational hermeneutics or a conversational model for truth: By conversing with each other we can step beyond our limitations; in fact, this is the only human way to do so. That such conversation between utterly different and limited visions of truth is possible cannot be proven. It is always a matter of trust, of hope. But such hope, it would seem, is imperative. As Gregory Baum puts it: "To negate the existence of human nature [as a basis for crosscultural conversation], to deny that people in different religions and different cultures hold some values in common, to reject dialogue across the boundaries on principle and to regard as illusory all utopias of emancipation—leaves no hope for humanity" (Baum 1994, 10). So if Christian theologians are going to share in this hope for humanity, if they are going to recognize and step beyond the limits of their own tradition, they will also have to converse with other traditions.

This cultural awareness that all religious traditions, including Christianity, are limited and therefore cannot claim to be "the whole truth" confirms and is confirmed by recent clarifications in Christian belief and theology. I think that most mainline Christians, and even many Evangelicals, would recognize that divine revelation extends beyond the borderlines of Christianity, that God's "eternal power and deity have been clearly perceived in the things that have been made" (Rom 1:20). For Christians, the God they trust is a power of universal and self-communicating love; therefore, there is a *universal revelatory presence* of God within all creation. If Christian belief includes an affirmation of a "universal revelation," if they claim that God has indeed "spoken in sundry forms" to all their brothers and sisters (Heb 1:1), then what has been made known to others must be respected by Christians, and it must have meaning for them too.

In other words, if Christians truly believe that God has spoken to others, they must also enter into a conversation with these "other Words." To hold up Christian tradition as the sole source or norm for theology is to disrespect what God has revealed elsewhere. The Christian Word is *incomplete* without other Words. Or in more contemporary terms, if it is the nature of any classic, including religious classics, to speak publicly and not just to members of its parent culture or religion, then this applies to *all* religious classics. If Christians would hold that the Bible can also, in some analogous form, be a classic for Hindus, they must also recognize that the Upanishads can be a classic for them. And that means that, in some way and degree, the Upanishads must also be part of the data that Christian theologians make use of.

There are other insights of contemporary hermeneutical theory which show why the Christian tradition, if taken only by itself, is *inaccessible*. These insights call upon theologians to expand their procedure for establishing what is called the appropriateness of a theological argument. For a theological interpretation to be appropriate, the theologian must be able to show that what he or she is proposing is grounded in a valid, faithful understanding of the past tradition, especially of the original witness in the New Testament (Ogden 1972).

But as Francis Schüssler Fiorenza points out, Christian theologians can no longer draw the criteria for establishing the appropriateness of Christian claims by making use only of the earliest Christian witness (Ogden) or traditional Christian classics (Tracy) (Fiorenza 1991, 131). This is so not simply for the general reason that we can understand ourselves and the meaning of our own kerygma only in conversation with others and their kerygmas; it is also because in order to comprehend and interpret the meaning of a text (i.e., what it *meant* and what it *means*), we must also understand the text within its historical *life-practice*.

By "life-practice" is meant the various social-economic-cultural circumstances that helped produce the text and the variety of social-economic-cultural effects that resulted from and continue to result from the text. "This emphasis on the life-praxis that produces texts and the life-praxis that flows from texts raises the issue of the relationship between diverse life-practices and the meaning and truth of religious classics" (Fiorenza 1991, 132-33). Such life-practices involve others, especially other believers, then and now. Thus, we cannot understand the meaning and truth of our religious classics unless we also analyze and evaluate the life-practices that they produce—including those practices that affect, positively and negatively, other religious communities and their classics. And we will be able truly to comprehend such practices only if we hear directly from those religious communities. This means that only in a conversation with other religious communities, not only about the meaning of their classics but also about how the life-practices produced by *our* classics have affected *them*—perhaps excluded or subordinated or marginalized them—only then can we move forward to an appropriate interpretation of the meaning of our classics and tradition.

Theology and Religious Studies: A Globally Responsible Marriage

If the case we have been making for theology *as* dialogue makes any sense, if theology, like the church's outward mission in general, will have to be carried out in conversation with other religious persons, then the long-standing, strictly guarded fence between theology and religious studies (or comparative religions), both within the university and the religious education classroom, will not be as menacing as it has been. In fact, the fence may well have to be dismantled, for if theology is going to be dialogical, then what was previously separated will now have to cohabitate. To ply their trade properly, theologians are going to have to know something about other religions. (And if scholars of religious studies or comparative religions want to be part of this dialogue, they will have to do more than simply describe objectively or classify nonjudgmentally the material they are studying.)[4]

Paul Tillich was one of the first to try to remove the fence between theology and religious studies and, in a sense, to call for their marriage. In the last lecture of his life he expressed his desire to rewrite his *Systematic Theology* "oriented toward, and in dialogue with, the whole history of religions" (Tillich 1966, 31, 91). Wilfred Cantwell Smith has gone even further and disturbed many a comfortable theology professor with his call for a union that transcends the conjugal: "The true historian [of religions] and the true theologian are one and the same . . . To speak truly about God means henceforth to interpret accurately the history of human religious life on earth . . . The new foundation for theology must become the history of religion" (Smith 1987b, 55; also 1984, 52-68). Leonard Swidler endorses Smith's call when, just as provocatively, he warns that the choice between a "monological" or a "dialogical" theology is the choice between a religion's life or death (Swidler, et al. 1990, vii-viii).

Perhaps these calls for a merging or marriage between theology and religious studies are somewhat hasty or overly enthusiastic. The relationship between the two is much more complex and the need for recognizing and living with differences more extensive than would appear at first sight (see Knitter 1992). But whatever the image we do eventually affirm, what is clear now is that theologians must work at changing their relationship with the study of other religious traditions. The twain, though so different, do have to meet—or, they have to struggle for a new kind of relationship. I have a suggestion for making that struggle more easy and the envisioned new relationship more promising.

This suggestion is taken from a theme that runs throughout the fabric of this book and its predecessor, *One Earth Many Religions* (Knitter 1995): the relationship between Christianity and other religions, as between all religions, today needs to be not only *dialogical* but also *globally responsible*. This then would be a means for initiating, nurturing, and guiding the new dialogical or marital relationship between theology and the study of other religions. Insofar as they are *human* beings, theologians and scholars of religions can share the same concern and commitment that Christians and other believers can as *religious* beings: as human and religious beings they want to respond to the horrendous amount of unjust human suffering in our world and do something about the endangered state of our planet.

Here is the uniting and stimulating context in which the marriage between theology and religious studies can be worked out day by day. Concrete issues and pressing problems of human suffering, social or gender injustice, environmental devastation can provide the meeting points at which the theologian can make contact between beliefs and practices in Christianity and those in other traditions. The context in which the relationship is worked out would be primarily, or initially, ethical. Coming together on ethical issues would eventually lead to conversations on the doctrinal and ritual levels. The hope is that where there has been a constructive dialogue (which doesn't necessarily require mutual agreement) on ethical issues, the same can be possible on more complex differences in belief and philosophy. Francis Fiorenza sees the same hope and promise:

> In facing shared political oppression, economic domination, race and gender exploitation as well as death, isolation, and loneliness, we encounter issues that retroductively make possible areas of communicative discourse and even agreement . . . What I am suggesting is precisely where humanity is threatened, there exist [sic] the challenge of diverse religious beliefs and practices to bring resources of their religious traditions to bear on these threats to humanity. In confronting these challenges, possibilities for religious self-transcendence and for conversation exist (Fiorenza 1991, 136).

Marriages generally are nurtured and strengthened by common concerns that arise from outside the marriage.

To Make It Work

If there is any validity to this call for a dialogical model for theological education, then it will require significant changes in theological programs of seminaries, universities, and religious education offices. Such practical restructuring can, of course, best be worked out *in situ*, according to varying individual contexts. What follow are a few concluding practical, though still general, suggestions.

Clearly, as has often been noted, the restructuring of theological or religious education requires much more than tinkering with the curriculum, yet my first suggestion has to do with curricular changes. If the conversation with other traditions has to enter into the theological process in some significant degree, then there will have to be more opportunities for taking up that conversation than are presently available in most seminary, college, or religious education programs. Simply put, Christian students need opportunities to learn about traditions which, for the most part, will be thoroughly foreign to them. This will call for courses, required courses, in Islam, Asian religions, indigenous spiritualities, and such courses will have to form an integral part of the educational program.

To teach these courses in a genuinely dialogical manner will require a special and demanding methodology. Teachers will have to meld both scholarship and personal involvement and so enable students not only to understand but also to appreciate and be challenged by other religious ways of being in the world. It would be ironic to teach other religions in a theology program with a method that is increasingly recognized as outmoded within religious studies programs. Even teachers of comparative religions in secular universities are admitting that to present the contents of religious traditions in a detached (*epoché*), objective, and nonjudgmental way is both impossible and, for most students, a waste of time. Religions make claims about reality, and we don't respect those claims unless we ask questions not only of their meaning but of their truth (Farley 1988, chap. 4). So must religions be taught in theological or religious educational curricula—in a conversational, rather than in a purely informational, mode and in an attempt to mediate between the religions and contemporary culture.

This, of course, is more easily said than done. If such courses must avoid a purely disinterested approach, they must also steer clear of the other extreme, more common in seminaries, of forming Christian judgments before one has been attentive to and intelligent about what the religions are really saying. Such an approach is usually predetermined to see the religions as either inferior to or as a preparation for Christ and Christianity. The multireligious model for theological education we are calling for must enable conversation, not monologue.

But such conversation requires more than the careful, sensitive, involved study of another religious tradition; it also calls for a personal entrance into the other's world of experience. Common sense and recent scholarly proposals tell us that we cannot really study and get to know other religions if all we do is "read about" them and pass objective tests on them. We must also try to "walk in their moccasins," "pass over" personally into their world of story and ritual, allow ourselves to be carried along by an "analogical imagination" as we try to feel as they feel (Dunne 1972; Tracy 1981; Knitter 1982). To carry out this personal-existential process, theology courses on other traditions will have to provide their students with opportunities genuinely to feel and to experiment with the truth of other ways. In a sense, students are to be encouraged, provisionally and always in a limited sense, *to be* Hindu or Buddhist or Muslim.

How this can be done will depend on the ingenuity and boldness of the teacher. Passing over to another religious world can be facilitated, for instance, through some form of actual conversation with followers of other faiths, whether this takes place in the classroom or coffee shop; Christian students can be greatly helped by the I-Thou experience of existentially hearing the personal witness and feeling the committed praxis of someone who is following a different way of being religious. Besides such personal encounters, passing over to another religious world can also be fostered through experimenting with the truth of—or at least observing—the spiritual practices of other religions. This can best take place in zendos or ashrams or temples where students can participate in forms of meditation, or chanting, or the puja sacrifice, or daily prayers. Religions must be studied as lived realities, not only as cherished teachings.

Another way of passing over to other religious ways of being in the world can be realized though the praxis-oriented, globally responsible methodology suggested earlier. After a basic introductory course in comparative religions, further courses, rather than dealing simply with more specific areas (e.g., the "history of Zen" or "Islamic mysticism"), could be issue-oriented. They could combine the ingredients of pluralism and oppression and use areas of needed liberation as the starting points or shared context for establishing the common ground of genuine conversation. Courses on "Religions and Peace" or "Buddhism, Christianity, and Ecology," or "Feminist Voices in Muslim-Christian Dialogue" would be more engaging of student interest and would provide a more effective hermeneutical link for both entering into and being challenged by other religious worlds.

Merely to add quality, theologically oriented courses on other religious traditions to the curriculum will not, in itself, achieve the intended goal of a multireligious restructuring of theological education. If the conversation with other religions cannot, understandably, be the exclusive or dominant concern in theological reflection, neither can it be shunted off to the side track of a few required courses. What is needed and hoped for is that a conversation with other traditions may, to some extent, be mainlined into all courses in a Christian curriculum, especially those courses traditionally identified as systematic or ethical. By this I mean that in teaching a standard course on evil or redemption or church or the question of God, teachers will inject into the discussions what other religious perspectives hold, how they sometimes radically differ, and how they provoke Christian tradition to further reflection. Naturally, given the expertise and general background of most theological faculties, such dreams of mainlining an interreligious conversation into the general curriculum cannot be realized overnight. But they will never be realized at all unless the ideal is affirmed.

Although we cannot realistically expect either students or professors to be proficient in all the major religious traditions of the world, we can entertain more modest yet nonetheless helpful ideals. What can be expected—eventually of professors, more immediately of students—is that every Christian theologian have, as it were, a minor in one religious tradition other than Christianity. After taking a broad, introductory course in comparative religions, students of Christian theology should be encouraged (required?) to sub-specialize in the history, beliefs, and spirituality of another non-Christian religious path. The goal would be for students to become so at home in another religious tradition that it would become a conversation partner for the students as they go about their study of Christian theology. Thus a student who has sub-specialized in Buddhism would not be able to interpret and evaluate Christian beliefs such as Trinity or incarnation, or Christian rituals such as baptism or eucharist, without hearing or feeling what a Buddhist might say to such a belief or practice, or what might be its Buddhist equivalent. Such a conversation partner can enhance, challenge, perhaps even invigorate the study of Christian theology.

In order to move toward this goal of providing conversational courses on other traditions and of including other religious perspectives in mainline courses, changes in the composition of a theological faculty are also required. No seminary or university faculty should feel itself complete or properly balanced unless it includes one or more faculty members specifically trained in one or other non-Christian traditions. This would require someone who knows the language(s) of the sacred texts and who has been steeped in the parent culture of the religion. Ideally, such persons should be able to represent the other tradition(s) not only academically but personally, not only with scholarly expertise but also with existential commitment. To have such a person or persons available for advice to the entire faculty, present at faculty meetings, in chapel, in the lounge, and at Christmas parties would contribute mightily to overcoming the mono-religious mentality of most theology programs and to mainlining an awareness of other religious perspectives into the school's courses and activities.

For the above practical suggestions to be assessed properly and eventually implemented, faculties and administration of seminaries, divinity schools, theology departments, and even parish education programs will first have to undergo a fundamental attitudinal shift (a conversion). They will have to recognize intellectually and feel existentially that the theological enterprise must move from a mono-religious to a multireligious structure. On such a conversion depends the future health of theological education—and of Christianity and its mission.

AFTERWORD

Running through the reflections and proposals in this book is what can be called a Kingdom-centered (or soteriocentric) approach to interreligious dialogue and to our efforts to understand Jesus Christ, his mission, and his church. Such an approach presumes that only if Christians are truly about the *work* of Jesus will they be able to understand the *person and the mission* of Jesus; only if they are faithfully given to the praxis of trying to bring about God's Reign of love, unity, and justice "on earth as in heaven" can they carry on the theological task of understanding Jesus, the world, and other religions. "Seek first the Kingdom of God and its justice and all things [including a more effective dialogue and a more relevant christology and missiology] will be given to you" (Mt 6: 33).

If I'm interpreting that text correctly, then I trust that other Christians will find this book helpful. Whether they do or don't will determine the validity of what I have been proposing.

NOTES

1. My Dialogical Odyssey

1. As I will explain later in this chapter, I do not think the term "pluralism" properly expresses what this approach is reacting against and trying to achieve.

2. Brahman is the Hindu symbol for the Universal Spirit or Ultimate Reality, and Atman indicates the expression of that Universal Spirit in the individual spirit of creatures; this seemed to me to illuminate richly Rahner's efforts to explain that our existence or existential situation as humans was thoroughly supernatural—that our "nature" was imbued with "supernature" or the divine life.

2. Addressing the Other Names

1. For a more elaborated picture of the correlational, globally responsible approach to dialogue see *One Earth Many Religions,* chapter 2.

2. In *One Earth Many Religions,* I try to listen to, and then respond to, the postmodern claims that religions can't really understand and judge each other, especially in chapters 3-5. See Knitter 1995.

3. In chapter 4 of *One Earth Many Religions,* I try to describe the reality and the moral challenges of such suffering, and in chapter 5, I make a case that religions can and do have a "saving word" to speak to this state of global suffering.

4. One might make a philosophical objection to these sweeping implications of historical consciousness. Granting that all religions are limited and relative, cannot there be something like a "first among equals"—or better, a "first among the limited"? Could there not be one religion that, though rooted in the soil of historical contingency, still stands above all the other religions as closest to the fullness of Divine Truth? It would be, in a sense, the least limited of all the limited religions. Indeed, the suggestion is logically possible. "But how would it be known?" asks John Hick. Such claims for being the best among the limited could not be based on a priori assumptions or on divine revelation given to the one "superior" religion. Somehow these claims would have to be grounded on an "examination of the facts"—data available to all. Such facts, however, are not available. Even if we were to try to evaluate the relative superiority of any religion on the broad basis of how well it promotes the welfare of humanity as compared to others, Hick concludes that "it seems impossible to make the global judgment that any one religious tradition has contributed more good or less evil, or a more favorable balance of good and evil, than the others . . . As vast complex totalities, the world traditions seem to be more or less on a par with each other. None can be singled out as manifestly superior" (Hick 1987, 30).

5. To be honest, I must add: at least at this moment. Given my experience and my understanding of the world, Christianity, and the nature of religion, this is what I feel deeply. Perhaps there will be other experiences, insights, discoveries that will change my conviction and faith. At the moment, that is unimaginable.

6. Of course, this still leaves the question of how to understand and integrate the affirmations of the Easter-christology with those of a Wisdom christology. Can Jesus as the constitutive cause of salvation be reconciled with Jesus as the representation of salvation? Such questions are taken up in chapters 4 and 5.

3. IT ISN'T CHRISTIAN

1. In associating the names of Hick and Knitter, I certainly want to acknowledge our shared commitment to the pluralist path and the common features of our theological responses, but I would also want to acknowledge clear and important differences between us, especially in issues of how to understand and ground the uniqueness of Jesus, the role of "mission" for the Christian churches, and the soteriocentric or liberative method of dialogue.

2. Griffiths goes on to point out that many other religions have developed doctrines "that are, *prima facie* at least, particularist and exclusivist." Other religions, too, tie truth to particular events or statements. When pluralists demand that such absolute, exclusivist claims have to be set aside for dialogue, they are, again, continuing the old Western tactic of "setting the agenda and the terms of interreligious dialogue" (Griffiths 1990, 157-58).

3. "The presence of God in Jesus was not first a matter of Christian experience, but a claim of Jesus himself and this claim involved eschatological finality. It is this claim that lies at the roots of the incarnational Christology that was developed in the church. The Christian claim to uniqueness is not based on any Christian experience. If this were so, it would be fair to argue that there are other experiences of uniqueness within the world religions" (Pannenberg 1990, 101).

4. These critics seem to presuppose that full and final commitments are necessary (and possible) in the human condition. Or they are supposing that in order to be fully and definitively *committed* to a truth, we must *know* it fully and definitively. We will explore these presuppositions in coming chapters.

5. Such distinctions seem to me to be highly questionable, more verbal than actual. Can one really claim to have God's final and definitive word without claiming superiority over others and without excluding other final words?

6. In a personal letter to me, Monika Hellwig expressed this concern sensitively yet firmly: "I theologize decidedly from inside the tradition, and am unwilling to set out any theory which I think the Catholic community of believers . . . cannot possibly accept as consonant with its faith . . . We come to the anchor of Christian faith when we speak of the uniqueness of Jesus . . . If I were to say that Christians do not really, ultimately, see Jesus as central or unique, this would not, I think, be true in fact."

7. In face of such a criticism, I feel perplexed and helpless. The immediate response I would like to make, and which I hope will be felt in subsequent chapters, is to suggest to the Carmodys that we break bread together and that

we join basic Christian communities in their struggles for justice. Perhaps in this way they can see that I, and other pluralist theologians, are trying to live (and think) as disciples of Christ.

8. Of course, in the order of causality, Christians first appeal to their experience of Jesus, on the basis of which their claims about his divinity and his decisive difference make sense.

9. When I called for a nonnormative christology I had in mind the traditional understanding of normativity: that Christ is a *norma normans non normata*—a norm that norms all others but is not normed itself. I should have said more clearly than I did that I would endorse an understanding of Jesus as a *norma normans et normata*—a norm that norms others but can also be normed itself. I will try to lay out what this means in chapter 4.

4. Uniqueness Revised

1. As is clear from this citation, what Panikkar means by the "work of Christ" is not to be identified with or limited to the work of Jesus. He elaborates that when he wrote his book about "the Hidden Christ of Hinduism," he did not mean the Christ known to Christians but unknown to Hindus; rather, he was referring to "that Mystery unknown to Christians and known to Hindus by many other names, but in which Christians cannot but recognize the presence of God. The same light illumines different bodies polychromatically" (Panikkar 1990b, 122).

2. Kelsey holds that the authority of the Bible is not to be found in any unchangeable content but rather in its power "to shape individual and communal life and thereby author new identities" (Kelsey 1985, 51). This power can be described as "the power of God's kingly rule" (ibid., 57), which means that the new identities will be according to the values of what in the gospel is described as the Kingdom of God (ibid., 58). Sallie McFague finds biblical authority in the same process: "Our primary datum is not a Christian message for all time, which becomes concretized in different contexts; rather, it is experiences of women and men witnessing to the transforming love of God interpreted in a myriad of ways" (McFague 1987, 44; see also Haight 1990, 211-12). What these theologians are describing is the experience in the Christian community of what Gadamer calls "effective history"; the truth of a text is not to be found in a given, unchangeable meaning but in the way in which it continues to be true, in a variety of expressions, throughout history (see Schneiders 1992).

3. Some will say that I am inverting the scholastic adage *Agere sequitur esse*, "action follows being." Not really. Rather, I am suggesting an identification: *Esse est agere*, "to be is to act." I think such a statement is much closer to the way we are and the way we experience ourselves and the world.

4. "The metaphor of underlying is appropriate here; the experience of Jesus as salvation bringer is prior to and the basis of the various interpretations of his identity and how salvation was won. This priority need not be conceived as a chronological priority, as though it were formless and inarticulate before taking shape through symbolic mediation and expression. Rather the priority here may be seen in the ability to generalize it: a saving encounter with God mediated through Jesus is distinguishable from the large variety of different articulations of the 'how' and the 'why' of it" (Haight 1992, 264).

5. This *universal claim* within the New Testament love language about Jesus is something I should have recognized more explicitly in what I had to say in *No Other Name?*. I am grateful to E. Schillebeeckx for pointing this out (see Schillebeeckx 1990, 162).

6. This understanding of New Testament language about Jesus as action or performative language is very similar to, if not essentially the same as, George Lindbeck's well-known reinterpretation of the nature of doctrine. In fact, Lindbeck's insights offer further guidance for the difficult task of reinterpreting Christian beliefs in the light of dialogue with other religions. He urges us to view and make use of doctrine as rules rather than as propositions—as "instantiations of rules rather than as having a statable, fixed propositional content" (Lindbeck 1984, 104). What he means by "rules" has to do with what I'm trying to get at with "praxis," for he holds that his view "makes doctrines more effectively normative by relating them more closely to praxis" (ibid., 91). If doctrines are to be understood primarily as rules of life rather than as fixed statements of belief, then we will go about the job of interpreting a given doctrine by asking not whether it is faithful to what was *said* in the past but rather whether it is faithful to what was *done* in the past. And to comprehend what was done in the past, we will have to understand the context of the past and relate it creatively to our own. "Perhaps the best way to sum up the practical difference between propositional and regulative approaches is by considering the contrast between interpreting a truth and obeying a rule . . . If the doctrine . . . is taken as a rule, attention is focused on the concrete life and language of the community. Because the doctrine is to be followed rather than interpreted, the theologian's task is to specify the circumstances, whether temporary or enduring, in which it applies" (Lindbeck 1984, 107).

Applying Lindbeck's views to our efforts to elaborate a theology of religions, we will understand the New Testament language about the uniqueness of Christ or about "other names" not as fixed, propositional formulae but as rules of life. Fidelity to belief in the uniqueness of Jesus, then, is primarily not a matter of words concerning his nature, but of acting in a certain way.

7. We shouldn't think that they rejected it all, for as the early Palestinian communities of Jesus-followers moved into the Greco-Roman world, they were transformed from an essentially Jewish religion into a Greco-Roman one. They absorbed, that is, learned from, much of this pluralism. The particular formulation of the doctrine of the Trinity that we have today was born of this cultural union of Jewish and Hellenistic religious and philosophical images and constructs.

8. Leonard Swidler and Paul Mojzes have proposed the basic content of what follows in this chapter as the subject matter for a discussion among Christian theologians; see *The Uniqueness of Jesus: A Dialogue with Paul Knitter* (Swidler and Mojzes 1996).

9. The isolated instances where the New Testament seems to term Jesus God are, as Raymond E. Brown has pointed out, highly ambiguous. In general, the New Testament avoids any simple identification of Jesus and God (see Brown 1967, 23-38).

10. Justin, *I Apologia,* 46; *II Apologia,* 10, 13; Clement of Alexandria, *Stromata,* 1,13; 5,87, 2; idem, *Protreptikos, 6,* 68, 2ff.; Origen, *Commentarium in Joanem,* I, 39.

11. "The power of a divine person is infinite and cannot be contained by anything created. Therefore, we cannot say that the divine person, in assuming one human nature, could not assume another . . . for the uncreated cannot be limited by the created. It is therefore evident that, whether we consider a divine person according to its divine power, which is the principle of union, or whether we consider the divine person according to its personality, which is the goal of the union, we must say that the divine person can assume another human nature besides the one that it did assume" (ST 3, q.3. a. 7).

12. Here I have some problems with the way Hans Küng, in his eagerness to promote dialogue, seems to restrict the transforming power of Jesus' truth only to Christians. With his distinction between "outside" and "inside" perspectives on religions, he suggests that it is only "inside" or within Christianity that Christians would proclaim Jesus as savior. Küng compares allegiance to Christ with allegiance to the constitution of one's own country; just as one would not claim that one's own national constitution is valid for others, one would not claim that one's religion is valid for others. This, it seems to me, contradicts the New Testament affirmation of the *universal* relevance of what God has done in Jesus Christ (see Küng 1991, 99-100).

13. So I want to clarify and qualify—which means change—the terminology I used in *No Other Name?*, when I struggled to formulate the characteristics of a theocentric christology. No longer do I advocate a "nonnormative christology," for that seems to imply that the encounter with God through Jesus cannot be decisive insofar as it cannot give us norms with which to direct our lives and take our stands (see Knitter 1985, chap. 9). What I was opposing at that time was a christology that holds up Jesus as the absolute, final, full, unsurpassable norm for all times and all religions. So, today, while I want to affirm clearly that Jesus *is* normative, and universally so, I still am questioning whether he is, or can be, the only such norm.

14. Schillebeeckx seems to admit this indirectly when, after proclaiming Christ's truth as normative and definitive, he adds: "Whether this revelation is also normative for other religions is another matter . . . Christians confess what in their experience God has done for them in Jesus of Nazareth. In itself, this does not imply any judgment on how those of other religions experience salvation" (Schillebeeckx 1990, 145-46).

15. Here, however, as Haight himself points out, one must be extremely careful not to identify too hastily what is genuinely different with what is contradictory. Many of the differences between Christianity and Buddhism that often have been held up as contradictions are turning out to be complementarities. An example might be the difference between the Buddhist notion of the No-Self and the Christian ideal of the new person in Christ. Thus, when Christians say that Jesus is a norm that can be applied to all religions, they are also open to the possibility or probability that other religions may present Christians with norms that prove to have power over Christian self-understanding.

16. See especially the warnings of Wolfhart Pannenberg, summarized in chapter 3, page 49.

17. As we shall see in the next chapter, the popular scholarly view that Jesus expected the end of the world within his lifetime has been exposed to widespread doubt (see chapter 5, note 5).

18. This notion of indispensability is what Schillebeeckx is getting at in his conviction that the early Christians claimed a "constitutive significance" for Jesus. "To believe in Jesus as the Christ means at its deepest to confess and at the same time to recognize that Jesus has an abiding and constitutive significance for the approach of the Kingdom of God and thus for the comprehensive healing of human beings and making them whole (Schillebeeckx 1990, 121). And he holds that this indispensability can be found in the "historical self-understanding of Jesus: there is a connection between the coming of the Kingdom of God and the person of Jesus of Nazareth" (ibid., 144). I think that many Buddhists would make similar claims that there is "a connection between the coming of Enlightenment and the person of Siddhartha Gautama."

19. As I suggested, the same could be said of the Christian who comes to know "the saving truth" of Buddha. Perhaps in this case, the analogy might be not that the illiterate person learns to read, but the distracted person learns how to feel the present moment.

20. In *Is There Only One True Religion?* Schubert Ogden's main criticism of the pluralists is that they too hastily conclude to the *actuality* of many true religions when they should affirm only the *possibility*. Ogden's admonitions are appropriate and, I hope, well taken, for many pluralists much too facilely and a priori announce that because all other religions *are* true, Christians must acknowledge and dialogue with them. Still, I would ask Ogden whether he is faithful to his own Christian starting point when he admits only the possibility that there are other true religions besides Christianity. Given the God of pure, unbounded love, whom Ogden finds at the heart of the Christian message, and given the anthropological necessity of this love having to take historical-cultural form in order to be real in the lives of men and women, should he not recognize that it is *probable* that God's love will be found in and through other religions, thus rendering them, at least to some extent, true? In order truly to affirm the actuality and efficacy of God's saving love for all people, Ogden needs to affirm the *probability* of many true religions. That means he enters the dialogue, like the pluralists, *expecting* to find God's truth revealed in other religious traditions.

21. While agreeing basically which what I have presented in this section, Haight still wants to preserve the traditional terms "decisiveness, definitiveness, finality, and even absoluteness of Jesus as God's medium of salvation." But he immediately adds, "provided that these determinations are not construed exclusively, as negating the possibility that God as Spirit is at work in other religions" (Haight 1992, 282).

22. Therefore, even when Christians claim that they have the "full" revelation of God in Jesus, as long as they also recognize that this "fullness" cannot, as it were, be unpacked unless they carry on a dialogue with other Words in other religions, I would not argue with them. Even when they insist that any truth they might learn from others was implicitly contained in the Bible, they are also admitting that the "full truth" of the Bible is a relational or dialogical fullness. It can't be understood by itself, without conversation with others (see Cobb 1990, 87).

23. Cobb goes even further in the demands of what it means to be faithful to Christ: "In faithfulness to Christ I must be open to others . . . I must be ready to learn even if that threatens my present beliefs . . . I cannot prede-

termine how radical the effects of that learning will be . . . I cannot even know that, when I have learned what I have to learn here and been transformed by it, I will still see faithfulness to Christ as my calling. I cannot predetermine that I will be a Christian at all. That is what I mean by full openness. *In faithfulness to Christ I must be prepared to give up even faithfulness to Christ.* If that is where I am led, to remain a Christian would be to become an idolater in the name of Christ. That would be blasphemy" (Cobb 1984, 174-75, emphasis mine). I find myself saying yes and no to what Cobb is proposing here. Theoretically he's right. The God I have known through Christ could, hypothetically, lead me away from Christ. But personally and existentially, that's inconceivable. Cobb is proposing an "impossible possibility." It's like saying that my wife has helped me achieve such an openness to and appreciation for others that I would be willing to leave her for another woman. My head tells me that that is possible; my heart assures me that it is not.

5. UNIQUENESS REAFFIRMED

1. "Though we cannot ever be certain that we have direct and exact quotations from Jesus, we can be relatively sure of the *kinds* of things he said, and of the main themes and thrust of his teaching. We can also be relatively sure of the kinds of things he did: healings, association with outcasts, the deliberate calling of the twelve disciples, a mission directed to Israel, a final purposeful journey to Jerusalem" (Borg 1987, 15).

2. "The most historical aspect of the historical Jesus is his practice and the spirit with which he carried it out. By 'practice' I mean the whole range of activities Jesus used to act on social reality and transform it in the specific direction of the Kingdom of God. The 'historical' is thus primarily what sets history in motion, and this practice of Jesus, which in his day set history in motion, is what has come down to our times as a history set in motion to be continued" (Sobrino 1994, 51).

3. Pope Paul VI was in agreement with this understanding of what was Jesus' absolute: "As an evangelizer, Christ first of all proclaims a kingdom, the Kingdom of God; and this is so important that, by comparison, everything else becomes the rest, which is given in addition. Only the Kingdom therefore is absolute, and it makes everything else relative" (*Evangelii nuntiandi* AAS 68 [1975], 5-76, no. 8).

4. This recognition that Jesus intended not only eternal life after death but also a changed society in this world has been enforced by the growing communal change of mind among New Testament scholars regarding Jesus' own eschatology and view of the end of the world. As Marcus Borg observes: "The consensus regarding Jesus' expectation of the end of the world has disappeared. The majority of scholars no longer thinks that Jesus expected the end of the world in his generation" (Borg 1987, 14). "Over the last ten years, the image of Jesus as an eschatological prophet, which dominated scholarship through the middle of this century, has become very much a minority position" (Borg 1994, 29). Therefore, the final crisis that Jesus was warning against was not the end of time, as has been commonly thought and taught. "Though Jesus did speak of a last judgment, there is no reason to believe that he thought it was imminent. Instead, like the predestruction prophets before

him, the crisis he announced was the threat of historical catastrophe for his society" (Borg 1987, 157; see also Borg 1988 and 1991).

5. Segundo's hermeneutical key is essentially the same as the "revelatory canon" urged by Elisabeth Schüssler Fiorenza in her feminist critical hermeneutics of the Bible. What she calls the "advocacy stance for the oppressed"—commitment to further Jesus' original vision of a community of equals—becomes "the criterion of appropriateness for biblical interpretation and evaluation of biblical authority claims" (Schüssler Fiorenza 1983, 32-35).

6. What I am proposing as unique to Christianity is for the most part, with different emphases, unique to Christianity's parent religion, Judaism. Therefore, in the discussion on whether the relationship between Christianity and Judaism is best understood on a "one covenant" or "two covenants" model, I would lean toward the one covenant perspective; that is, that Jews and Christians, in their different ways, are still carrying on the covenant that the God of history made on Mount Sinai.

7. Mark Taylor seeks to express the same nonduality when he holds that "material practice" is an essential aspect of what it means to "be in Christ." "Human agents are presented as 'in Christ' . . . when they are given to a life of meeting the material needs of the hungry, the thirsty, the stranger, the naked, the imprisoned. This is not simply a divine imperative from Christ to go into faithful service; no, more accurately, the message is that to serve in this way is to serve the Christ . . . Christians come to life in Christ by being at work with and for the material needs of the least of these. Doing unto these is not a second act, occurring after or in addition to knowing and being in Christ. The latter is the kind of spirituality that permits many of us North Americans to call ourselves Christians without resisting the systems that wreak material suffering upon so many of the world's poor" (Taylor 1990, 234-35).

8. This is the position of Schubert Ogden, who hesitates to base the claims of liberation theology directly on the historical Jesus. For Ogden, a commitment to the poor and their liberation is a modern-day application and requirement of the Christian law of love (see Ogden 1979, 43-65).

9. Nolan is even more specific: "There is a power that can resist the system and prevent it from destroying us. There is a motive that can replace, and can be stronger than, the profit motive. There is an incentive that can mobilise the world, enable the 'haves' to lower their standard of living and make us only too willing to redistribute the world's wealth and its population. It is the same drive and incentive that motivated Jesus: *compassion and faith.* It has generally been called faith, hope, and love; whatever you choose to call it, you must understand it as the unleashing of the divine but thoroughly 'natural' power of truth, goodness, and beauty" (Nolan 1978, 141).

10. By Asian religions in this reference, I include Hinduism, Buddhism, Jainism, and Taoism, but not Confucianism. By primal religions, I am speaking of older, usually indigenous religions, such as Native American, African, and Australian Aborigine spiritualities.

11. The Semitic religions are those stemming, in their scriptures if not historically, from Abraham. Charlene Spretnak ranks Judaism, Christianity, and Islam in the category of world-affirming or historically oriented traditions. She does not recognize the differences, even tensions, in the way each of these

traditions understands and seeks to realize God's vision for history (Spretnak 1991, chap. 5).

12. With these statements, Spretnak intends to describe all the Semitic religions—Islam, as well as Judaism and Christianity—though her references to the Qur'an and Muslim practice are few in comparison to her references to the Bible. I think a case can indeed be made that the Abrahamic religions are more historical, and much more concerned with questions of social justice, than are the Indic or primal religions. But the differences in the reasons and way that Jews, Christians, and Muslims are so committed to this-worldly well-being are such that one should not place them in the same liberative pot; they have much to learn from each other (see Engineer 1990; Cohn-Sherbok 1987).

6. MISSION REVISED

1. This inclusive or fulfillment model of christology is also part of the foundation for *Dialogue and Proclamation,* the document issued shortly after *Redemptoris Missio* by the Pontifical Council for Interreligious Dialogue and the Congregation for the Evangelization of Peoples. The document states clearly that since there is "one plan of salvation for humankind, with its center in Jesus Christ" (DP 28), any presence of God and grace in other religions will see "its fulfillment in Jesus Christ in whom is established the new and definitive Covenant for all peoples" (DP 19). Therefore, whatever positive elements Christians may find in their dialogue with other believers, they must continue to affirm "the necessity of the missionary activity of the Church in order to perfect in Christ those elements found in other religions" (DP 18). The *New Catechism* is even clearer in insisting that the revelation given in Christ is final; it even holds that no other public revelations from God are to be expected and that the truth found in other religions cannot go beyond that of Christ, or even serve to confirm Christian revelation (see 66-67). Other religions, therefore, must be seen as a "preparation for the Gospel" and are called to fulfillment in the one Roman Catholic Church (843-45, 839).

2. Personal letter to the author, February 11, 1993.

3. Modalism was an early trinitarian heresy which argued that the differences among the three divine persons are merely "modes" of action of the one and same God, as if God sometimes acts like a Father, sometimes like a Word, sometimes like a Spirit. The early community wanted to affirm real differences.

4. The *"Filioque"* controversy between the Western and Eastern church dealt with whether the Spirit proceeds only from the Father or from the Father "and the Son" (*Filioque*). Such a seemingly abstract debate has a practical pay-off: by questioning the *"Filioque,"* Eastern theologians want to stress the real difference between the Spirit and the Son. That's the point Khodr is making in his essay.

5. It is telling that in the earlier drafts of DP, this statement about other religions as ways of salvation was even more explicit. Only after the more conservative influence of Cardinal Tomko and his Congregation for the Evangelization of Peoples became part of the composing process of DP was the phrase "and by following the dictates of their conscience" added. There was, as Dupuis (who was part of the earlier stages of drafting) observes, "a certain

fear on the part of some to concede too much to other religions as constituting ways of salvation" (Dupuis 1994, 136).

A ROMAN CATHOLIC INTER-MISSION

1. As is so often the case with Vatican II, this particular perspective on the apparent identification of church and Kingdom in *Lumen Gentium* is qualified by perspectives in other documents. In *Gaudium et Spes* the growth of the Reign of God and Christ in history and its eschatological fulfillment are recognized without explicit reference to the church and with reference to the whole of humanity (GS 39).

2. The pope has to be careful of not leaning to the other extreme of a *spiritual* reduction. On the one hand, he pointedly states that the church must work "for the liberation from evil in all its forms" (RM 15) and that missioners must be on the "side of those who are poor and oppressed in any way" (RM 60). But he seems to place so much stress on the spiritual component of liberation that it seems that once the spiritual piece is in place, the job is done. When he tells us, for example, that the church's mission "consists essentially in offering people not opportunity to 'have more' but to 'be more'" (RM 58), he gives the impression that the *campesinos* who need to *have more* in order to feed their children should be content because they *are more*. Also, in declaring that development "does not derive primarily from money, material assistance or technological means, but from the formation of conscience and the gradual maturing of ways of thinking and patterns of behavior" (RM 58), one runs the danger of implying that what is primary is sufficient; the formation of conscience does not automatically bring urgently needed material assistance.

7. MISSION REAFFIRMED

1. In the Thirteenth General Chapter, 1988, as stated in *Following the Word*, no. 1 (August 1988), p. 17.

2. In the case of DP, this is due to a large extent to the need to inject the concerns of the Congregation for the Evangelization of Peoples and of the Doctrine of the Faith into the earlier drafts of the document made by the Council for Interreligious Dialogue. Dupuis notes the confusion or tension this caused in the final draft (Dupuis 1994, 146-47).

3. Jacques Dupuis points out the tensions and ambiguities in the way DP, after calling both dialogue and proclamation "integral" and "necessary" parts of the church's mission, then subordinates dialogue to proclamation. He seeks to resolve these tensions by urging that the authors of the documents should have recognized that "dialogue informed by witness *as it must be in all circumstances* . . . is by itself a form of evangelization, even in the absence of proclamation" (1994, 148). But if dialogue must be "informed by witness . . . in all circumstances," how can proclamation be absent? What is the difference between witness and proclamation?

4. I therefore agree with those for whom the difference between theology and religious studies cannot be reduced simply to the difference between subjective *vs.* objective or advocacy *vs.* scholarship. Rather, *both* areas or contents for study include advocacy *and* scholarship, subjective engagement *and* objective data. Both theology and religious studies seek to mediate between

religion and culture. Religious studies does so with an understanding of religion as a pluralistic phenomenon and so recognizes the possible truth or validity of many religious traditions and forms of religious experience; religious studies, therefore, does not operate with a priori criteriological preferences for any one religious tradition. Envisioning a more modest goal, theology seeks to mediate between the Christian religion and culture, convinced as it has been that this mediation can take place from within the Christian tradition *by itself*. By calling for a marriage between theology and religious studies, I am questioning this "by itself" (see Fiorenza 1991; Ogden 1986, 102-20).

WORKS CITED

Amaladoss, Michael. 1985. "Faith Meets Faith." *Vidyajyoti* 49: 109-17.
———. 1986. "Dialogue and Mission: Conflict or Convergence?" *Vidyajyoti* 50: 62-86.
———. 1989. "The Pluralism of Religions and the Significance of Christ." *Vidyajyoti* 53: 401-20.
———. 1992a. "Liberation as an Interreligious Project." In Wilfred 1992, 158-74.
———. 1992b. "Mission and Missioners in Today's Global Context." *Discovery: Jesuit International Ministries* 1: 1-14.
Anderson, Gerald H., and Thomas F. Stransky, eds. 1981a. *Christ's Lordship and Religious Pluralism*. Maryknoll, NY: Orbis Books.
———. 1981b. *Mission Trends No. 5: Faith Meets Faith*. New York: Paulist Press.
"Attitude of the Church toward the Followers of Other Religions." 1984. Issued by the Vatican Council for Interreligious Dialogue. In *Bulletin Secretariatus pro non-Christianis* 56: 126-41. Also in *Acta Apostolicae Sedis* 76 (1984): 816-28.
Ayrookuzhiel, A. M. Abraham. 1994. "The Dalits, Religions, and Interfaith Dialogue." *Hindu-Christian Studies Bulletin* 7: 13-19.
Balasuriya, Tissa. 1980. "Towards the Liberation of Theology in Asia." In Fabella 1980, 16-27.
Baum, Gregory. 1974. "Introduction." In Ruether 1974, 1-22.
———. 1987. "The Grand Vision: It Needs Social Action." In Lonergan and Richards 1987, 51-56.
———. 1994. "Religious Pluralism and Common Values." *The Journal of Religious Pluralism* 4: 1-16.
van Beeck, Frans Jozef. 1979. *Christ Proclaimed: Christology as Rhetoric*. New York: Paulist Press.
———. 1985. "Professing the Uniqueness of Christ." *Chicago Studies* 24: 17-35.
———. 1991. "Professing the Creed among the World's Religions." *The Thomist* 55, 539-68.
Bernstein, Richard. 1983. *Beyond Objectivism and Relativism*. Philadelphia: University of Pennsylvania Press.
Bevans, Stephen B. 1992. *Models of Contextual Theology*. Maryknoll, NY: Orbis Books.
Bingemer, Maria Clara. 1990. "The Holy Spirit as Possibility of Universal Dialogue and Mission." In Mojzes and Swidler 1990, 34-41.
Boff, Leonardo. 1978. *Jesus Christ Liberator: A Critical Christology for Our Times*. Maryknoll, NY: Orbis Books.

Borg, Marcus. 1987. *Jesus, A New Vision: Spirit, Culture, and the Life of Discipleship.* HarperSanFrancisco.

_____ . 1988. "A Renaissance in Jesus Studies." *Theology Today* 45: 280-92.

_____ . 1991. "Portraits of Jesus in Contemporary North American Scholarship." *Harvard Theological Review* 84: 1-22.

_____ . 1994. *Meeting Jesus Again for the First Time: The Historical Jesus and the Heart of Contemporary Faith.* HarperSanFrancisco.

Bosch, David J. 1991. *Transforming Mission: Paradigm Shifts in Theology of Mission.* Maryknoll, NY: Orbis Books.

Braaten, Carl E. 1981. "The Uniqueness and Universality of Jesus Christ." In Anderson and Stransky 1981b, 69-89.

_____ . 1985. *The Apostolic Imperative: Nature and Aim of the Church's Mission and Ministry.* Minneapolis: Augsburg.

_____ . 1987. "Christocentric Trinitarianism *vs.* Unitarian Theocentrism." *Journal of Ecumenical Studies* 24: 17-21.

_____ . 1990. "The Triune God: The Source and Mode of Christian Unity and Mission." *Missiology* 18: 415-27.

_____ . 1992. *No Other Gospel! Christianity among the World's Religions.* Minneapolis: Augsburg Fortress Press.

_____ . 1994. "Interreligious Dialogue in the Pluralistic Situation." *Dialog* 33: 294-98.

Brown, Raymond E. 1967. *Jesus, God and Man.* Milwaukee: Bruce.

Burrows, William R., ed. 1994. *Redemption and Dialogue: Reading Redemptoris Missio and* Dialogue and Proclamation. Maryknoll, NY: Orbis Books.

Carmody, Denise Lardner, and John Tully Carmody. 1990. *Christian Uniqueness and Catholic Spirituality.* New York: Paulist Press.

Cobb, John B., Jr. 1984. "The Meaning of Pluralism for Christian Self-Understanding." In Rouner 1984, 161-79.

_____ . 1990. "Beyond 'Pluralism.'" In D'Costa 1990, 81-95.

Cohn-Sherbok, Dan. 1987. *On Earth as It Is in Heaven: Jews, Christians, and Liberation Theology.* Maryknoll, NY: Orbis Books.

Cox, Harvey. 1988. *Many Mansions: A Christian's Encounter with Other Faiths.* Boston: Beacon Press.

Croatto, J. Severino. 1987. *Biblical Hermeneutics: Toward a Theory of Reading as the Production of Meaning.* Maryknoll, NY: Orbis Books.

Crossan, Dominic. 1991. *The Historical Jesus: The Life of a Mediterranean Jewish Peasant.* HarperSanFrancisco.

D'Costa, Gavin. 1985. *Theology and Religious Pluralism: The Challenge of Other Religions.* Oxford: Basil Blackwell.

_____ , ed. 1990. *Christian Uniqueness Reconsidered: The Myth of a Pluralistic Theology of Religions.* Maryknoll, NY: Orbis Books.

Dean, Thomas. 1987. "The Conflict of Christologies: A Response to S. Mark Heim." *Journal of Ecumenical Studies* 24: 24-31.

"Dialogue and Proclamation." 1991. Issued by the Vatican Council for Interreligious Dialogue and the Congregation for the Evangelization of Peoples, in *Bulletin of the Pontifical Council on Interreligious Dialogue* 26, no. 2.

Driver, Tom F. 1987. "The Case for Pluralism." In Hick and Knitter 1987, 203-18.

Dulles, Avery. 1977. *The Resilient Church: The Necessity and Limits of Adaptation.* New York: Doubleday.

Dunne, John. 1972. *The Way of All the Earth.* Notre Dame, IN: University of Notre Dame Press.

Dupuis, Jacques. 1993. "The Church, the Reign of God, and the 'Others.'" *Federation of Asian Bishops Conference Papers,* no. 67, 1-30.

———. 1994. "A Theological Commentary: Dialogue and Proclamation." In Burrows 1994, 119-58.

Eddy, Paul R. 1993. "Paul Knitter's Theology of Religions: A Survey and Evangelical Response." *The Evangelical Quarterly* 65: 225-45.

Engineer, Asghar Ali. 1990. *Islam and Liberation Theology: Essays on Liberative Elements in Islam.* New Delhi: Sterling Publishers.

Fabella, Virginia, ed. 1980. *Asia's Struggle for Full Humanity.* Maryknoll, NY: Orbis Books.

Farley, Edward. 1988. *The Fragility of Knowledge: Theological Education in the Church and University.* Philadelphia: Fortress Press.

Fiorenza, Francis Schüssler. 1975. "Critical Social Theory and Christology: Toward an Understanding of Atonement and Redemption as Emancipatory Solidarity." *Proceedings of the Catholic Theological Society of America* 30: 63-110.

———. 1984. *Foundational Theology: Jesus and Church.* New York: Crossroad.

———. 1991. "Theological and Religious Studies: The Contest of the Faculties." In Wheeler and Farley 1991, 119-50.

Fowler, James. 1981. *Stages of Faith: The Psychology of Human Development and the Quest for Meaning.* San Francisco: Harper & Row.

Geffré, Claude. 1990. "Christian Uniqueness and Interreligious Dialogue." In Mojzes and Swidler 1990, 61-76.

Geffré, Claude, and J. P. Jossua, eds. 1980. *True and False Universality of Christianity (Concilium 135).* New York: Seabury.

Gilkey, Langdon. 1987. "Plurality and Its Theological Implications." In Hick and Knitter 1987, 37-53.

Gittens, Anthony J. 1994. "A Missionary's Misgivings: Reflections on Two Recent Documents." In Burrows 1994, 216-22.

Gremillion, Joseph. 1976. *The Gospel of Peace and Justice.* Maryknoll, NY: Orbis Books.

Griffiths, Paul. 1990. "The Uniqueness of Christian Doctrine Defended." In D'Costa 1990, 157-73.

Gutiérrez, Gustavo. 1984. *We Drink from Our Own Wells: The Spiritual Journey of a People.* Maryknoll, NY: Orbis Books.

Habermas, Jürgen. 1979. *Communication and the Evolution of Society.* Boston: Beacon Press.

———. 1984. *The Theory of Communicative Action.* Vol. 1. Boston: Beacon Press.

Haight, Roger. 1988. "The Mission of the Church in the Theology of the Social Gospel." *Theological Studies* 49: 477-97.

_____ . 1989. "Towards an Understanding of Christ in the Context of Other World Religions." *East Asian Pastoral Review* 3/4: 248-65.

_____ . 1990. *Dynamics of Theology.* New York: Paulist Press.

_____ . 1992. "The Case for Spirit Christology." *Theological Studies* 53: 257-87.

_____ . 1994. "Jesus and Salvation: An Essay in Interpretation." *Theological Studies* 55: 225-51.

_____ . 1995. "Jesus and Mission: An Overview of the Problem." *Discovery: Jesuit International Ministries* 5:1-23.

Hastings, Adrian. 1990. *The Theology of a Protestant Catholic.* London: SCM Press.

Hearne, Brian. 1993. "New Models for Mission." *Furrow* 64: 91-98.

Heim, S. Mark. 1985. *Is Christ the Only Way? Christian Faith in a Pluralistic World.* Valley Forge, PA: Judson Press.

_____ . 1987. "Thinking about Theocentric Christology." *Journal of Ecumenical Studies* 24: 1-16.

_____ . 1994. "Salvations: A More Pluralistic Hypothesis." *Modern Theology* 10: 341-59.

_____ . 1995. *Salvations: In Search of Authentic Religious Pluralism.* Maryknoll, NY: Orbis Books.

Hellwig, Monika. 1983. *Jesus the Compassion of God: New Perspectives on the Tradition of Christianity.* Wilmington: Michael Glazier.

_____ . 1989. "Re-emergence of the Human, Critical, Public Jesus." *Theological Studies* 50: 466-80.

_____ . 1990. "Christology in the Wider Ecumenism. In D'Costa 1990, 107-16.

_____ . 1992. *The Eucharist and the Hunger of the World.* Rev. ed. Kansas City, MO: Sheed & Ward.

Hick, John. 1973. *God and the Universe of Faiths.* New York: St. Martin's Press.

_____ . 1980. "Whatever Path Men Choose Is Mine." In Hick and Hebblethwaite 1980, 171-90.

_____ . 1987. "The Non-Absoluteness of Christianity." In Hick and Knitter 1987, 16-36.

_____ . 1989. *An Interpretation of Religion.* New Haven: Yale University Press.

_____ . 1993. *The Metaphor of God Incarnate.* London: SCM Press.

Hick, John, and Brian Hebblethwaite, eds. 1980. *Christianity and Other Religions.* Philadelphia: Fortress Press.

Hick, John, and Paul F. Knitter, eds. 1987. *The Myth of Christian Uniqueness: Toward a Pluralistic Theology of Religions.* Maryknoll, NY: Orbis Books.

Hill, Brennan, Paul Knitter, and Wm. Madges. 1990. *Faith, Religion and Theology: A Contemporary Introduction.* Mystic, CT: Twenty-Third Publications.

Hillman, Eugene. 1975. *Polygamy Reconsidered: African Plural Marriage and the Christian Churches.* Maryknoll, NY: Orbis Books.

_____ . 1993. *Toward an African Christianity: Inculturation Applied.* New York: Paulist Press.

Hodgson, Peter C., and Robert King, eds. 1985. *Readings in Christian Theology*. Philadelphia: Fortress Press.

Hoekendijk, J. C. 1960. *The Church Inside Out*. Philadelphia: Westminster Press.

Horsely, Richard A. 1985. *Bandits, Prophets, and Messiahs: Popular Movements in the Time of Jesus*. Minneapolis: Winston Press.

Irudayaraj, Xavier, ed. 1989. *Liberation and Dialogue*. Bangalore: Claretian Publications.

Kelly, Anthony. 1989. *A Trinity of Love: A Theology of the Christian God*. Wilmington: M. Glazier.

Kelsey, David. 1985. "The Function of Scripture." In Hodgson and King 1985, 50-59.

Kermode, Frank. 1975. *The Classic: Literary Images of Permanence and Change*. New York: Viking.

Khodr, George. 1991. "An Orthodox Perspective of Inter-Religious Dialogue." *Current Dialogue* 19: 25-27.

Klostermaier, Klaus. 1991. "Religious Pluralism and the Idea of Universal Religion(s)." *Journal of Religious Pluralism* 1: 45-64.

Knitter, Paul F. 1975. *Toward a Protestant Theology of Religions: A Case Study of Paul Althaus and Contemporary Attitudes*. Marburg: N.G. Elwert Verlag.

_____ . 1978. "World Religions and the Finality of Christ: A Critique of Hans Küng's *On Being a Christian*." *Horizons* 5: 151-64.

_____ . 1982. "Religious Imagination and Interreligious Dialogue." In Masson 1982, 97-112.

_____ . 1985. *No Other Name? A Critical Survey of Christian Attitudes toward World Religions*. Maryknoll, NY: Orbis Books.

_____ . 1987. "Spirituality and Liberation: A Buddhist-Christian Conversation" (with Masao Abe). *Horizons* 15: 347-64.

_____ . 1988. "Dialogue and Liberation: Foundations for a Pluralist Theology of Religions." *The Drew Gateway* 58: 1-53.

_____ . 1990a. "Interreligious Dialogue: What? Why? How?" In Swidler, et al. 1990a, 19-44.

_____ . 1990b. "Interpreting Silence: A Response to Miikka Ruokanen." *International Bulletin of Missionary Research* 14: 62-63.

_____ . 1990c. *Pluralism and Oppression: Theology in World Perspective*. Lanham, MD: University Press of America.

_____ . 1991. "A New Pentecost? A Pneumatological Theology of Religions." *Current Dialogue* 19: 32-41.

_____ . 1992. "Religious Pluralism in Theological Education." *Anglican Theological Review* 74: 418-37.

_____ . 1995. *One Earth Many Religions: Multifaith Dialogue and Global Responsibility*. Maryknoll, NY: Orbis Books.

Küng, Hans. 1976. *On Being a Christian*. New York: Doubleday.

_____ . 1986a. *Christianity and the World Religions: Paths of Dialogue with Islam, Hinduism, and Buddhism*. New York: Doubleday.

_____ . 1986b. "Towards an Ecumenical Theology of Religions: Some Theses for Clarification." *Concilium* 183, 119-25.

_____ . 1991. *Global Responsibility: In Search of a New World Ethic.* New York: Crossroad.

Kuschel, Karl Josef. 1991. "Christologie und interreligiöser Dialog: Die Einzigartigkiet Christi im Gespräch mit den Weltreligionen." *Stimmen der Zeit* 209: 387-402.

Lane, Dermot. 1991. *Christ at the Centre: Selected Issues in Christology.* New York: Paulist Press.

Ledd, Mary Jo, ed. 1987. *The Faith that Transforms: Essays in Honor of Gregory Baum's Sixtieth Birthday.* New York: Paulist Press.

Lindbeck, George. 1984. *The Nature of Doctrine: Religion and Theology in a Postliberal Age.* Philadelphia: Westminster Press.

Lochhead, David. 1988. *The Dialogical Imperative.* Maryknoll, NY: Orbis Books.

Lonergan, Anne, and Caroline Richards, eds. 1987. *Thomas Berry and the New Cosmology.* Mystic, CT: Twenty-Third Publications.

Lonergan, Bernard. 1973. *Method in Theology.* New York: Herder & Herder.

Maguire, Daniel C. 1993. *The Moral Core of Judaism and Christianity: Reclaiming the Revolution.* Minneapolis: Fortress Press.

Masson, Robert, ed. 1982. *The Pedagogy of God's Image: Essays on Symbol and the Religious Imagination.* Chico: Scholars Press.

Maurier, Henri. 1976. "The Christian Theology of the Non-Christian Religions." *Lumen Vitae* 21: 59-74.

McFague, Sallie. 1987. *Models of God: Theology for an Ecological, Nuclear Age.* Philadelphia: Fortress Press.

Meier, John P. 1991. *A Marginal Jew: Rethinking the Historical Jesus.* Vol. 1: *The Roots of the Problem and the Person.* New York: Doubleday.

Mercado, Leonardo N., and James J. Knight, eds. 1989. *Mission & Dialogue: Theory and Practice.* Manila: Divine Word Publications.

Merton, Thomas. 1968. *Zen and the Birds of Appetite.* New York: New Directions.

_____ . 1969. *The Way of Chuang Tzu.* New York: New Directions.

Mojzes, Paul, and Leonard Swidler, eds. 1990. *Christian Mission and Interreligious Dialogue.* Lewiston: Edwin Mellen Press.

Moran, Gabriel. 1992. *Uniqueness.* Maryknoll, NY: Orbis Books.

Mudge, Lewis S., and James N. Poling, eds. 1987. *Formation and Reflection: The Promise of Practical Theology.* Philadelphia: Fortress Press.

New Universal Catechism. 1994. Washington, D.C.: U.S. Catholic Conference.

Newbigin, Lesslie. 1990. "Religion for the Marketplace." In D'Costa 1990, 135-48.

Nolan, Albert. 1978. *Jesus before Christianity.* Maryknoll, NY: Orbis Books.

O'Brien, John. 1992. *Theology and the Option for the Poor.* Collegeville, MN: Liturgical Press.

O'Donnell, John. 1989. "In Him and Over Him: The Holy Spirit in the Life of Jesus." *Gregorianum* 70: 25-45.

Ogden, Schubert. 1972. "What Is Theology?" *The Journal of Religion* 52: 22-40.

_____ . 1979. *Faith and Freedom: Toward a Theology of Liberation.* Nashville: Abingdon Press.

_____ . 1982. *The Point of Christology.* New York: Harper & Row.

_____ . 1986. *On Theology.* San Francisco: Harper & Row.

_____ . 1992. *Is There Only One True Religion or Are There Many?* Dallas: Southern Methodist Press.

_____ . 1994. "Some Thoughts on a Christian Theology of Interreligious Dialogue." *Criterion* 11: 5-10.

Omann, Thomas B. 1986. "Relativism, Objection, and Theology." *Horizons* 13: 291-305.

Panikkar, Raimon, ed. 1977. *The Vedic Experience—Mantramanjarli: An Anthology of the Vedas for Modern Man and Contemporary Celebration.* Berkeley: University of California Press.

_____ . 1978. *The Intrareligious Dialogue.* New York: Paulist Press.

_____ . 1981. *The Unknown Christ of Hinduism.* Maryknoll, NY: Orbis Books.

_____ . 1987. "The Jordan, the Tiber, and the Ganges: Three Kairological Moments of Christic Self-Consciousness." In Hick and Knitter 1987, 89-116.

_____ . 1990a. "Can Theology Be Transcultural?" In Knitter 1990c, 3-22.

_____ . 1990b. "The Christian Challenge to the Third Millennium." In Mojzes and Swidler 1990, 113-25.

_____ . 1993. *The Cosmotheandric Experience: Emerging Religious Consciousness.* Maryknoll, NY: Orbis Books.

Pannenberg, Wolfhart. 1990. "Religious Pluralism and Conflicting Truth Claims." In D'Costa 1990, 96-106.

Pawlikowski, Paul. 1982. *Christ in the Light of the Christian Jewish Dialogue.* New York: Paulist Press.

Pieris, Aloysius. 1987. "Jesus and Buddha: Mediators of Liberation." In Hick and Knitter 1987, 162-77.

_____ . 1988a. *An Asian Theology of Liberation.* Maryknoll, NY: Orbis Books.

_____ . 1988b. *Love Meets Wisdom: A Christian Experience of Buddhism.* Maryknoll, NY: Orbis Books.

Pinnock, Clark. 1992. *A Wideness in God's Mercy.* Grand Rapids: Zondervan.

Placher, William. 1989. *Unapologetic Theology: A Christian Voice in a Pluralistic Conversation.* Louisville: Westminster/John Knox Press.

Pushparajan, A. 1992. "Whither Interreligious Dialogue? A Reflective Response to the Vatican Document on 'Dialogue and Proclamation.'" *Vidyajyoti* 56: 224-32.

Puthiadam, Ignatius. 1980. "Christian Faith and Life in a World of Religious Pluralism." In Geffré and Jossua 1980, 99-112.

_____ . 1992. "Dialogue and Proclamation? Problem? Challenge? Grace-filled Dialectic? *Vidyajyoti* 56: 289-308.

Race, Alan. 1983. *Christian and Religious Pluralism: Patterns in Christian Theology of Religions.* Maryknoll, NY: Orbis Books.

Rahner, Karl. 1964. *The Dynamic Element in the Church.* New York: Herder & Herder.

_____ . 1966a. "Christianity and the Non-Christian Religions." In *Theological Investigations V*, 115-34.

_____ . 1966b. "The Concept of Mystery in Catholic Theology." In *Theological Investigations IV*, 36-73.

_____ . 1978a. *Foundations of Christian Faith: An Introduction to the Idea of Christianity.* New York: Crossroad.

_____ . 1978b. "Thomas Aquinas on the Incomprehensibility of God." *Journal of Religion* 58: 107-25.

_____ . 1979. "Towards a Fundamental Theological Interpretation of Vatican II." *Theological Studies* 40: 716-27.

_____ . 1983. *The Love of Jesus and the Love of Neighbor.* New York: Crossroad.

Rayan, Samuel. 1989. "Spirituality for Inter-faith Social Action." In Irudayaraj 1989, 64-73.

_____ . 1990. "Religions, Salvation, Mission." In Mojzes and Swidler 1990, 126-39.

Robinson, John A. T. 1979. *Truth Is Two-Eyed.* London: SCM Press.

Rouner, Leroy S., ed. 1984. *Religious Pluralism.* Notre Dame, IN: University of Notre Dame Press.

Ruether, Rosemary Radford. 1974. *Faith and Fratricide: The Theological Roots of Anti-Semitism.* New York: Seabury.

_____ . 1981. *To Change the World: Christology and Cultural Criticism.* New York: Crossroad.

_____ . 1987. "Feminism and Jewish-Christian Dialogue." In Hick and Knitter 1987, 137-48.

Ruokanen, Miikka. 1990. "Catholic Teaching on Non-Christian Religions at the Second Vatican Council." *International Bulletin of Missionary Research* 14: 56-61.

Samartha, Stanley J. 1991. *One Christ—Many Religions: Toward a Revised Christology.* Maryknoll, NY: Orbis Books.

Sanders, E. P. 1985. *Jesus and Judaism.* Philadelphia: Fortress Press.

Sanders, John. 1992. *No Other Name: An Investigation into the Destiny of the Evangelized.* Grand Rapids: Eerdmans.

Sanneh, Lamin. 1989. *Translating the Message: The Missionary Impact on Culture.* Maryknoll, NY: Orbis Books.

Schillebeeckx, Edward. 1963. *Christ the Sacrament of Encounter with God.* New York: Sheed & Ward.

_____ . 1979. *Jesus: An Experiment in Christology.* New York: Crossroad.

_____ . 1980. *Christ: The Experience of Jesus as Lord.* New York: Crossroad.

_____ . 1990. *The Church: The Human Story of God.* New York: Crossroad.

Schneiders, Sandra. 1992. "Living Word or Deadly Letter: The Encounter between the New Testament and Contemporary Experience." *Catholic Theological Society of America Proceedings,* 45-60.

Schneller, Peter. 1990. *A Handbook on Inculturation.* New York: Paulist Press.

Schreiter, Robert J. 1985. *Constructing Local Theologies.* Maryknoll, NY: Orbis Books.

Schüssler Fiorenza, Elisabeth. 1983. *In Memory of Her.* New York: Cross-road.

Segundo, Juan Luis. 1984. *Faith and Ideologies.* Maryknoll, NY: Orbis Books.

_____ . 1985. *Jesus of the Synoptic Gospels.* Maryknoll, NY: Orbis Books.

Smith, Wilfred Cantwell. 1981. *Towards a World Theology.* Philadelphia: Westminster Press.

_____ . 1984. "The World Church and the World History of Religion: The Theological Issue." *Proceedings of the Catholic Theological Society of America* 39: 52-68.

_____ . 1987a. "Idolatry in Comparative Perspective." In Hick and Knitter 1987, 53-68.

_____ . 1987b. "Theology and the World's Religious History." In Swidler 1987, 51-72.

Sobrino, Jon. 1984. *The True Church and the Poor.* Maryknoll, NY: Orbis Books.

_____ . 1987. *Jesus in Latin America.* Maryknoll, NY: Orbis Books.

_____ . 1988. *Spirituality of Liberation: Toward a Political Holiness.* Maryknoll, NY: Orbis Books.

_____ . 1994. *Jesus the Liberator: An Historical-Theological Reading of Jesus of Nazareth.* Maryknoll, NY: Orbis Books.

Spretnak, Charlene. 1991. *States of Grace: The Recovery of Meaning in the Postmodern Age.* HarperSanFrancisco.

Starkey, Peggy. 1982. "Biblical Faith and the Challenge of Religious Pluralism." *International Review of Mission* 71: 68-74.

Stendahl, Krister. 1981. "Notes on Three Bible Studies." In Anderson and Stransky 1981a, 7-18.

Suchocki, Marjorie. 1987. "In Search of Justice: Religious Pluralism from a Feminist Perspective." In Hick and Knitter 1987, 149-61.

Swidler, Leonard. 1990. *After the Absolute: The Dialogical Future of Religious Reflection.* Minneapolis: Augsburg-Fortress Press.

_____ , ed. 1987. *Toward a Universal Theology of Religion.* Maryknoll, NY: Orbis Books.

Swidler, Leonard, John B. Cobb, Jr., Paul F. Knitter, and Monika K. Hellwig. 1990. *Death or Dialogue? From the Age of Monologue to the Age of Dialogue.* Philadelphia: Trinity International Press.

Swidler, Leonard, and Paul Mojzes, eds. 1996. *The Uniqueness of Jesus: A Dialogue with Paul Knitter.* Maryknoll, NY: Orbis Books.

Taylor, Mark Kline. 1990. *Remembering Esperanza: A Cultural-Political Theology for North American Praxis.* Maryknoll, NY: Orbis Books.

Thompson, William M. 1985. *The Jesus Debate.* New York: Paulist Press.

_____ . 1987. "Jesus' Uniqueness: A Kenotic Approach." In Ledd 1987, 16-30.

_____ . 1994. "'Distinct But Not Separate': Historical Research in the Study of Jesus and Christian Faith." *Horizons* 21: 130-41.

Tillich, Paul. 1957. *Systematic Theology.* Vol. 2. Chicago: University of Chicago Press.

_____ . 1966. *The Future of Religions.* Ed. Jerald C. Brauer. New York: Harper & Row.

Tippit, Alan. 1987. *Introduction to Missiology.* Pasadena: Wm. Carey Library.

Tomko, Jozef. 1990. "Christian Mission Today." In Mojzes and Swidler 1990, 236-62.

_____ . 1991. "On Relativing Christ: Sects and the Church." *Origins* (April 4), 753-54.

Tracy, David. 1975. *Blessed Rage for Order: The New Pluralism in Theology.* New York: Seabury.

_____ . 1980. "Particular Questions within General Consensus." In *Consensus in Theology? A Dialogue with Hans Küng and Edward Schillebeeckx.* Ed. Leonard Swidler. Philadelphia: Westminster Press, 33-39.

_____ . 1981. *The Analogical Imagination: Christian Theology and the Culture of Pluralism.* New York: Crossroad.

_____ . 1986. "On Crossing the Rubicon and Finding the Halys: Religious Pluralism and Christian Theology—Some Reflections." Paper delivered at the Blaisdell Conference on Religion, Claremont, California (March).

_____ . 1987a. *Plurality and Ambiguity: Hermeneutics, Religion, Hope.* New York: Harper & Row.

_____ . 1987b. "Practical Theology in the Situation of Global Pluralism." In Mudge and Poling 1987, 139-54.

_____ . 1990. *Dialogue with the Other: The Inter-Religious Dialogue.* Grand Rapids: Eerdmans.

Wheeler, Barbara G., and Edward Farley, eds. 1991. *Shifting Boundaries: Contextual Approaches to the Structure of Theological Education.* Louisville: Westminster/John Knox Press.

Whitehead, Alfred North. 1957. *Process and Reality: An Essay in Cosmology.* New York: Free Press. (Original: 1929.)

Wilfred, Felix. 1987. "Dialogue Gasping for Breath? Toward New Frontiers in Interreligious Dialogue." *Federation of Asian Bishops Conference Papers,* no. 49, 32-52.

_____ . 1994. "Liberating Dialogue in India." German translation in *Befreiender Dialog—Befreite Gesellschaft: Politische Theologie und Begegnung der Religionen in Indien und Europa.* Sybille Fritsch-Oppermann, ed. Loccum: Evangelische Akademie, 29-40.

_____ , ed. 1992. *Leave the Temple: Indian Paths to Human Liberation.* Maryknoll, NY: Orbis Books.

Yagi, Seiichi. 1987. "'I' in the Words of Jesus." In Hick and Knitter 1987, 117-34.

Yates, Tim. 1994. *Christian Mission in the Twentieth Century.* New York: Cambridge University Press.

INDEX

Acts 4:12, 69-70

Acts 12:4, 43-44

Amaladoss, Michael, S.J., 109

Analogical Imagination, The (David Tracy), 30

Anti-Kingdom, 123

Aquinas, Thomas, 74-75

Atman, 167 n.2

Autobiography, theological, 2-22

Baptism, as goal of mission, 58-59; priority for missionaries, 129-30

Baum, Gregory, 56, 158

Benjamin, Walter, 32

Bible, authority of the, 169 n.2; human experience and the, 64-65; incentives for a correlational, globally responsible theology of religions in the, 40-44

Boff, Leonardo, 75

Borg, Marcus, 92-93, 173 n. 4

Bosch, David, 110, 111

Braaten, Carl, 48-49, 51-52, 57

Brahman, 167 n.2

Buddhism, 8

Captivity, Latin, 149

Christ, belief in, 47-52; of faith, 87-88; following, 52-55; proclaiming the name of, 57-60; resisting evil in the name of, 55-57

Christianity, efforts toward liberation, 99-101; monocultural, 147-48; revelation and, 150; role of suffering in, 100

Christians, anonymous, 120; attitudes of, toward other believers, 39; contemporary awareness of, 27-36; dialogue and, 15-16; truth and, 33-34; view of Jesus as one-and-only Savior among early, 48-49; views of other religions among, 39

Christology, 88; correlational, 105; correlational, globally responsible, 61-83; exclusive claims of traditional, 133; inclusivist, 61-62, 146; John Paul II's, 134; Logos/Wisdom *vs.* Paschal/Easter, 42; mission and, 103

Church, crosscultural approach to culture in the, 152-54; Kingdom of God and, 108-9, 125-26; reform and the, 124; as servant, 110; Spirit and, 111-14; supercultural approach to culture in the, 149; supracultural approach to culture in the, 150-52; world, 147-48

Cobb, John, 81-82, 172 n.23

Commission, Great, 58

Commitment, Christian, 104-8

Communication, God's mission of self-, 144-45

Community, Christian, 104-8, 132; church, 116; necessity of, 87-88

Conversation, rules for, 33

Conversion, 121-24, 132-35

Covenant, 174 n.6

Cox, Harvey, 55

Croatto, J. Severino, 96-97

Crossan, Dominic, 87

Culture, church approaches to, 148-54; incentives for a correlational, globally responsible theology of religions within, 38-40

Dean, Thomas, 48

Dialogue and Proclamation (DP), 118-19, 122, 125-35, 136-39, 144, 146

Dialogue, component of mission, 138; in a correlational, globally responsible theology of religions, 23-24; in *Dialogue and Proclamation*, 139-40; egalitarian community as requirement for interreligious, 17-18;

globally responsible, 12-14, 160-61; Hindu-Christian, 11; inter-class, 156-57; interreligious, 13-14, 16-19; Jesus and, 61-62; mission as, 136-64; moral imperative of, 31-34; normative claims and, 51; Pope John Paul II's christology and, 134; proclamation and, 141; soteriocentric, 18-19; theology as, 154-64; within Trinity, 145

Discipleship, 105

Divine, historical mediation and the, 94-95; universality of the, 106

Doctrine, incentives for a correlational, globally responsible theology of religions in, 36-38; nature of, 170 n.60

Dupuis, Jacques, 126

Earth, authentic religion and the, 35-36; as suffering Other, 11-12

Ecclesiology, 111-14; Kingdom-centered, 126; Vatican concerns about Kingdom-centered, 130-35; Vatican objections to Kingdom-centered, 127-30

Education, theological, 161-64

Eucharist, 115

Evangelii Nuntiandi, 137

Evil, resisting in Christ's name, 55-57

Exclusivism, 4-5

Experience, the Bible and human, 64-65; I-Thou, 162; role in knowing Christ, 53-54; as source for theology, 27, 155-56

Faith, 63-71; Christ of, 87-88; of Christians, 44; committed, 104-6; cosmological, 35-36; mature, 106-8

Fidelity, to Jesus the Christ, 63-71

Filioque, 175 n.4

Fiorenza, Francis, 161

Gaudium et Spes, 109

Geffré, Claude, 110

Gilkey, Langdon, 29-30, 56

God, as dialogical, 145; of history, 94-95; as Mystery, 36-37; of the oppressed, 96-97; of promise, 97-98; self-communication of, 144-45; in teaching of Jesus, 89-90

Griffiths, Paul, 49

Haight, Roger, 77, 79, 85, 90, 136

Hastings, Adrian, 47-48

Hearne, Brian, 144

Heim, S. Mark, 49

Hellwig, Monika, 53-54, 115, 168 n.6

Hermeneutics, conversational, 157-58; of suspicion, 121

Hick, John, 43, 167 n.4

Hinduism, 8

History, awareness of, 29-30; God of, 94-95; Jesus as definitive difference in, 53-55

Humanism, 130-31

Identity, Christian, 93-94

Ideology, truth and, 32

Imagination, analogical, 112

Imperative, dialogical, 31-34

Incarnation, 37-38

Inclusivism, 5-7

Inseparability, 134-35; of the church and the Kingdom of God, 128-29

Ipsissima verba, 87

Jesus, Christian pluralism and, 104-6; as a definitive Word of God, 74-75; as definitive difference in history, 53-55; dialogue and, 61-62; as eschatological prophet, 49-50, 173 n.4; exclusive language about, 43-44; exclusivity for salvation, 133-35; exclusivity of the name of, 69-70; fidelity to, 63-71; as God's sacrament, 105; historical, 86-93; identification of Kingdom of God and, 128; images of, 87; incarnation of, 37-38; New Testament language and, 67-69; practice of, 173 n.2; primary message of, 89-92; as prophet, 117; relational uniqueness of, 80-83, 98-101; as saving word, 73-76; as social prophet, 93; as Spirit-filled prophet, 92-93, 131; spirituality and, 53; teaching about God, 89-90; titles and images of, 42-43, 67, 107; truly/only distinction, 73-74; as Truth, 49-50; uniqueness of, 47, 72-83, 84-101; as universal, decisive, indispensable word, 76-80; universal and particular, 41; words of, 87

John Paul II, Pope, 57-58, 58-59; christology and dialogue in views of, 134

Judaism, 100, 174 n.6

Justice, 91, 96-97, 100, 117, 131; eco-human, 12-14, 17, 35-36

Kelly, Anthony, 80

Kelsey, David, 65
Key, hermeneutical, 91-92, 174 n.5
Khodr, George, 112-14
Kingdom of God, church and, 108-9, 125-26; conversion to, 121; identification between Jesus and, 128; religions as agents of the, 118-21; seeking the, 115-18; in the world, 116-17. *See also* Reign of God
Klostermaier, Klaus, 29
Küng, Hans, 8-9, 51, 52, 56; global ethic of, 12,
Kuschel, Karl Josef, 50-51
Land and the Human Presence Conference, The, 11
Lane, Dermot, 89, 98
Language, 170 n.6; of early Christians, 48-49; about Jesus, 43-44; New Testament, regarding Jesus, 67-69; performative, 68-69, 93, 107
Lex orandi, 52-53
Liberation, 98, 116-17; pluralism and, 9-12; unique characteristics of Christian efforts toward, 99-101
Lindbeck, George, 30, 56-57, 170 n.6
Listening, as part of mission, 145-46
Logos, 74, 80
Love, 116; Christian, 95-96; priority of, in Christianity, 99; universality of God's, 41-42
Lumen Gentium, 126
Matthew 6:33, 115-18, 165
Mediation, historical, 94-95
Medium, message and, 48
Merton, Thomas, 8
Message, medium and, 48
Ministry, incentives for a correlational, globally responsible theology of religions within, 44-45
Missio Dei, 111-12, 115, 144
Missiology, Reign of God as center of, 108-11
Mission, 102-24; Christian, 57-60; dialogical church and, 136-54; dialogue as, 136-64, 142-47; proclamation and dialogue as components of, 138; revised and reaffirmed, 108-24; role of listening in, 145-46; transcendence and, 131-32; Vatican views of, 125-35
Missionaries, role of, 129
Modalism, 175 n.3

Moran, Gabriel, 105
Mystery, Paschal, 97
Myth of Christian Uniqueness, The, 9-10
Native Americans, 11
Nature of Doctrine, The (George Lindbeck), 30
Neo-Gnosticism, 52
Newbigin, Lesslie, 51-52
No Other Names? 2
Nolan, Albert, 66, 98
Norms, absolute, 56-57
Ogden, Schubert, 172 n.20
One Faith Many Religions, 1
Oppressed, God of the, 96-97
Orthodoxy, orthopraxis and, 65-67
Orthopraxis, orthodoxy and, 65-67
"Other," meaning of, 2-3
Other, suffering: Earth as, 11-12
Others, awareness of, 28-29; Christian attitudes toward religious, 39; religious and suffering, 3, 13-14
Panikkar, Raimon, 8, 35, 38, 42, 62-63, 143, 148-49, 151, 152
Pannenberg, Wolfhart, 49-50
Paul VI, Pope, 137
Pieris, Aloysius, 42, 99
Pluralism, 7-9; criticism of, 46-60; early Christian rejection of, 70-71; Jesus and, 104-6; liberation and, 9-12; missionary critique of, 57-60; New Testament world and religious, 70-71; Reign of God and, 105; threat to mission by, 57-58
Pluralists, 172 n.20
Plurality and Ambiguity (David Tracy), 30
Pneumatology, 88, 111-14
Polanyi, Michael, 76
Poor, preferential option for the, 96-97
Prayer, law of (*lex orandi*), 52-53
Proclamation, 139-40, 143-44, 145; as component of mission, 138; dialogue and, 141
Promise, God of, 97-98
Prophet, Jesus as eschatological, 49-50, 173 n.4; Jesus as, 117; Jesus as social, 93; Jesus as Spirit-filled, 92-93, 131
Prophets, 52
Pushparajan, A., 141-42
Puthiadam, Ignatius, 143-44

Rahner, Karl, 5-6, 38, 46, 119, 144-45, 147-48
Rayan, Samuel, 62, 114
Redemptoris Missio (RM), 57-58, 102-3, 109, 125-39, 144
Reduction, christological, 75; spiritual, 176 n.2
Reform, the church and, 124
Reign of God, 89-92; as center of missiology, 108-11; pluralism and the, 105. *See also* Kingdom of God.
Religion, superiority of one, 167 n.4
Religions, Abrahamic, 41; as agents of the Kingdom, 118-21; Asian and Semitic compared, 99-100; Christian intolerance of other, 34; Christian view of other, 4-9, 39; correlational, globally responsible model's view of, 24-26; the Earth and, 35-36; globally responsible correlational dialogue among, 16-19; liberative theology of, 16; plurality of, 17; salvation and other, 118; theology of, 113-14, 118
Responsibility, global: dialogue and, 12-14
Revelation, 85-86, 175 n.1; Christianity as, 150; fullness of, 73-74
Ruether, Rosemary Radford, 43
Sacrament, Jesus as God's, 105
Salvation, 133; other religions and 118; outside the church, 118; the world and, 96
Samartha, Stanley, 42
Sanctuary Movement, 10
Schillebeeckx, Edward, 15, 28-29, 37, 54-55, 68, 69, 73, 77, 90-91, 96, 97, 116, 117, 172 n.18
Schüssler Fiorenza, Elisabeth, 174 n.5
Scripture, 64-65; authority of, 65; hermeneutical key to, 91-92; incentives for a correlational, globally responsible theology of religions in, 40-44; Jesus and his message in, 67-68
Segundo, Juan, 35, 90, 91-92
Servant, church as, 110
Smith, Wilfred Cantwell, 160
Sobrino, Jon, 66, 68-69, 75-76, 78, 89, 95, 111
Soteriology, 130-31; mission and, 103
Sovereignty, superiority *vs.*, 51
Spirit, church and, 111-14; Holy, 88;

Word and the, 111-12
Spirituality, Jesus' uniqueness and, 53
Spretnak, Charlene, 100
Stendahl, Krister, 68
Studies, religious, 159-61, 176 n.4
Suffering, cause of, 99-100; role of, in Christianity, 100
Superiority, sovereignty *vs.*, 51
Suspicion, hermeneutics of, 121
Swidler, Leonard, 160
Taylor, Charles, 66
Taylor, Mark, 88-89, 174 n.7
Theologians, Christian, 47; liberation, 156; task of, 155-56
Theology, dialogue as, 154-64; liberation, 10, 15-21; mono-religious character of Christian, 157; religious studies and, 159-61, 176 n.4; sources for, 27, 64, 155-56; trinitarian, 112-13, 145
Theology of religions, 15-21; Christian supports for a correlational, globally responsible model, 36-45; constructing a, 26-27; a correlational, globally responsible, 23-45; cultural incentives for a correlational, globally responsible model, 38-40; cultural supports for a correlational, globally responsible model, 27-36; doctrinal incentives for a correlational, globally responsible model, 36-38; pastoral incentives for a correlational, globally responsible model, 44-45; scriptural incentives to a correlational, globally responsible model, 40-44
Thompson, William, 81
Tillich, Paul, 160
Titles, of Jesus, 67, 107
Tomko, Cardinal, 58-59, 102-3
Tracy, David, 27, 30, 31, 33
Tradition, as source for theology, 27, 155-56
Transformation, 116-18, 122, 131
Truth, 31-32, 55; Christians and, 33-34; classicist view of, 48-49; ideology and, 32; person of Jesus as, 49-50; plurality of, 28
Unique, meaning of, 84-86
Uniqueness, of Jesus, 84-101; relational, 98-101

Universality, correlational, globally responsible theology of religions and, 25-26; of the Divine, 106; of Jesus, 76-78

van Beeck, Frans Jozef, 51, 71, 81

Vatican, views of mission, 125-35

Vatican II, 5-6

Whitehead, Alfred North, 25-26

Wilfred, Felix, 45

Wisdom, priority of, in Buddhism, 99

Word, Spirit and the, 111-12

Words, of Jesus, 87; other, 158

World, correlational, globally responsible theology of religions' view of, 26; Kingdom of God in the, 116-17; responsibility for the, 34-36; salvation and the, 96

Yagi, Seiichi, 42